The Theory of
Environmental
Policy

WILLIAM J. BAUMOL

Princeton and New York Universities

WALLACE E. OATES

Princeton University

with contributions by

V. S. BAWA *and* DAVID BRADFORD

THE THEORY OF ENVIRONMENTAL POLICY

externalities, public outlays,
and the quality of life

PRENTICE-HALL, INC., Englewood Cliffs, New Jersey

Library of Congress Cataloging in Publication Data

BAUMOL, WILLIAM J

The theory of environmental policy; externalities,
public outlays, and the quality of life.

Includes bibliographical references.
1. Environmental policy. 2. Externalities
(Economics) 3. Expenditures, Public. I. Oates,
Wallace E., joint author. II. Title.
HC79.E5B375   301.31'01   74-11205
ISBN   0-13-913673-8

Printed in the United States of America

Prentice-Hall International, Inc., *London*
Prentice-Hall of Australia, Pty. Ltd., *Sydney*
Prentice-Hall of Canada, Ltd., *Toronto*
Prentice-Hall of India Private Limited, *New Delhi*
Prentice-Hall of Japan, Inc., *Tokyo*

For Hilda and Mollie

Contents

PART III

Preface

This book is one of a pair of companion volumes devoted to the study of economic policies to enhance the quality of life. Our willingness to embark on so considerable a subject only reflects our conviction that economists as a body have already made sufficient headway on these problems to make such an undertaking worthwhile. We believe, in short, that this is a subject on which economists have a great deal to say that is useful; these books are intended both to bring that material together and to carry the investigation some stages further.

This volume is primarily theoretical and is consequently addressed to our fellow economists. However, it is not meant to be theory for theory's sake. Here our prime concern is policy; we are interested in the theory as a means of understanding the complexities of environmental programs.

The orientation of the other book is primarily empirical; there we will present and evaluate pertinent data and experience for guidance in the choice of policies for environmental protection and for the improvement of other aspects of the quality of life. Though it will be less technical than the theoretical volume and will consequently address itself to a broader audience, we intend it to provide the empirical counterpart to the theoretical structure developed in this book.

Our most direct debt is that to the National Science Foundation, whose support has made our work on the two volumes possible. In particular, the collection and analysis of the empirical materials in the companion volume has, predictably, proved to be a long and difficult undertaking which would have been impossible without the Foundation's generosity.

Happily, intellectual debt does not necessarily carry with it the threat of bankruptcy, for in writing this volume the debts we have accumulated have been numerous and heavy. Our deepest obligations for help above and beyond what might reasonably be asked of anyone, are those to our colleagues, David Bradford and Elizabeth Bailey. Their painstaking reading of the entire manuscript and their extensive and valuable suggestions and comments have resulted in enormous improvements both in substance and in exposition (and, incidentally, have added considerably to the labor of revision).

Professor Bradford also contributed more directly by his co-authorship of an article which served as the basis for Chapter 8 and by his authorship of Appendix B to Chapter 8. A second such contribution was provided by Dr. V. S. Bawa of Bell Laboratories, who in his very illuminating appendix to Chapter 11 solved some basic problems underlying our discussion in that chapter.

We also owe special thanks to Lionel Robbins for urging us to undertake this project (though there have been moments when we doubted whether this was cause for gratitude) and to Robert Dorfman and a number of advanced students at the Stockholm School of Economics for detecting some critical errors in our arguments.

For their very useful comments on particular parts of the analysis, we are also most grateful to Polly Allen, Hourmouzis Georgiades, Peter Kenen, Harold Kuhn, Edwin Mills, Herbert Mohring, Richard Musgrave, Fred Peterson, Robert Plotnick, Michael Rothschild, Ralph Turvey, and Edward Zajac. The opportunity to work through these materials in two separate lectures delivered by one of us at the Stockholm School served as a stimulus for our ideas and the completion of this book, and for this too we are most grateful.

Finally, for patience, good humor, skill at deciphering our hieroglyphics, and for ability to produce order out of chaos, we want to thank Sue Anne Batey who has acted as research assistant, secretary, and a repository of sanity, and who, we trust, will not be excessively embarrassed as she types these words.

The Theory of Environmental Policy

chapter I

Introduction: Economics and the Quality of Life

Man's influence on the quality of the environment depends on two things: the damage he does and the effort devoted to undoing that damage. This statement is hardly more than a tautology. Yet, most discussions in the theoretical literature treat only the first of these activities. Focusing upon the problem of externalities, they examine systematically why man's activities are likely to have deleterious consequences for the quality of life, and why, moreover, they are likely to go beyond anything that can be defended on grounds of economic efficiency. But they typically have not considered the other side of the matter: the resources devoted to the public services that are designed to improve the quality of life at the same time that external costs continue to eat away at it.

We believe that to understand some of the most urgent problems besetting our environment we must consider both these elements. For, if there is continuing environmental degradation, it must be attributed not only to a compounding of external effects but also to growing problems in the supply of those public services that are largely independent of the externalities; moreover, analysis suggests that difficulties concerning public outlays are likely to continue and perhaps become increasingly serious. In short, it is at least possible that the quality of life is threatened from both sides: first, by increasing damage from activities imposing external costs, and second, by decreasing effectiveness in public-sector activities devoted to improvement of the quality of life.

Because emphasis upon public services in a discussion of environment and the quality of life is relatively novel, it is well to say a bit more about its pertinence. For example, the cleanliness of a city's streets depends both upon the rate at which trash is dropped and the speed and thoroughness with which it is removed. The trash dropping is an issue of externalities. The cleanup is a matter of supply of public services: the amount budgeted for the department of sanitation and the effectiveness with which the funds are used. If we are interested in explaining the state of public sanitation or its trends, we must consider both these elements.

External effects and the levels of public services can serve simultaneously to determine the state of the environment; the condition of a particular area depends both on the extent of private activities that damage the locality and on the public resources expended to maintain it. More generally, the quality of the environment depends both on individual, private decisions and on collective action undertaken through the public sector (that is, on the provision of public services). This is only to be expected because *environmental quality*, broadly interpreted, is a public good consumed jointly by all members of society.

It is easy to supply more examples in which these two influences significantly affect the quality of life. Obvious cases are municipal waste treatment services and dams constructed to increase the flow of streams as a means of reducing the effects of impurities introduced into those waterways as external consequences of other human activities. But the range of application of this notion is considerably broader. Slums as well as relatively limited private investments in education and the prevention of communicable diseases are attributable, at least in part, to the external incidence of their damages and benefits. The influence of public outlays in these areas is obvious enough.

Our approach, therefore, will be to reexamine, in Parts I and II of this book, the pure and then the applied portions of the theory of externalities. We believe this treatment offers some new and significant results reached within a theoretical framework differing somewhat from that typical of much of the recent literature. Part III turns to the theory of public-goods supply; here we find that the nature of the problem and its policy implications are altogether different in character from those associated with the externalities issue.

Finally, we want to emphasize that the bulk of the analysis in this book is theoretical. Although we will consider explicitly the policy implications of the theory and provide some fragmentary evidence where appropriate, our primary objective is to offer a conceptual analysis of the problems at issue. We will, for example, provide no survey of the successes and failures of various policies for environmental protection, nor will we seek to document the rising costs in the public sector. There will be a companion volume containing a series of systematic empirical studies intended to complement the theoretical analysis in this book. The second book will be less technical analytically and is intended for a broader audience. Here, however, we want to explore in a more rigorous way the economic theory of the environment.

part **I**

ON THE THEORY
OF
EXTERNALITIES

chapter 2

"Relevance" in the Theory of Externalities

By bringing to light sources of error in the formulation of both actual and potential policy, and by helping us to deal with the critical problem of allocative efficiency, externalities theory can provide significant guidance to the practitioner. Part II of this book explores some of the more concrete policy issues to which the analysis can be applied; in doing so, it deals with several topics that have not been the subject of much formal analysis.

But before coming to these applications, we first reexamine the theoretical underpinnings of the analysis. We shall argue in Part I that a number of widely held views about the theory of externalities are unfounded. The analysis also points out several (frequently undetected) booby traps that threaten the unwary in the use of the theory. We believe that Part I includes a number of novel results, most of them with implications for policy.

We have not tried in this book to provide a comprehensive review of the externalities literature. Because we are interested primarily in materials relevant to the pressing problems attributable to externalities, we have deliberately avoided some of the theoretical issues that have received a great deal of attention. More will be said about these omissions later in this chapter.

1. OUTLINE OF PART I

In Chapter 3, we define what we mean by the term *externalities*. Explicit definitions will be offered for several subcategories of operational significance, notably those corresponding to the distinction between *technological* and *pecuniary* externalities and between "private" and "public goods" externalities. We show that these distinctions continue to be of considerable significance for public policy.

Chapter 4 describes a number of basic externalities models[1] of considerable generality (although, because they are designed to represent the large-numbers case, they are restricted by the assumption of pure competition). These models serve as prototypes for the sort of construct needed for the analysis of policy in the presence of externalities. They lead at once to several policy conclusions, some of them confirming Pigou's results but going beyond Pigou in the use of formal analysis and in explaining the mechanism of the tax-subsidy approach. In particular, the theorems indicate the role that must be assigned to the victims (beneficiaries) of externalities if a Pareto optimal resource allocation is to be attained; they examine, under a Pareto optimal tax-subsidy scheme, whether recipients of external effects should be compensated for the damage they suffer (forced to pay for the benefits they receive) or whether, in line with the well-known Coase analysis, the victims of externalities may need to be taxed for the sake of improved resource allocation.[2]

It should be noted that, with one or two exceptions, our analysis of welfare maximization will utilize the weak criterion of Pareto optimality, which sweeps under the rug the issue of distribution. At a later point, distributive problems will be considered explicitly and the dangers of the Paretian approach will be commented upon. Yet, as has so often proved true, the Pareto criterion will permit us to draw a considerable number of conclusions of greater significance than the weakness of the underlying premise might lead us to expect.

Chapter 5 is a digression, exploring briefly the problem of the optimal pricing of exhaustible resources that, although it may have little to do with externalities, has recently drawn a considerable degree of attention as an issue affecting the quality of life. Here we find that conventional analysis indicates a number of interesting propositions about intertemporal pricing

---

[1] We should emphasize that, in contrast to much of the literature (see E. J. Mishan, "The Postwar Literature on Externalities: An Interpretive Essay," *Journal of Economic Literature* IX (March, 1971), 8), we shall utilize general-equilibrium models in most of the analysis. Although they are sometimes simplified by substantial aggregation, our models indicate at all times the effects of a development in, or upon, the remainder of the economy. There are, incidentally, some noteworthy exceptions to Mishan's partial-equilibrium characterization. See, for example, R. V. Ayres and A. V. Kneese, "Production, Consumption and Externalities," *American Economic Review* LIX (June, 1969), 282–97; R. A. Meyer, Jr., "Externalities as Commodities," *American Economic Review* LXI (September, 1971), 736–40; and Karl-Göran Mäler, *Environmental Economics*, forthcoming in 1974.

[2] See R. H. Coase, "The Problem of Social Cost," *Journal of Law and Economics* III (October, 1960), 1–44.

patterns for resources that are fixed in supply. Some of the theorems seem counterintuitive at first glance; we show, for example, that, under certain fairly general conditions, an optimal pattern of usage for an exhaustible resource requires a declining price over time.

Chapters 6 and 7 examine a number of additional topics in the theory of externalities. We explore the problem that market imperfections create for the implementation of tax-subsidy policies to correct for the distortions caused by external effects. We also provide a formal proof of the proposition that, with convexity of production and utility functions, the presence of external costs in a particular activity leads unambiguously to a competitive equilibrium with activity levels exceeding those that are optimal,[3] and that the reverse holds for external benefits.

However, Chapter 8 shows that, if externalities are sufficiently strong, the second-order concavity-convexity conditions must necessarily be violated, so that a world in which externalities are important may be expected to be characterized by a multiplicity of local maxima. This may, of course, complicate enormously, and perhaps render totally impractical, attempts to reach even a state of Pareto optimality, whether through global tax-subsidy measures or via central planning and direct controls.

2. OMITTED AREAS: a. EXISTENCE THEORY

As we suggested earlier, our exclusive concern with the theory of policy dictates the omission of a number of interesting theoretical topics. Two of these have received so much attention in the literature that some justification seems necessary.

The first is the issue of the existence of a general equilibrium solution in the presence of externalities; this is a subject that has given rise to a small, but very sophisticated, body of materials.[4] It is clear that, in an ultimate sense, the issue of existence is highly relevant. If no solution exists, theoretical discussion of policy is basically pointless. It is possible also that the necessary or sufficient conditions for existence will themselves turn out to have some direct policy implications. So far, however, no such connection seems to have emerged and so we will do no more than acknowledge the issue and make sure to build at least some of our models so that they satisfy sufficient conditions for existence of an equilibrium.

[3] Here is one case in which the Paretian approach is insufficient to get us where we want to go. Part of Chapter 6 consequently utilizes stricter but more questionable approaches, such as the Hicks-Kaldor criterion of increases in social welfare.

[4] See, for example, K. J. Arrow and F. H. Hahn, *General Competitive Analysis* (San Francisco: Holden-Day, 1971).

3. OMITTED AREAS: b. SMALL NUMBERS AND THE VOLUNTARY SOLUTION CASE

We have also omitted a second noteworthy topic in externalities theory from our analysis: the small-numbers case in which a very few decision makers are involved in the generation of an externality *and* few are affected by it. With all of the complexities that beset the theory of oligopoly and other small-numbers models, this case has proved an irresistible subject for theoretical analysis. The result is an extensive literature focusing on the small-number situation, a literature which, we are convinced, is disproportionate to its importance for policy.

Many of these analyses reach the conclusion that, in the circumstances postulated, the affected parties, if left to themselves, will negotiate a voluntary set of bribes to induce those who generate the social damage to adjust their behavior, perhaps even nearly to optimal levels.[5] The farmer, whose crops are damaged by runoff from the field above his, will find it profitable to offer a side payment to his unwitting tormentor sufficient to induce him to reduce the runoff appropriately.[6] All this rests on the assumption that the number of parties to such a situation is sufficiently small to make negotiation possible. It is generally recognized that where the number of individuals concerned is large, the likelihood of voluntary negotiation becomes small, because the administrative costs of coordination become prohibitive and because "as the number of participants becomes critically large, the individual will more and more come to treat the behavior of 'all others' as beyond his own possible range of influence" (p. 116).[7]

The important point for us is that most of the major externalities problems that concern society so deeply today *are* large-number cases.[8] *Even where the number of polluters in a particular neighborhood is small, so long as the number of persons affected significantly by the emissions is substantial,*

---

[5] See Coase, "The Problem of Social Cost," *Journal of Law and Economics*; J. M. Buchanan and W. C. Stubblebine, "Externality," *Economica* XXIX (November, 1962), 371–84; and Ralph Turvey, "On Divergences Between Social Cost and Private Cost," *Economica* XXX (August, 1963), 309–13.

[6] The argument does assume away the problems of oligopolistic indeterminancy. If both sides to such a negotiation try to outsmart one another by devious strategies, an optimal outcome is by no means certain. Moreover, a recent paper by J. M. Marchand and K. P. Russell, "Externalities, Liability, Separability and Resource Allocation," *American Economic Review* LXIII (September, 1973), 611–20, argues that, even in the small-numbers case, negotiation may result in *systematic* deviations from optimality. However, in an unpublished note, A. J. Lee and R. F. Settle have questioned the Marchand-Russell argument.

[7] J. M. Buchanan, "Cooperation and Conflict in Public-Goods Interaction," *Western Economic Journal* V (March, 1967), 109–21.

[8] For a related comment see A. V. Kneese, "Environmental Pollution: Economics and Policy," *American Economic Review*, LXI, no. 2 (May, 1971), 153–66.

the process of direct negotiation and agreement will generally be unmanageable.[9] The same point, obviously, applies to all other types of externality. It thus seems to us that the role of voluntary negotiation among individual decision makers is of limited applicability for environmental policy.[10]

Once asserted, the point is almost obvious. Yet it is important to nail it down, because it seems to get lost in so much of the discussion. For example, it is surprising how many casual readers of the literature one encounters who feel that Coase's shafts have dealt a fatal blow to the Pigouvian solution in practice because, if negotiation moves resource allocation toward the ideal, the imposition of the optimal Pigouvian taxes on top of this will prove too much of a good thing. The argument, so far as it goes, is valid. But if, in most important externalities problems, negotiation is impractical and virtually nonexistent, the damage to the Pigouvian position inflicted by this point can hardly be very serious.

We want to be clear on this assertion. No one can possibly sustain against Coase, Buchanan, or Turvey the accusation that he does not understand the significance of the large-numbers case. For example, the preceding quotation from Buchanan makes his grasp of the issue abundantly clear and the same is true of Turvey.[11] Moreover, all three surely recognize its importance in practice. Indeed, the sentence immediately preceding our quotation from Buchanan asserts, "To be at all relevant for public-goods problems in the real world, the analysis must be extended from the small-number to the large-number case." [12] This does not mean that our discussion attacks a straw man. At the least, it indicates which portions of the recent theoretical

---

[9] This does not mean to imply that the number of polluters makes no difference for policy. For example, Lerner observes that ". . . where the firm is large enough to be able to influence the price of pollution by varying its own output, we have a kind of monopolistic distortion 'in reverse' . . . As the additional pollution raised the price per unit . . . he would have to pay not only the higher price of the additional unit but the *price increase* on each unit he was previously producing . . . so that he would be producing *too little pollution.*" A. P. Lerner, "The 1971 Report of the President's Council of Economic Advisors; 'Priorities and Efficiency,'" *American Economic Review* LXI (September, 1971), 527–30. (Quote from 529–30). This issue is discussed in detail in Chapter 6.

[10] An instructive exception is a case reported in the Swedish newspapers. On the outskirts of Göteborg in Sweden, an automobile plant is located next to an oil refinery. The automobile producer found that, when the refining of lower quality petroleum was underway and the wind was blowing in the direction of the automobile plant, there was a marked increase in corrosion of its metal inventory and the paint of recently produced vehicles. Negotiation between these two parties *did* take place. It was agreed to conduct the corrosive activities only when the wind was blowing in the other direction *toward the large number of nearby inhabitants who, naturally, took no part in the negotiation.* See "BP och Volvo, jättarna som kom överens," *Medecinska Föreningens Tidsskrift* (March, 1969), p. 114. We are grateful to Peter Bohm for this illustration.

[11] See, for example, Turvey's discussion of a large-numbers case in "Optimization in Fishery Regulation," *American Economic Review* LIV (March, 1964), 64–76.

[12] Buchanan, "Cooperation and Conflict in Public-Goods Interaction," *Western Economic Journal*, p. 116

literature are of central "relevance" for environmental policy. In addition, it deals with a misplaced emphasis (if not an error) that is widespread among those who have read the literature without sufficient care.

The point may be brought home most effectively by a simple listing of pervasive externalities problems that the majority of observers would consider to be among the most serious:

a. Sulfur dioxide, lead, and other contaminants of the atmosphere,

b. Various degradable and nondegradable wastes that pollute the world's waterways,

c. DDT and other pesticides, which, through various routes, become imbedded in food products,

d. Deterioration of neighborhoods into slums,

e. Congestion along urban highways,

f. High noise levels in metropolitan areas.

Other important illustrations will occur to the reader, but this list is representative. It should be clear that the number of individuals involved in each of these cases is typically very substantial. In considering the list, we want to stress again that negotiation is usually precluded by the presence of a large number of individuals *either* on the side that generates the externalities *or* on the side that suffers from them. That is, if pollution is emitted only by a small number of sources but affects a great many individuals, the small-numbers analysis simply does not apply.

To illustrate the issues raised by the concrete problems in the preceding list, we conclude by offering a few comments on one of them: the pesticides problem. DDT and other chemical insecticides have been used by millions of farmers in the United States alone. Certainly, their number is sufficiently large to make negotiation impractical. It may perhaps be surmised that the pesticide used by a farmer only affects persons living in his immediate neighborhood, and that therefore effective negotiations can be conducted by small groups of farmers and their neighbors. Unfortunately, this simply is not true. The mechanism whereby a pesticide is transported beyond its point of origin is fairly well-known. Agricultural runoff carries it into rivers from which it is borne by winds and by ocean currents and spread throughout the globe. When the pesticide is sprayed by airplanes, only a small portion (in one study, only 13 to 38 percent) ends up on the plants or in the local soil; a substantial proportion is transported enormous distances by air currents. That is how it gets into the organs of arctic animals, as the newspapers have reported. One striking observation illustrates the point: "Rain falling on the agriculturally remote Shetland Islands has been found to have about the same level of pesticide concentrations as is found in the San Joaquin River even where that river received drainage directly from irrigated fields." [13] Thus, the number of persons affected by a pesticide spraying (though each one will sustain a negligible amount of damage from any one spraying) is likely to be enormous. Moreover, they are likely to be spread over huge distances with the sources of the spray affecting any particular individual difficult, if not impossible, to identify. It would seem clear that the pesticides are hardly promising subjects for control by spontaneous negotiation. It is equally hard to see much of a role for resolution through individual bargaining for any of the other environmental problems on our list.

[13] These and other interesting materials on the movements of pesticides can be found in Justin Frost, "Earth, Air, Water," *Environment* XI (July-August, 1969), 14–33.

chapter 3

Externalities: Definition, Significant Types, and Optimal-Pricing Conditions

The externality is in some ways a straightforward concept; yet, in others, it is extraordinarily elusive. We know how to take it into account in our analysis, and we are aware of many of its implications, but, despite a number of illuminating attempts to define the notion,[1] one is left with the feeling that we still have not captured all its ramifications. Perhaps this does not matter greatly. The definitional issue does not seem to have limited seriously our ability to analyze the problem and so it may not be worth a great deal of effort. Certainly, we do not delude ourselves that this discussion will be the last word on the subject.

Classification of types of externalities is another matter. Although we are inclined to agree with those who feel that taxonomy often yields sharply diminishing returns, there are classes of externalities whose formal properties and policy implications differ significantly. Moreover, as we hope to show, failure to recognize those distinctions has led to errors in the past and continues to do so. Therefore, it is important to discuss these categories and their implications with care. Consequently, we will examine Viner's distinction between technological and pecuniary externalities fairly thoroughly; although

---

[1] See, for example, F. M. Bator, "The Anatomy of Market Failure," *Quarterly Journal of Economics* LXXII (August, 1958), 351–79; J. M. Buchanan and W. C. Stubblebine, "Externality," *Economica*, as well as the classic discussion by James E. Meade in his "External Economies and Diseconomies in a Competitive Situation," *Economic Journal* LXII (March, 1952), 54–67; and his more recent book, *The Theory of Economic Externalities* (Geneva: Institut Universitaire de Hautes Études, 1973), especially Chapters 1 and 2.

writers generally accept Viner's distinction and its implications, propositions that overlook this point still appear periodically and yield misleading conclusions. For example, in a later section of this chapter we enlarge upon the recent argument by some authors that the imposition of a set of Pigouvian taxes upon the generators of externalities (that is, taxes per unit of activity equal to their net marginal social damage) will themselves become the source of a difference between private and social costs, and will thus *lead to* resource misallocation. It will be shown, however, that (at least under some circumstances) these effects of Pigouvian taxes are in the nature of *pecuniary* externalities, and, hence, produce no misuse of resources.

We will also distinguish between two other categories of externality, apparently first recognized explicitly by Bator and Head.[2] Bator refers to them as public and private goods externalities. We will show that these two cases require rather different analytic approaches and that they have significantly different implications, both in terms of theory and for public policy. In particular, we will demonstrate that the level of compensation of the victims of externalities required for Pareto optimality varies with the type of externality.[3] In the case of public externalities, taxation of those who generate externalities with neither compensation nor taxation of the victims (beneficiaries) is necessary for optimal resource allocation, but for private externalities, taxation of the generators *and* compensation of the victims, determined on competitive pricing principles, is normally required. The discussion will also suggest why, in practice, it is so difficult to find significant cases of private externalities (a scarcity noted by Bator).

Perhaps most important, the discussion will also indicate more clearly the role of the price system in the control of externalities. We will show that, *where externalities are of the pure or even the impure public goods variety, the optimal-pricing vector exhibits a fundamental asymmetry, requiring one level of price for consumers (victims) of the externality and a different level of price for its producers.* In the absence of taxes, no normal market price can fulfill this asymmetry requirement (in the market, if the buyer of an item pays p dollars per unit for it, the seller will receive p dollars per unit). Thus, one must qualify the wide spread attribution of misallocations resulting from these types of externalities to the failure to charge a price for the resource or the service in question.

[2] Bator, "Anatomy of Market Failure," *Quarterly Journal of Economics*; and J. G. Head, "Public Goods and Public Policy," *Public Finance* XVII, No. 3 (1962), 197–219.

[3] Some writers have argued for the payment of compensation to those who suffer, say, smoke damage, but others [among them R. H. Coase, "The Problem of Social Cost," *Journal of Law and Economics* III (October, 1960), 1–44; and H. Mohring and J. G. Boyd, "Analyzing 'Externalities': 'Direct Interaction' vs. 'Asset Utilization' Frameworks," *Economica*, New Series XXXVIII (November, 1971), 347–61] argue that efficient resource allocation may require a tax on those who are harmed by the smoke. In correspondence, Professor Mohring has since revised his views on the subject.

In this chapter, we will present and discuss these propositions rather heuristically; we postpone more rigorous derivations to the following chapter where they easily fall out of the analysis of the formal models.

1. DEFINITION: *EXTERNALITY*

Ultimately, definitions are a matter of taste and convenience. Bator, who makes no attempt to define the externalities concept very formally, nevertheless proposes to interpret the concept so broadly that it includes most major sources of what he calls "market failure." [4] He even includes in this category cases of increasing returns to scale in which "natural monopoly" may be the most efficient market form and in which marginal-cost pricing does not permit the firm to cover its costs. One can only object that this broad connotation is not what most writers have in mind when they discuss externalities. The analysis of the increasing-returns problem is ultimately quite different from that of the more conventional externalities[5] that constitute the primary threat to the environment and to the quality of life more generally. It therefore seems preferable to hold to a narrower, more conventional interpretation of the term.

Buchanan and Stubblebine do just that, though, as has been suggested elsewhere; the concept they call the "Pareto-relevant externality" corresponds to what is meant in most of the literature when the term *externality* is used

[4] Bator, "Anatomy of Market Failure," *Quarterly Journal of Economics.*

[5] For a rather heterodox approach to the concept of externalities that also distinguishes them from increasing returns, see K. J. Arrow, "The Organization of Economic Activity: Issues Pertinent to the Choice of Market Versus Nonmarket Allocation," in Congress of the United States, Joint Economic Committee, *The Analysis and Evaluation of Public Expenditures: The PPB System,* I, (Washington, D.C.: Government Printing Office, 1969), 47–64.

Increasing returns were, at one point, considered to be an externalities problem in the conventional sense, because *A*'s purchase of such an item may make it cheaper for *B* to obtain. This led to a long and confusing controversy that was only settled when J. Viner—in his "Cost Curves and Supply Curves," *Zeitschrift für Nationalökonomie,* III (1931–I), 23–46— showed that what was involved was just a pecuniary externality. For a review of the literature see H. S. Ellis and W. Fellner, "External Economies and Diseconomies," *American Economic Review,* XXXIII (September, 1943), 493–511. Of course, increasing returns do give rise to a number of analytic and policy problems: the unsustainability of competition (if the increasing returns are not produced by external economies), the losses resulting from marginal cost pricing in these circumstances, and the danger of breakdown of the second-order maximum conditions. None of these is, however, an externalities problem in the conventional sense, and each has given rise to a distinct body of literature. For a review of the discussion of increasing returns and monopoly, see Alfred E. Kahn, *The Economics of Regulation* (Wiley: New York, 1970), especially Volume II, Chapter 4. On the literature on marginal cost pricing and decreasing costs, see W. Baumol and D. Bradford, "Optimal Departures from Marginal Cost Pricing," *American Economic Review,* LX (June, 1970), 265–83.

without modifiers.[6] Their approach is, in general, unobjectionable as an operational concept. By and large, they define externalities not in terms of what they are but what they do. That is, they assert, in effect, that a (Pareto-relevant) externality is present when, in competitive equilibrium, the (marginal) conditions of optimal resource allocation are violated. Perhaps this is all that need be said. However, it is not fully satisfying. One is tempted to look for a definition that starts earlier in the process, one that identifies the economic phenomenon leading to the postulated violation of the optimality conditions. Somehow, one is happier if the violation of these requirements can be *deduced* from the economic conditions that one takes as a definition, rather than just assuming that the violation occurs in some unspecified way.

Let us then attempt to provide an alternative definition of our own. We may define:[7]

Condition 1. An externality is present whenever some individual's (say *A*'s) *utility* or *production* relationships include real (that is, nonmonetary) variables, whose values are chosen by others (persons, corporations, governments) without particular attention to the effects on *A*'s welfare.[8]

This definition should not be misunderstood to be a simple equation of externalities with economic interdependence. When I rely on the farmer for my food, no externality need be involved, for he does not decide for me how many zucchini I will consume, nor does my consumption enter directly into his utility function.[9] Note also that the definition rules out cases in which someone *deliberately* does something to affect *A*'s welfare, a requirement Mishan has emphasized.[10] If I purposely maneuver my car to splatter mud on a pedestrian whom I happen to dislike, he is given no choice in the amount of mud he "consumes," but one would not normally regard this as an externality.

---

[6] "Externality," *Economica.*

[7] This definition is, of course, very similar in spirit to many others found in the literature. See, for example, E. J. Mishan, "The Postwar Literature on Externalities, An Interpretive Essay," *Journal of Economic Literature,* IX (March, 1971), 2–3.

[8] The reason the definition has been confined to effects operating through utility or production functions will become clear in a later section. We should also append to this definition the condition that the relationship holds in the absence of regulatory pressures for the control of the activity. One might argue that the threat or presence of government intervention can force the polluter to concern himself with the effects of his emissions on those whom he harms, but we would not want to say that his newly awakened concerns disqualify his emissions as an externality.

[9] Of course my *payment* to him does affect his utility. This already brings in the distinction between pecuniary and technological externalities that will be discussed later in this chapter.

[10] E. J. Mishan, pp. 342–3 of his "The Relationship between Joint Products, Collective Goods and External Effects," *Journal of Political Economy* LXXVII (May/June, 1969), 329–48.

It has also been suggested that for a relationship to qualify as an externality it must satisfy a second requirement:

Condition 2. The decision maker, whose activity affects others' utility levels or enters their production functions, does not receive (pay) in compensation for this activity an amount equal in value to the resulting (marginal) benefits or costs to others.

This second proviso is required if the externality is to have all of the unpleasant consequences, including inefficiencies and resource misallocation, that are associated with the concept. It has long been recognized that, at least in some cases, proper pricing or tax-subsidy arrangements will eliminate the misallocations, though, as we will see later in this chapter, matters here are not as simple as has sometimes been supposed.[11]

Nevertheless, as was suggested to us by Professor Dorfman, one may prefer to define an externality to be present whenever condition 1 holds, whether or not such payments occur. If optimal taxes are levied, smoke generation by factories will no doubt be reduced, but it will not be reduced to zero. In that case, it seems more natural to say that the externality has been reduced to an appropriate level, rather than asserting that it has been eliminated altogether. Perhaps more important, the use of condition 1 alone as our definition has the advantage that, instead of postulating in advance the pricing arrangements that yield efficiency and Pareto optimality,[12] we can *deduce* from it what prices and taxes are compatible with these goals and which are not. These calculations will, as a matter of fact, be carried out in this and the following chapters. At any rate, we will say that an externality is present if the activity satisfies condition 1.[13]

---

[11] Thus, condition 1 may be taken to correspond roughly to what Buchanan and Stubblebine, in "Externality," *Economica*, have called *an externality* and conditions 1 and 2 together constitute what they call "a Pareto-relevant externality," (that is, an externality that prevents the necessary conditions for Pareto optimality from being satisfied). On the role of condition 2 in previous discussions of the definition of *externality*, see Mishan, "Relationship between Joint Products, Collective Goods and External Effects," *Journal of Political Economy*, p. 342.

[12] In this volume, we will define a vector of outputs to be *efficient* if it involves the largest *output* of some arbitrarily chosen good that can be attained without reducing the output of any other good. A vector of output values, *and its distribution among consumers*, is, as usual, defined to be *Pareto-optimal* if it yields the largest value of some one consumer's *utility* that can be obtained without a reduction in the utility of any other consumer. Clearly, any Pareto-optimal arrangement must also be efficient, but the converse is not necessarily true.

[13] The omission of condition 2 from our definition may appear to leave us with a problem in some cases of private external benefits that, as we will see, come extremely close to being services provided very much like other services, except that, for them, for one of a variety of reasons, the pricing system has gone wrong. Charge an appropriate price and the external benefit becomes simply another commodity purchasable on the market in quantities determined by the consumer. More will be said on this shortly.

2. DEPLETABLE (PRIVATE) AND UNDEPLETABLE (PUBLIC) EXTERNALITIES

It is generally recognized that the resource misallocation attributable to an externality will occur only when an appropriate price is not charged by (to) the *supplier* of some such services (or disservice). But we have yet to explain why such services will, in fact, be present in the economy. Why should there be some activities whose producers escape the workings of the price system?

Bator, in his "Anatomy of Market Failure," points out that many externalities partake of the character of public goods. If the air in a city is polluted, it deteriorates simultaneously for every resident of the area and not just for any one individual. Air pollution, then, is a clearly a public "bad." Similarly, landscaping of a garden that can be seen by all and sundry passers is a public good. It is by now a commonplace that, where a public good is involved, the ordinary price system just will not do. The reasons and the implications will perhaps become clearer in the next section.

Rather than referring to these as public-goods externalities, a concept that has acquired so many implications, many of them not altogether clear or relevant for our purposes, we prefer to call them *undepletable* externalities. This is meant to emphasize the *one* characteristic of a public good that is most directly pertinent to us here: the fact that an increase in the consumption of the good by one individual does not reduce its availability to others. My breathing of polluted city air can (to a reasonable degree of approximation) be taken to leave unaffected the quality of the air available to others.

Note that an externality may be undepletable and yet satisfy the excludability requirement that is often taken to be violated by public goods.[14] I can exclude passers-by from enjoying the sight of my garden by fencing it in, and if the garden is really spectacular, I may even be able to charge an admission price. However, it still remains true that, at least within some range, an increase in the number of persons who see it need not affect its ability to please others.[15] Of course, if congestion eventually sets in, the externality will then change its character from the one type to the other.

---

[14] For the classic discussion of these two attributes of public goods, depletability and excludability, see Head, "Public Goods and Public Policy," *Public Finance*. Head refers to undepletability as the "jointness of supply" of public goods.

[15] Thus exclusion may be possible even when depletion is not. Note that the converse is also true: depletion does not require the exclusion property, though we will suggest presently (as a bit of casual empiricism) that such cases are exceptional. The standard example is the case of *n* petroleum suppliers exploiting the same oil field. None can really prevent the others from drawing off oil, but every barrel obtained by one of them means that there will be that much less for the others. Head shows very clearly that depletion may occur in the absence of exclusion and vice versa, (*ibid.*, pp. 206–7). He also notes that this was recognized by Samuelson in "The Pure Theory of Public Expenditure," *Review of Economics and Statistics* XXXVI (November, 1954), 387–89; Musgrave in "The Voluntary

For reasons that will soon be noted, it is not easy to provide a convincing example of a depletable externality. To get a clear illustration that may also begin to suggest the nature of the difficulty, we go back to an item of recent economic history. In the postwar period, when there was a severe shortage of fuel, it is reported that in several parts of Europe many persons spent a good part of their time walking along railroad tracks looking for coal that had been dropped by passing trains. It is clear that this is a depletable externality because every additional bit of coal found by gatherer *A* meant that so much less was available to *B*.

In this case, undoubtedly, the reason coal was left along the tracks is that the railroad did not find it worth the cost of gathering the coal and selling it at a price. In principle, if there were enough money to be made, the railroad might even have been able to hire the self-employed gatherers and put them to work collecting the coal for sale. We know very well that business firms are prepared to spend large amounts on the accumulation of bits of material when they are precious enough (for example, in the working of gold and platinum).[16]

The point is quite, but not completely, general. Where there are no legal or institutional restrictions inhibiting the pricing process, a depletable externality will usually be permitted to persist only if the cost of collecting a price for it exceeds the potential gains. For although a depletable externality need not always have the exclusion property (note the oil field illustration mentioned in footnote 15), *usually* individuals can (with sufficient outlays for the purpose) be prevented from acquiring additional quantities of such items and can therefore be charged an appropriate price.

In such cases, then, either the externality must be insignificant or the cost of collecting an appropriate fee must be very high. *Otherwise, private enterprise will find it profitable to take the measures necessary to eliminate the externality.* Thus it is hardly an accident that Bator found a dearth of depletable externalities that constitute critical policy issues.[17] If they are sufficiently important economically (that is, if their potential price is sufficiently high), private enterprise will generally eliminate them. Or, looked at the other way, if the cost of their elimination is high relative to their economic

---

Exchange Theory of Public Economy," *Quarterly Journal of Economics* LIII (February, 1939), 213–37; and Bator, "Anatomy of Market Failure," *Quarterly Journal of Economics.*

[16] It is not easy to find examples of *detrimental* externalities that are of the private-goods variety. If its effects are undesirable, there must be some way to force its victims to accept it. A standard example is the dumping of garbage on someone's (unguarded) property. Given the initial amount to be deposited, the more that is thrown onto *C*'s land, the less there will be to dump on *D*'s. Garbage dumped on streets or in other public areas is quite another matter. This is obviously a *public* bad.

[17] We owe this observation to Assar Lindbeck and Jacob Mincer (in conversation).

significance, the advantage may be just as questionable from the viewpoint of society as it is from that of private enterprise.[18]

In practice, the major source of depletable externalities lies in institutional impediments that effectively prevent the assignment of property rights permitting the implementation of normal market exclusion and pricing procedures. One interesting example is the training of unskilled labor (a complex case which for our purposes need be considered only at its most superficial level).[19] Suppose a company hires a number of persons every year and provides them, on the job, with skills that increase their marginal productivity for the remainder of their working lives. Assume, moreover, that, on the average, such a person has a working life of h years, but usually changes jobs every $w < h$ years, and that the training contributes b dollars for the next h years. The discounted present value of the b dollars over the individual's entire working life is obviously greater than the marginal social benefit to the firm, which realizes only the discounted value of a stream of receipts of b dollars for w years. The firm will therefore train persons only up to the point where the marginal training cost equals $\sum_{t=1}^{w} b/(1 + r)^t$, (that is, its marginal private yield), and the number of persons trained may well be below the optimal level. The remainder of the lifetime benefits, $\sum_{t=w+1}^{h} b/(1 + r)^t$, will presumably accrue to the worker in the form of wages higher than he would otherwise have gotten in his future jobs or possibly will go entirely or in part to his future employers in the form of lower costs for skilled personnel.

Here we have an externality that has drawn increased attention as scarcity of skills in urban slums becomes more noticeable. Moreover, it is of the depletable variety: given the resources to be used in on-the-job training, the hiring of individual A implies the displacement of some other candidate.

Why, then, is an appropriate price apparently not charged for the training process? The reasons seem to be institutional. The prohibition of slavery prevents the trainee from signing a contract to remain for the rest of his working life in the employment of the company that teaches him skills. This obstacle could be circumvented if, during the training period, the worker were to accept a wage so low that the surplus of his product over his wage

---

[18] In principle, an exception may occur where a government agency can collect payments more economically than a private firm because other activities happen to be complementary to the payments collection. It is not easy to think of examples.

[19] This case has given rise to a considerable discussion in the writings of labor economics. For the basic reference, see G. S. Becker, *Human Capital: A Theoretical and Empirical Analysis with Special Reference to Education*, National Bureau for Economic Research (New York: 1964).

covers his training cost. However, that may be prevented by the minimum wage laws. A further alternative is for the company to open a school that provides training for a fee sufficient to cover the training costs. But that will work only if the skills do not require experience on the job. Where learning by doing is the only effective training process, the minimum wage laws and the laws against slavery may be responsible for the persistence of this depletable and apparently significant externality.

A second important example of a depletable externality, whose source also is institutional obstacles to the assignment of property rights, is the usage of exhaustible common-property resources.[20] One example that has received some attention in the literature is the economics of the fisheries.[21] Consider a body of water (a lake) to which all fishermen have free access. The haul of one fisherman reduces the expected size of the catch of others, a clear case of a depletable externality. The result of individual maximizing behavior in this setting is an excessive level of fishing activity. This is easily illustrated. If W in Figure 3–1 represents the wage (and marginal product) in activities other than fishing, the number of fishermen in equilibrium will

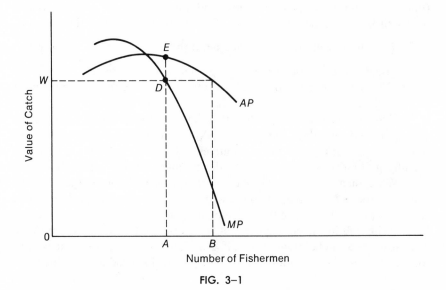

FIG. 3–1

[20] The earlier illustration, several oil producers drawing on the same oil field, is another case of this type. The problem has long been recognized. "In this country, for instance, when the only common property consists in hedge-nuts and blackberries, how seldom are they allowed to ripen?", Mrs. J. Marcett, *Conversations on Political Economy* (London, 1819), p. 61.

[21] See, for example, Ralph Turvey, "Optimization and Suboptimization in Fishing Regulation," *American Economic Review* LIV (March, 1964), 64–76.

be *OB*, where the average product (in money terms) of a fisherman equals the wage he can obtain elsewhere. This is obviously too large a number of fishermen, because an individual's fishing activity imposes costs on others and thereby generates a marginal social yield lower than the value of marginal product in other activities.[22] What is required to generate an optimal level of fishing activity is control of entry to the body of water; if this were effected through private ownership, the profit-maximizing firm would hire only *OA* fishermen making the wage equal to the value of the marginal product. Alternatively, a price of admission to the lake equal to *DE* could be charged; this would also yield the efficient level of fishing activity.

The preceding two illustrations suggest that we may prefer to think of depletable externalities not as externalities at all, but as cases where institutional impediments make it impossible to impose the appropriate prices. For this reason we may want to include condition 2 as part of our definition. We emphasize, however, that this ambiguity does not arise in the undepletable and the mixed cases that will occupy the bulk of our attention and, that, for the reasons just discussed, encompass most of the significant cases for public policy; the reader may verify this by reexamining our list of serious environmental problems in Section 3 of the preceding chapter.

3. PARETO-OPTIMAL PRICING OF DEPLETABLE AND UNDEPLETABLE EXTERNALITIES

As we will show formally in the next chapter, in a competitive economy, an inefficiency or misallocation of resources resulting from the presence of a depletable externality can be corrected simply by charging an ordinary price equal to marginal social cost (benefit). We stress, however, that a depletable externality need not cause inefficiencies: as illustrated by the case of the coal collectors, it may be that the transactions costs (costs of exclusion or collection) are sufficiently high to make pricing of the externality unprofitable both socially and privately. In such cases, the continuation of an "uncorrected" externality obviously may be consistent with Pareto optimality.

Where, however, administrative (transactions) costs are not excessive, an appropriate price can prevent any misallocations induced by the presence of depletable externalities. If such a price (reduced wage) were offered for on-the-job training, there would be no undersupply of training opportunities; similarly, if the proper admission fee were charged, there would not be excessive fishing activity in our illustrative lake. For the case of depletable ex-

---

[22] This is admittedly a highly simplified representation of the fishing case. We are assuming, for example, that the catch in one period is independent of that during earlier periods and also that the supply of fish from the lake is sufficiently small to have no impact on the market price of fish.

ternalities, the usual explanation is quite correct: if there is a misallocation, it arises simply because we have failed to put an appropriate price on the relevant resources or services.

However, for the undepletable externality, the matter is quite different. Consider the familiar case of the local flower garden: suppose a number of competitive firms raise flowers for sale to commercial florists and by their industry's custom admit visitors to their uncrowded gardens without admission charge. Obviously the number of gardens supplied in these circumstances is likely not to be optimal. The potential marginal private yield of a garden will typically be less than its marginal social yield, for the private returns do not include the value it brings to the visitors who will see it each day. Firms will provide an optimal number of gardens only if they charge an admission price to visitors in addition to the price they obtain from the sale of their crop. The difficulty is that *any nonzero price must also produce an inefficiency.* The fee will generally discourage some visitors from coming to the garden, and, because the marginal social cost of an additional visitor is zero, this clearly is undesirable.

This, then, is the dilemma. The optimal price to the *supplier* of an external benefit is positive, just as that for the *supplier* of a detrimental externality is negative (a charge for the social damage he inflicts). But the optimal price to the *consumer* of an undepletable externality is zero, because an increase in the number of consumers of such externalities has, by definition, neither costs nor benefits to others.[23] Obviously, no price can simultaneously be zero and nonzero; the price system is thus inherently incapable of dealing with such cases.[24]

4. SHOULD THE VICTIMS OF EXTERNALITIES BE TAXED OR COMPENSATED?

Before pursuing the role of the price system in this matter, we must consider the case of undepletable externalities a bit further. Smoke is a familiar and clear-cut case of an undepletable externality; the fact that my

[23] Arrow ("Organization of Economic Activity," Congress Joint Economic Committee, *The Analysis and Evaluation of Public Expenditures*, p. 58) offers an observation that may perhaps be the obverse of our conclusion here. He points out that, where an externality is present, "we can determine a shadow price for the buyer; this will differ from the price, zero, received by the seller. Hence, formally, the failure of markets for externalities to exist can also be described as a difference of prices between buyer and seller." This observation corresponds to condition 2 in our discussion of the definition of externalities, rather than as a characterization of the difficulty in dealing with them via the normal price mechanism, the subject we are now considering.

[24] Arrow (*ibid.*, p. 59) seems to ascribe externalities to "(1) inability to exclude [and] (2) lack of necessary information to permit market transactions to be concluded." It strikes us that these come closer to characterizing the depletable than the undepletable case.

house is enveloped by smoke does not, in general, reduce (or increase) the damage to my neighbor. The preceding discussion seems to imply that my neighbor and I should be charged a zero price (receive no compensation) for the smoke damage we consume. How would some misallocation result if he and I were both to receive compensation (a negative price for smoke inhalation) to cover our loss? Coase has supplied the answer to this question.[25] In this case, optimality generally requires some degree of geographic separation between smoky factories and private residences. If all neighbors of factories were paid amounts sufficient to compensate them fully not only for the unpleasantness, but for their increased laundry bills, the damage to their health, and so on, obviously no one would have any motivation to live away from the factory. Too many persons would choose to live in smoky conditions, for they would, in effect, have been offered an economic incentive to accept the ill effects of smoke with no offsetting benefits to anyone. The resulting inefficiency should be clear enough.

Looked at another way, the problem we are considering can be taken to involve two variables that together determine the magnitude of the total social damage. These variables are the amount of smoke emitted by the factory and the number of persons who locate themselves close to the factory. An excessive amount of smoke emission and an excessive number of nearby residents should both be avoided. Excessive smoke emission can be curbed by a Pigouvian tax on the producer. Now Coase's analysis has suggested that, to prevent too many nearby residents, it may be necessary to impose a tax on those who live nearby. Far from compensating the victims of the externality, Coase's view is that they should be charged for the smoke they inhale.

However, as the analysis of the next chapter confirms, neither compensation nor taxation of the victims is compatible with optimal resource allocation. No tax upon the victims is necessary; the smoke itself will keep residents away. Because smoke is an undepletable externality, A's inhalation of smoke will affect no one but himself and, so, at a zero price (tax) he will absorb the full social cost of his location decision. The decision that is optimal privately will be optimal socially as well. On the other hand, if he were to be compensated for smoke damage, he would be relieved of the real cost of his decision and then Coase's problem would indeed arise: too many persons would end up living next to the factory.

This point has been recognized in the case of detrimental externalities by Olson and Zeckhauser: ". . . the commonplace suggestion that those who generate external diseconomies ought to have to compensate their victims for any losses they suffer, can work against Pareto optimality. When such a suggestion is adopted, those injured by the diseconomy have no in-

[25] R. H. Coase, "Problem of Social Cost," *Journal of Law and Economics*.

centive to protect themselves from it, even if this should be more economical than requiring adjustments on the part of those who generate the diseconomy." [26]

The undesirability of either compensation or taxation of victims (at least as an allocative matter) is fortunate from the administrative point of view, because in practice, the calculation and payment of compensation to the myriad persons affected by externalities would seem virtually impossible.

5. SUMMARY: PRICING, TAXATION, AND DEPLETABILITY OF EXTERNAL EFFECTS

We see then that only in the case of depletable externalities can an extension of the ordinary price system serve as an effective allocation mechanism. In that case alone, it is true that the levying of a price for the social resources involved can assure their efficient utilization. In other words, this is the one case where taxes upon the generator of the externalities together with compensation of the victims *at the same rate per unit* will produce the desired results.

In contrast, where the externalities are undepletable, no price can do the job. It has long been recognized that no ordinary price system will produce a satisfactory allocation of resources to public goods. We have now found a slightly different way of looking at the matter. The trouble in this case is that optimality requires a pricing asymmetry: a nonzero price to the supplier of the externality (a positive price for an external benefit and a negative price for one that is detrimental) and a zero price for the consumption of the externality. This is the general requirement for the pricing of any pure public good.

Now, as has already been noted, no ordinary price can meet this requirement. *However, a Pigouvian tax (subsidy) can.* Indeed, one of the remarkable properties of this device is that it can assume either the symmetry required in the depletable case or the asymmetry called for when externalities are undepletable. The tax or subsidy to the supplier serves as the required

---

[26] M. Olson, Jr. and R. Zeckhauser, "The Efficient Production of External Economies," *American Economic Review* LX (June, 1970), 512–17. The allocative problems that can be produced by full compensation are well-known in other contexts. Full payment by an insurance company for all losses from theft removes any incentive for precautions against robbery; it makes for an inadequate allocation of resources to burglary prevention devices. Or to bring the matter out more sharply with the aid of a rather grizzly example, suppose workers, *on the average*, were known to feel fully compensated for the loss of a finger by the payment of one million dollars. Imagine the horror that might result if industrial insurance were to offer this compensation to anyone suffering from such a loss! In each of these cases, the *absence* of full coverage is essential for the prevention of what may conservatively be described as great economic waste.

nonzero price for the externalities he generates. Symmetry can then be achieved in the depletable case by using the proceeds (positive or negative) to compensate those who are affected by the externality, for example, the tax charged to those who employ workers trained by others can be used to subsidize the suppliers of the training. Similarly, the asymmetry in the important undepletable case can be attained by simple absorption of the tax proceeds into the public treasury, so that the charges to consumers of the external effect are then zero, as optimality requires.

So much for the polar cases corresponding roughly to the pure public and pure private goods. What about the mixed cases? One difficulty here is that there is some ambiguity about the definition of an "impure public good." For our purpose, this term may be taken to have two meanings.[27]

a.   The Case of Eventual Congestion.   This involves activities in which there is zero depletion of the external effect at modest values of the relevant variables, but where depletion (congestion) may set in at increased utilization levels.[28] Thus, with a hundred visitors a day to our illustrative garden, an additional visitor does not reduce any other person's pleasure or add to anyone's costs; however, with five thousand visitors per day matters may change significantly, with marginal visitors imposing nontrivial costs on others.

b.   Mixed Externalities.   The other intermediate case is one in which an economic activity can be taken to generate two externalities: one depletable and one undepletable (even though the two may not be distinguishable physically). An example is an expansion in output that increases the availability of on-the-job training (a depletable externality) and simultaneously improves the social climate (reduces crime rates, and so on) in impoverished areas.

A moment's reflection shows how our results can be adapted to these two cases.

a.   The case of eventual congestion remains an instance of a pure public good so long as *marginal* depletion remains zero. When congestion does finally materialize, a price should be charged to all of those receiving benefits from the externality. In terms of our garden example, there should

---

[27] Our discussion of this subject here and in the next chapter has benefited from ideas offered by Sally E. Holtermann, "Externalities and Public Goods," *Economica* N.S. XXXIX, no. 153 (February, 1972), 78–87.

[28] For a formal treatment of congestion as a source of "impurity" in public goods, see J. M. Buchanan, "An Economic Theory of Clubs," *Economica*, XXXII N.S. (February, 1965), 1–14; and J. M. Litvack and W. E. Oates, "Group Size and the Output of Public Goods: Theory and an Application to State-Local Finance in the United States," *Public Finance* XXV, No. 1 (1970), 42–58.

be no admission fee charged to visitors so long as they are sufficiently few
to impose no costs of congestion (perhaps on weekdays), but during periods
when the number of visitors rises to a level at which they impose such costs
(say on weekends), then an admission fee should be charged to all visitors
to the garden. However, until congestion occurs, because an additional unit
of consumption imposes no costs on others, it is inappropriate to stimulate
or discourage an additional unit of consumption by a positive or negative
price.[29]

   b. The mixed case, in effect, requires the imposition of two sets of
prices: one for the private depletable externality and another for the public
undepletable externality. The former requires a price, p_d, upon each unit of
the externality generated and an identical price, p_d, per unit of the externality
consumed. The latter, as before, calls for a nonzero price, p_u, per unit of
the externality supplied and a price of zero on each unit consumed. Hence
the total optimal price is $(p_d + p_u)$ to the producer of the externality and
$(p_d + 0) = p_d$ to its consumer (victim). Thus, although the latter price is no
longer zero, as in the case of pure public externalities, the fundamental asymmetry in the optimal price structure remains. This sort of asymmetrical
pricing can be achieved by means of a Pigouvian tax with partial compensation or by a combination of an ordinary price, p_d, plus a Pigouvian subsidy
(tax), p_u, upon the generator of the externality.

   Thus, either in the case of the externalities that are undepletable or in
the mixed cases, which between them seem to encompass the bulk of externalities that significantly affect public policy, the imposition of an ordinary
price is not an appropriate remedy. All such cases are characterized by the
fundamental pricing asymmetry requiring either zero or, at most, partial
compensation of the victims.

6.   TECHNOLOGICAL AND PECUNIARY EXTERNALITIES

   In a paper that is now one of the classics of economic literature, Jacob
Viner showed that not all relationships that appear to involve externalities
will produce resource misallocation.[30] There is a category of pseudoexternal-
ities, the *pecuniary externalities*, in which one individual's activity level affects
the financial circumstances of another, but which need not produce a mis-

---

   [29] As we will see in the next chapter, the relevant price is the dual structural variable
corresponding to the constraint (resource limitation) responsible for the congestion. A
standard result of duality theory tells us that this shadow price must be zero so long as the
corresponding capacity is not utilized fully.
   [30] Viner, "Cost Curves and Supply Curves," *Zeitschrift für Nationalökonomie.*

allocation of resources in a world of pure competition. Viner brought the distinction to our attention to clear up an error in Pigou. The nature of the error is now largely a matter of doctrinal history and does not particularly concern us here. However (despite some recent assertions to the contrary), the distinction remains of great relevance for current discussions of externalities.

Pecuniary externalities result from a change in the prices of some inputs or outputs in the economy. An increase in the number of shoes demanded raises the price of leather and hence affects the welfare of the purchasers of handbags. But unlike a true externality (Viner called it a *technological externality*), it does not generate a *shift* in the handbag production function.

It should be emphasized that, whether an externality is pecuniary or technological, the ultimate comparative static effects are likely to involve changes both in prices *and* in the values of the relevant real variables. In the case of technological externalities (for example, the increased real resource cost of laundry output resulting from an enlarged volume of smoke), prices will almost certainly be affected (laundry prices will rise) and even input prices may well be altered as their usage is changed. Similarly, in the pecuniary case, say in the case of a rise in the price of leather produced by an increased demand for shoes, the handbag manufacturers may well modify their manufacturing processes by, for example, the substitution of labor for leather through more careful cutting of the raw materials.

The essence of the distinction then is *not* that a pecuniary externality affects only the values of monetary, rather than real, variables. The point is that the introduction of a technological externality produces a *shift* in the functions relating quantities of resources as independent variables and output quantities or utility levels of consumers as dependent variables. Consequently, it means—comparing two otherwise identical states in which there is a technological externality in one, but not in the other—that a given vector of real inputs allocated identically in both cases will *not* leave all members of the economy indifferent between the two states. In contrast, the introduction of a pecuniary externality permits all members of the economy to remain at their initial utility levels *if all inputs are used as before* and if there is an appropriate redistribution of income to compensate for the income effects of the price changes that are the instrument of that externality.

The smoke that increases the soap and labor costs of the laundry means that, if one were to employ the same quantities of inputs as would be used in the absence of the externality, either fewer clothes must be laundered or the clothes cannot come out as clean. But with the enhanced demand for shoes, it need take no more leather than before to produce a handbag. The higher price of handbags represents, in effect, only a transfer of income from purchasers of handbags or from handbag manufacturers to the suppliers of leather, or perhaps, in the long-run competitive equilibrium, from handbag purchasers to the owners of land for cattle grazing. But the initial collection of inputs will still be capable of producing the initial bundle of outputs and, hence, of leaving everyone as well off as he would have been in the absence of the increased demand for shoes.

This immediately suggests why pecuniary externalities need produce no resource misallocation under conditions of pure competition. For they do not constitute any change in the real efficiency of the productive process viewed as a means to transform inputs into utility levels of the members of the economy. Indeed, the price effects that constitute the pecuniary externalities are merely the normal competitive mechanism for the reallocation of resources in response to changes in demands or factor supplies.

Viewed another way, our increased demand for shoes, for example, may well induce a rise in the production (and in the relative cost) of shoes compared to pencils. However, this takes the form of a movement along the production-possibility frontier; it does not shift the frontier itself, as would a change in the output of smoke by our illustrative factory, that is, it causes no divergence between the slope (social marginal rate of transformation) and the private MRT at any point on this frontier. Similarly, because a pecuniary externality enters no utility function, it will produce no divergence between any social and private MRS.

This suggests the irrelevance of pecuniary externalities for the optimality of the market equilibrium of the competitive system. Equilibrium conditions for the competitive system consist (where the relevant functions are twice differentiable) of a set of equalities and inequalities involving only *private* marginal rates of substitution and transformation (that is, those of the decision maker to whose decision variables the marginal rates apply). Optimality of resource allocation, however, requires the satisfaction of precisely the same equalities and inequalities but this time involving the *social* marginal rates of substitution and transformation. Because pecuniary externalities produce no divergences between private and social marginal rates of substitution and transformation, they do not create any differences between the optimality conditions and those characterizing a competitive equilibrium. Consequently, despite the presence of pecuniary externalities, the competitive equilibrium will produce an optimal allocation of resources, provided, of course, that all of the other necessary conditions (existence, the appropriate convexity-concavity requirements, and so on) are fulfilled.

7. VARIATIONS IN PIGOUVIAN TAXES AS PECUNIARY EXTERNALITIES

The analysis of the preceding section can shed some light on the optimality of the Pigouvian tax measures. It has been argued recently that the imposition of such a tax can itself introduce a set of externalities, for those who are protected by the tax can, by their own decisions, affect the magnitude of the payment. If a household moves near a smoke-generating factory or undertakes to do more laundry in its vicinity, the social damage caused by the smoke will be increased and this, in turn, will lead to an increase in the tax rate that will harm the factory owner; this rise in tax rate constitutes an externality caused by the decision of the household just as surely as the smoke produced by the factory. In the words of Professor Coase,

> An increase in the number of people living or of business operating in the vicinity of the smoke-emitting factory will increase the amount of harm produced by a given emission of smoke. The tax that would be imposed would therefore increase with an increase in the number of those in the vicinity. This will tend to lead to a decrease in the value of production of the factors employed by the factory, either because a reduction in production due to the tax will result in factors being used elsewhere in ways which are less valuable, or because factors will be diverted to produce means for reducing the amount of smoke emitted. But people deciding to establish themselves in the vicinity of the factory will not take into account this fall in the value of production which results from their presence. This failure to take into account costs imposed on others is comparable to the action of a factory-owner in not taking into account the harm resulting from his emission of smoke.[31]

This rising tax relationship that Professor Coase described is equivalent, analytically, to a *pecuniary*, not a *technological*, externality. It need produce no misallocation of resources. Again, this is not difficult to show. The generation of smoke increases the real resource cost of laundry production and perhaps influences the marginal utility of various types of consumption as well. However, the increase in the tax has no such effects. It merely changes the marginal *pecuniary* return to the activities of the factory. An increase in laundry activity that increases the tax rate is precisely analogous to an increase in shoe production that increases the cost of leather to handbag manufacturers. In each case, a resource (in one case, leather, in the other, clean air) has become more valuable and the price of the resource has increased commensurately, as proper resource allocation requires.

It is true that the rise in tax rates has some real effects and not just pecuniary consequences: it leads ". . . to a decrease in the value of production of the factors employed by the factory," but exactly the same is true in the handbag example. People formerly employed in handbag production may, because of higher leather prices, find themselves "being used elsewhere in ways which are [or, rather, formerly were] less valuable." But this is, of

[31] R. H. Coase, "Problem of Social Cost," *Journal of Law and Economics*, Section IX, p. 42.

course, a common property of pecuniary externalities, one that has already been emphasized. Price changes do have real effects on the equilibrium values of various economic variables but need not result in resource misallocation.

chapter 4

A Gallery of Externalities Models

In this chapter we construct and examine a series of basic models whose structures incorporate our various cases of externalities. With the aid of these models, we determine the conditions necessary and sufficient for the market mechanism to provide a Pareto-optimal allocation of resources in the presence of external effects. In particular, the models are used to derive formally the results we obtained in the previous chapter for the undepletable, the depletable, and the mixed cases. Moreover, we will use these basic models, not only to prove the results that were just arrived at on an intuitive basis, but also as prototypes for the constructs needed in the applications in later chapters. In much of this subsequent discussion, simpler versions of these models will suffice for our purposes, but, in each case, the manner in which the analysis can be modified to give it the degree of detail and generality of the constructs of this chapter should be clear.

Throughout the book we will utilize general equilibrium models almost exclusively. In welfare economics, perhaps as much as in any branch of our subject, there is real danger in partial analysis. When we consider expanding one sector of the economy, say, because of the net social benefits that it generates, it is essential that we take into account where the necessary resources will come from and what the consequences in other sectors will be. Interdependence among location decisions, levels of polluting outputs, and the use of pollution-suppressing devices are all at the heart of the problem. Indeed, the very concept of externalities implies a degree of interdependence sufficient to cast doubt upon the reliability of the partial analysis that, curiously, has most frequently characterized writings in this area.[1]

A general equilibrium analysis, however, need not bring with it the degree of complexity and abstraction that the nonspecialist often associates with the approach. One of Sir John Hicks's many significant contributions (and one that apparently is not always recognized) is what may be referred to as the "macro-general-equilibrium model," one in which all sectors of the economy are present but are so highly aggregated that the model becomes fairly easy to handle. The aggregation may, for example, proceed by dividing the economy into four sectors: the markets for goods, labor, money, and bonds; or (as will normally be most useful for us) it may separate explicitly two or three outputs and then employ one remaining portmanteau variable to represent "all other goods." This chapter makes little use of this simplification, but we will employ it in many of our discussions thereafter. The reader may well find it interesting to observe how easy this approach makes it to draw concrete conclusions from a model that has all the safeguards of a general equilibrium formulation.

1. PARETO OPTIMALITY IN THE UNDEPLETABLE (PUBLIC) EXTERNALITIES MODEL

As we will see, the model appropriate for the analysis of undepletable (public) externalities has basic differences from that which incorporates depletable (private) external effects; moreover, the two lead to results that are quite different. This section's model describes the undepletable case; later sections analyze the depletable and mixed cases. We examine the model for undepletable externalities in far greater detail than any of the others, because we consider it to be the case that is most important for policy. Indeed, the remainder of the book deals with this case almost exclusively. In any event, there is no need to go over all three cases with equal care, because the analysis is so similar.

Our strategy is to proceed in two steps. In this section, we derive necessary conditions for Pareto optimality. Then, in the two sections that follow, we can determine fairly easily, with the aid of simple models of the behavior of the individual and the firm, what prices and taxes are necessary to induce firms and individuals to behave in a manner compatible with the requirements for Pareto optimality.

---

[1] More recently, a number of general equilibrium models have appeared. See the references given in Chapter 2. See also the illuminating paper by H. Mohring and J. H. Boyd, "Analyzing 'Externalities': 'Direct Interaction' vs 'Asset Utilization' Frameworks," *Economica*, New Series, XXXVIII (November, 1971), 347–61.

Assume we have a perfectly competitive economy.[2] Let the productive activities of the firms generate an externality (for concreteness, it will be referred to as *smoke*) that increases the cost of (at least some) other production processes and constitutes a disutility to consumers. The choice of activity levels, including levels of outputs and input usage, are taken to influence the firm's output of smoke either directly or indirectly through the use of less polluting technological processes. Similarly, by the choice *both* of activity levels and of location, individuals and firms determine their vulnerability to smoke damage.

We use the following notation:

$$x_{ij} = \text{the amount of good (resource)}^3 \; i \text{ consumed by}$$
$$\text{individual } j, \; (i = 1, \ldots, n) \, (j = 1, \ldots, m),$$

$$y_{ik} = \text{the amount of good (resource) } i \text{ produced (used)}$$
$$\text{by firm } k, \; (i = 1, \ldots, n) \, (k = 1, \ldots, h)$$

$$r_i = \text{the total quantity of resource } i \text{ available to the}$$
$$\text{community}$$

$$s_k = \text{the emission of externality (smoke) by firm } k$$

$$z = \sum s_k = \text{total emissions in the community,}$$

$$u^j(x_{1j}, \ldots, x_{nj}, z) = \text{individual } j\text{'s utility function}$$

and

$$f^k(y_{1k}, \ldots, y_{nk}, s_k, z) \leq 0 = \text{firm } k\text{'s production function.}$$

Here the variable z in each utility and production function represents the possibility that the utility (production) of the corresponding individual (firm) is affected by the output of the externality in the community. This clearly represents the undepletable (public) externalities case in which any emission can enter into every utility and production function (that is, in which the amount of the externality consumed by one individual does not reduce the amount available to any other person or firm).

---

[2] The reader is reminded that, in accord with the Pigouvian tradition, our pure competition assumption is taken to involve both a "large number" of producers and a "large number" of consumers of the externality, in the sense that each one of them takes the magnitudes of the pertinent prices and taxes as given and beyond his influence. Thus, everyone in the economy is assumed to be a "price taker" in this extended sense. Without this premise, one gets into problems of monopolistic strategies designed to affect the levels of taxes and prices to be used to control externalities. This case is discussed briefly in Chapter 6.

[3] We do not distinguish here between manufactured goods and resources, such as land or labor. In the short run, even the consumption of a manufactured good can be constrained by the quantity of that item inherited from the past.

We assume that the feasible set of consumption complexes for each consumer is convex, closed, bounded from below in the x's, and contains the null vector, that the utility function that represents each person's preferences is twice differentiable, quasi-concave, and increasing in the x's, and that the feasible production set for each firm is defined by a set of technical constraints that are twice differentiable and define a convex production possibility set. Under these circumstances, as is well-known, the solution to the maximization problem that is about to be described exists and is unique.

To find a Pareto optimum, we maximize the utility of any arbitrarily chosen individual, say individual 1, subject to the requirements that there be no consequent loss to any other individual, and that the constraints constituted by the production functions and the availability of resources are satisfied. Our problem, then, is to

Maximize

$$u^1(x_{11}, \ldots, x_{n1}, z) \tag{1}$$

subject to

$$\left. \begin{aligned} u^j(x_{1j}, \ldots, x_{nj}, z) &\geq u^{*j} & (j = 2, \ldots, m) \\ f^k(y_{1k}, \ldots, y_{nk}, s_k, z) &\leq 0 & (k = 1, \ldots, h) \\ \sum_{j=1}^{m} x_{ij} - \sum_{k=1}^{h} y_{ik} &\leq r_i. & (i = 1, \ldots, n) \\ \text{all} \quad x_{ij} \geq 0, \quad s_k \geq 0, & \quad z \geq 0. \end{aligned} \right\} \tag{2}$$

Note that we do *not* require all $y_{ik} \geq 0$, for some firms may use the outputs of other firms as inputs (intermediate goods), and this is described by treating y_{ik} as a negative output when it is employed as an input.[4]

Because of our concavity-convexity assumptions we can use the Kuhn-Tucker theorem to characterize the desired maximum. We obtain the Lagrangian[5]

---

[4] Because y_{ik} is unrestricted in sign, as is well-known, the corresponding partial derivative of the Lagrangian will be set equal to zero, not less than or equal to zero as in the Kuhn-Tucker condition corresponding to a variable that is restricted to take only nonnegative values.

This assumption that y_{ik} is unrestricted in sign for all i is of course not always valid, for although every output can serve as an input in the form of inventory, the reverse is not true of inputs, such as "the original and indestructible powers of the soil" (land) that cannot be manufactured by firms. That is, the corresponding variable cannot take a positive value. The discussion would be complicated needlessly by taking this into account throughout and we provide the appropriate amendments in footnotes.

[5] Here we may, if we prefer, take $\lambda_1 = 1$ and $u^{*1} = 0$, so that the first term in L becomes $\sum_{j=1}^{m} \lambda_j[u^j(\cdot) - u^{*j})] = u^1 + \sum_{j=2}^{m} \lambda_j[u^j(\cdot) - u^{*j})]$, the latter, of course, being the

$$L = \sum \lambda_j[u^j(\cdot) - u^{*j}] - \sum \mu_k f^k(\cdot) + \sum_i \omega_i \left(r_i - \sum_j x_{ij} + \sum_k y_{ik}\right)$$

where the Greek letters all represent Lagrange multipliers. Differentiating in turn with respect to the x_{ij}, y_{ik}, and s_k we obtain the Kuhn-Tucker conditions given in the second column of Table 4-1. Here we use the notation $u_i^j = \partial u^j/\partial x_{ij}, f_i^k = \partial f^k/\partial y_{ik}$, and so on. It will be recalled also from an earlier footnote that there is only a single equality condition corresponding to the variable y_{ik}, because that variable is unrestricted in sign.

Conditions (3°)–(5°), together with the constraints[6] (2) and the concavity-convexity conditions described earlier, are necessary conditions for *any* Pareto optimum. That is, *no* candidate solution that violates *any* of these conditions can be a Pareto optimum.

2. MARKET EQUILIBRIUM: UNDEPLETABLE EXTERNALITIES

We will return presently to an economic interpretation of the Kuhn-Tucker conditions for a Pareto optimum, (3°)–(5°). However, it is more convenient to consider first the corresponding market equilibrium requirements. Specifically, our objective is to determine the characteristics of the prices and taxes (compensations), assuming that they exist,[7] that will induce the behavior patterns necessary (and sufficient) for the satisfaction of our Pareto-optimality conditions, and whether that set of prices and taxes is unique.

It is helpful to employ an admittedly artificial distinction between prices and compensatory taxes or subsidies. A *price*, in our competitive model, is a pecuniary quantity charged on each unit of some activity, whose magnitude is the same for all buyers and sellers. If a pair of gloves of some

---

form more usually encountered in the literature. With our concavity-convexity assumptions, the two forms are equivalent.

[6] Associated with the inequality constraints we also have the corresponding complementary slackness conditions

$$\lambda_j[u^j(\cdot) - u^{*j}] = 0, \qquad \mu_k f^k(\cdot) = 0, \quad \text{and}$$
$$\omega_i(r_i - \sum_j x_{ij} + \sum_k y_{ik}) = 0.$$

[7] As was noted in Chapter 1, we will not concern ourselves with the issue of the existence of a competitive solution that is consistent with any particular Pareto optimum. This subject has, of course, been explored in an extensive literature following Kenneth J. Arrow's classic paper. Our object here is to *describe* the prices and taxes that are part of such an equilibrium, on the premise that the existence issue has been settled. Of course, this is not meant to imply that the existence literature is either trivial or uninteresting, but only that it has not yielded any clear implications for policy, which are the primary concern of this volume. A noteworthy exception arises out of the relationship of externalities and violation of the convexity conditions, a subject that is examined in detail in Chapter 8.

TABLE 4–1

KUHN-TUCKER CONDITIONS: UNDEPLETABLE EXTERNALITIES

Variable	Pareto Optimality	Market Equilibrium	Prices
x_{ij}	(3°) $\begin{aligned} &\lambda_j \mu_4^j - \omega_i \leq 0 \\ &x_{ij}(\lambda_j \mu_4^j - \omega_i) = 0 \\ &\text{(all } i,j) \end{aligned}$	(3°) $\begin{aligned} &p_i - \alpha_j \mu_4^j + t_i^j \geq 0 \\ &x_{ij}(p_i - \alpha_j \mu_4^j + t_i^j) = 0 \\ &\text{(all } i,j) \end{aligned}$	$\begin{aligned} p_i &= \omega_i \\ t_i^j &= t_i^* \end{aligned}$
y_{ik}	(4°)ⓐ $\begin{aligned} &-\mu_k f_i^k + \omega_i = 0 \\ &\text{(all } i,k) \end{aligned}$	(4°)ⓐ $\begin{aligned} &p_i - \beta_k f_t^k - t_i^k = 0 \\ &\text{(all } i,k) \end{aligned}$	$\begin{aligned} p_i &= \omega_i \\ t_i^k &= t_i^* \end{aligned}$
$s_{\bar{k}}$	(5°)ⓑ $\begin{aligned} &-\mu_{\bar{k}} f_s^{\bar{k}} + \sum_j \lambda_j \mu_z^j - \sum_k \mu_{\bar{k}} f_z^k \leq 0 \\ &s_{\bar{k}}\Big(-\mu_{\bar{k}} f_s^{\bar{k}} + \sum_j \lambda_j \mu_z^j - \sum_k \mu_{\bar{k}} f_z^k\Big) = 0 \\ &\text{(all } \bar{k}) \end{aligned}$	(5°)ⓑ $\begin{aligned} &-t_s - \beta_{\bar{k}} f_s^{\bar{k}} \leq 0 \\ &s_{\bar{k}}(-t_s - \beta_{\bar{k}} f_s^{\bar{k}}) = 0 \\ &\text{(all } \bar{k}) \end{aligned}$	$\begin{aligned} t_s &= -\sum_j \lambda_j \mu_z^j \\ &+ \sum \mu_{\bar{k}} f_z^k \end{aligned}$

ⓐ For inputs that cannot be manufactured by the firm, (4°) and (4°) must be replaced by the pairs of Kuhn-Tucker conditions similar to those in (3°) and (3°).

ⓑ Here it is necessary to distinguish between the firm $\bar{k}$, that generates the externality, and the other firms, k, that are affected by it. The bar is omitted where this distinction is not pertinent.

specification sells for $5.80, then anyone can buy it for exactly that price, and, similarly, each seller will also receive $5.80 per pair.

A compensatory tax or a subsidy rate, however, will presumably depend on the smoke damage *to* the individual or firm and hence will differ from person to person and from firm to firm. If the optimal value of that tax turns out to be negative, it will represent a compensation payment to the victim. On the other hand, if it is positive, à la Coase, it will presumably represent an inducement to the victim to take measures to protect himself from the damage (for example, by moving away from the source of emissions).[8] We then assign to each consumer and firm a tax (compensation) payment for smoke damage he or it suffers, where we use t^j and t^k to designate the tax rate for individual j and firm k, respectively, the objective being to determine Pareto-optimal values for the t^j and the t^k.

The magnitudes of these tax-compensation rates must obviously depend on the victim's activity levels. If an exogenous shift in laundry demand leads to an increase in output, the damage caused the laundry by the polluter's smoke will necessarily increase. Hence, compensation payments to the laundry must rise correspondingly. Thus t^j and t^k cannot be treated as constants but must be considered functions of j's and k's respective decision variables.

We also impose on the emission of smoke a tax rate, t_s, per unit of emission whose optimal value is to be determined.

---

[8] In our model, the victim can, indeed, take such protective action. For example, if item i' is land in a smoky area and item i'' is land in an unpolluted neighborhood, a laundry (firm k) can reduce its vulnerability to smoke damage by increasing its use of i'' relative to i' (that is, by increasing the absolute value of $y_{i''k}$ and decreasing that of $y_{i'k}$).

It may seem at first glance that the ability of a consumer (producer) to reduce the damage he suffers from an undepletable (public) externality, for example, by relocation away from a smoky area or by investment in air conditioning, is inconsistent with the notion of a "public" externality. We sometimes think of a pure public good or bad as one that is available to all individuals (firms) in the same quantity. However, it is virtually impossible to think of a public good that is, in fact, available in equal quantity (or quality) in all locations, and whose consumption by the individual is unaffected by his various economic decisions. The quality of the air we breathe, for instance, obviously varies geographically and with the amount we spend on air conditioning. Even for the classic case of national defense, individuals located in particular areas (for example, away from priority enemy targets) may, in a sense, be better protected than others, though we can say that the same level of protection is available to everyone who makes a given location decision and whose other economic decisions are similar.

But the essential point is that all this is of little relevance to the argument. The only characteristic of a public good that is crucial for our analysis is that it is *undepletable:* the consumption of the good by an additional individual or firm *at any given location* does not reduce its availability to others at that or any other location. More formally, we can think of z in equation (1) (smoke emissions at a particular place) as entering all persons' utility functions, as we normally treat a public good, but with the disutility suffered depending also on the individual's location as indicated by his consumption of land, x_{i*}, in the $i*$th location. On public goods in a spatial setting, see Charles Tiebout, "An Economic Theory of Fiscal Decentralization," in *Public Finances: Needs, Sources, and Utilization.* (Princeton, 1961), pp. 79–96.

We can now proceed directly to examine the equilibrium of the consumer and of the firm. The consumer is taken to *minimize* the expenditure necessary to achieve any given level of utility,[9] u^{*i}, so that in Lagrangian form his problem is to find the saddle value of

$$L_j = \sum p_i x_{ij} + t^i + \alpha_j[u^{*i} - u^i(\cdot)], \tag{6}$$

(all $x_{ij} \geq 0$, where α_j is a Lagrange multiplier). We immediately obtain the Kuhn-Tucker conditions (3ᶜ) in Table 4–1.

Similarly, the objective of our (competitive) firm is taken to be maximization of profits after taxes subject to the constraint given by its production relation, $f^k \leq 0$. Its Lagrangian problem is to find the saddle value of

$$L_k = \sum p_i y_{ik} - t^k - t_s s_k - \beta_k f^k(\cdot) \tag{7}$$

$$s_k \geq 0, \qquad y_{ik} \text{ unrestricted,}^{10}$$

whose Kuhn-Tucker conditions are (4ᶜ) and (5ᶜ), in Table 4–1.

3. THE PRICE-TAX SOLUTION: UNDEPLETABLE CASE

Our objective now is to determine what values of emission taxes and damage-compensations (taxes) will induce consumers and firms to select Pareto-optimal activity levels. That is, we want to know what tax structure can sustain a competitive equilibrium that is Pareto-optimal. We will prove first that this *can* be achieved by setting

$$t_s = -\sum \lambda_j u_z^j + \sum \mu_k f_z^k, \qquad \text{all } t_i^j = t_i^k = 0. \tag{8a}$$

Note that (8a) calls for a zero derivative both of t^i with respect to any x_{ij} and of t^k with respect to y_{ik}. That is, even if damage from the externality varies with the victim's activity levels, it requires compensation payments to be completely unaffected by those activity levels (contrary to the concept of a compensation payment that we have just formulated).

To show that conditions (8a) are sufficient to induce the market to satisfy the Pareto-optimality requirements, note that competitive equilibrium

---

[9] We proceed in this manner rather than following the usual premise that the consumer maximizes the utility he derives from his income because our approach simplifies matters somewhat. First, it produces results more immediately comparable with (3°) because then the Lagrange multiplier multiplies the marginal utility rather than the price both in (3°) and in (3ᶜ). Moreover, our procedure evades the determination of the consumer's income which is clearly affected by the prices of the resources he holds. In any event, though, the two approaches are *not* quite equivalent, clearly either is valid for our purposes.

[10] With the exceptions noted in an earlier footnote.

is characterized by conditions (3^c) − (5^c) together with constraints (2) (including among them the market-clearance condition $\sum x_{ij} - \sum y_{ik} \leq r_i$) and the complementary slackness conditions corresponding to (2). Substituting the values of t_s, t_i^j and, t_i^k from (8a) into (3^c) − (5^c), we see that the system of inequalities and equations determining the competitive equilibrium (i.e., those determining the values of the variables x_{ij}^c, y_{ik}^c, s_k^c, α_j, β_k, and p_i) becomes identical with the system of inequalities and equations (2), (3°) − (5°) and the complementary slackness conditions for (2) that determine a Pareto-optimal solution: x_{ij}^o, y_{ik}^o, s_k^o, λ_j, μ_k, and ω_i. Thus, these systems will have the same solutions, so that if they are unique[11]

$$p_i = \omega_i \qquad \lambda_j = \alpha_j \qquad \mu_k = \beta_k \qquad \text{(all } i, j, k). \tag{8b}$$

Thus we have

Proposition One. Conditions (8a) are sufficient to render identical the competitive equilibrium and the Pareto-optimality conditions. That is, given the assumed convexity conditions, market behavior subject to this set of taxes will yield an optimal allocation of resources.

By (8a) and (8b) we have in fact proven that neither any tax nor any compensation of the victims of externalities is *necessary* to sustain *any* Pareto optimum, for $t^j \equiv 0$ and $t^k \equiv 0$ will obviously satisfy (8a) if t_s, the tax on the generation of the externality, is set appropriately. It may, however, be asked whether compensation or taxation of the victims is even possible without preventing the attainment of a Pareto optimum; that is, we may ask whether conditions (8a) are absolutely required for an optimum. The answer is that they are if we accept one plausible premise: that there exists one item, some of which is consumed by every individual.[12]

To deal with this issue, the uniqueness of the tax-compensation solution (8a), we must assume that there is a set of taxes and prices which yield equality between the market and Pareto-optimal activity levels [i.e., that there exist $x_{ij}^c = x_{ij}^o$, $y_{ik}^c = y_{ik}^o$, and $s_k^c = s_k^o$, which satisfy both (3^c) − (5^c) and (3°) − (5°)]. We then ask what values of the p_i, t_s, t^j, and t^k are consistent with these relationships.

For this purpose we can take leisure (labor) to be the item which is used by every individual (no one works 24 hours per day).

---

[11] It will be noted that even if the solution is otherwise unique, one can multiply all of the p_i, t_s, t^j, and t^k and all the Lagrange multipliers in any solution by the same constant without violating (3) − (5), the only relationships in which these variables appear. This gives us our one degree of freedom in the choice of absolute prices and taxes. Even if the solutions to the market equilibrium and optimality requirements were not otherwise unique, of course (8b) would still hold for *corresponding* solutions to the two systems.

[12] We also require the absence of discontinuities in derivatives. For, at such a kinked point, the slope of the budget line is not generally fixed and hence the corresponding taxes are not unique.

Let i^* represent leisure-labor. Because of our premise all $x_{i^*j} > 0$, the corresponding conditions (3°) and (3ᶜ) become equalities.[13] Taking i^* as our standard of value, we set arbitrarily[14]

$$\omega_{i^*} = p_{i^*}. \tag{9}$$

We then obtain from (3°) and (3ᶜ), both of which are now assumed to be satisfied,

$$\lambda_j = \omega_{i^*}/u_{i^*}^j = p_{i^*}/u_{i^*}^j = \alpha_j \qquad \text{(for every } j\text{)} \tag{10}$$

and[15]

$$\mu_k = \omega_{i^*}/f_{i^*}^k = p_{i^*}/f_{i^*}^k = \beta_k \qquad \text{(for every } k\text{)}. \tag{11}$$

That is, each $\lambda_j = \alpha_j$ and each $\mu_k = \beta_k$.

Then by (3°) and (3ᶜ), we must have, for any one item, i', if it is consumed by individual j' and consumed or produced by firm k',

$$\omega_{i'} = p_{i'} + t_{i'}^{j'} = p_{i'} - t_{i'}^{k'}. \tag{12}$$

It follows immediately, because $\omega_{i'}-p_{i'}$ takes the same value for every individual and every firm (that is, it is independent of j' and k'), that we must have

$$\text{for all } x_{i'j'} > 0 \quad \text{and all } y_{i'k'}, \tag{13}$$
$$t_{i'}^{j'} = -t_{i'}^{k'} = \omega_{i'} - p_{i'},$$

which is independent of j' and k'. That is, Pareto optimality requires the amount of tax paid or compensation received by any individual or firm subjected to an externality to vary by exactly the same amount in response to a given change in the level of any of the activities in which he or it is engaged, that is,

$$t_i^j \equiv \frac{\partial t^j}{\partial x_{ij}} = -\frac{\partial t^k}{\partial y_{ik}} \equiv -t_i^k, \qquad \text{for all } x_{ij} > 0$$
$$\text{and all } y_{ik}.$$

Writing $t_i^* = t_i^j = -t_i^k$ and

---

[13] With each firm using labor, the corresponding conditions (4°) and (4ᶜ) remain equalities even though y_{i^*k} is not unrestricted in sign because the firm cannot manufacture labor.

[14] This is where we use up our factor of proportionality. The reader will verify that if we had instead set $p_{i^*} = a\omega_{i^*}$, all other prices and taxes in (8) would simply be multiplied by a.

[15] To derive $\beta_k = \mu_k$, we do not have to find any item used or produced by every firm. We merely need some item that is *potentially* either an output or an input for every firm so that the corresponding variable is unrestricted in sign and the corresponding conditions (4°) and (4ᶜ) are equations.

$$p_i^* = p_i + t_i^j = p_i - t_i^k = p_i + t_i^* = \omega_i, \qquad (14)$$

we see that the $p_i + t_i^j$ and $p_i - t_i^k$ are merely disguised forms of the ordinary prices, given by (8b). Consequently,

Proposition Two. Aside from a lump-sum subsidy or tax, the Pareto-optimal solution [as described by (1) and (2)] can be sustained only by a financial arrangement that does not differ from a set of prices p_i^* for all activity levels and a set of zero (incremental) tax or compensation levels.

From (5°) and (5ᶜ) we deduce immediately[16] the remainder of the price-tax solution (8), that is, we deduce the postulated pollution tax rate, t_s. Thus we conclude

Proposition Three. Aside from a factor of proportionality and for all $x_{ij} > 0$, conditions (8) are necessary for achievement of a Pareto-optimal equilibrium through a system of prices and taxes under a regime of pure competition.

4. INTERPRETATION OF THE RESULTS AND THE KUHN-TUCKER CONDITIONS

We can characterize the preceding results succinctly:

Proposition Four. The price-tax conditions (8) necessary to sustain the Pareto optimality of a competitive market solution under the assumed convexity conditions are tantamount to the standard Pigouvian rules, with neither taxes imposed upon, nor compensation paid to,[17] the victims of externalities (except possibly for lump-sum taxes or subsidies).

---

[16] That is, assuming t^k are not assumed to vary with s_k, the firm's own emissions. Otherwise, we must repeat the preceding argument to show that t^k must be identical for all firms and is therefore simply a camouflaged component of t_s.

[17] The fact that these will be zero only for $x_{ij} > 0$ does not restrict the generality of these conclusions, because for any variable that is zero, the marginal payment must clearly be zero.

The reason tax and compensation payments must be zero for Pareto optimality should be clear. If these payments really are to correspond to the magnitude of the damage they *must* vary with the values of the victim's decision variables. The laundry whose output increases in response to an autonomous shift in demand suffers more damage as a result. Hence, a true compensation payment to the laundry *must* vary with the laundry's output level. But that will serve as an inducement to the laundry to increase its output on its own volition and, consequently, will produce a violation of the requirements of Pareto optimality.

If all that is at issue is a single state equilibrium it must be admitted that compensation can indeed be arranged without precluding a Pareto optimum. For this purpose one need only (!) calculate the damage that would be sustained by each victim if the Pareto optimum were somehow to be attained. The victim can then be given in compensation a

This is obviously true of the prices in (8). The only thing that remains to be shown is that the tax rate, t_s, per unit of smoke emissions is indeed equal to the marginal social damage of smoke. For that purpose we again use leisure-labor, $i*$, as the standard of evaluation. Assume now that every firm uses *some* labor and that every individual consumes some leisure so that all $x_{i*j} > 0$ and all $y_{i*k} > 0$. Then the corresponding inequalities (3°) and (4°) must be equations. We may then write

$$\lambda_j = \omega_{i*}/u^j_{i*}, \qquad \mu_k = \omega_{i*}/f^k_{i*}. \tag{15}$$

Substituting these into the tax relationship in (8) we obtain[18]

$$t_s = \sum - \lambda_j u^j_z + \sum \mu_k f^k_z = \omega_{i*} \left[-\sum_j (u^j_z/u^j_{i*}) + \sum_k (f^k_z/f^k_{i*}) \right]. \tag{16}$$

But keeping output and utility levels fixed we have[19]

$$u^j_z/u^j_{i*} = -\partial x_{i*j}/\partial z, \qquad f^k_z/f^k_{i*} = \partial \bar{y}_{i*k}/\partial z, \tag{17}$$

[writing $\bar{y}_{i*k}$ for the absolute value of the (negative) input y_{i*k}]. These expressions represent the increase in quantity of labor needed to keep utilities or outputs and use of other inputs constant when there is a unit increase in smoke output in the community. Hence substituting from (17) into (16), t_s becomes

$$t_s = \omega_{i*} \left[\sum_j (\partial x_{i*j}/\partial z) + \sum_k (\partial \bar{y}_{i*k}/\partial z) \right]. \tag{18}$$

Interpreting the dual variable ω_{i*} in the usual manner as the shadow price of labor,[20] we see that (18) is indeed the marginal smoke damage, measured in terms of the *value* of the labor needed to offset the various types of damage.

Having thus shown the economic implications of our solution, we may

---

payment that exactly offsets that Pareto-optimal damage level, a lump-sum payment absolutely immune to change by an act of the victim. However, that payment would at once become inappropriate if there were any autonomous change in tastes, technology, etc., which would change the nature of the Pareto optimum and the corresponding damage levels. As usual, lump-sum taxes have little relevance for policy—even for the *theory* of policy.

[18] Note the similarity of the *RHS* of (16) to the well known Samuelson condition for optimality in the output of a public good in which the *sum* of its marginal rates of substitution with respect to a private good is the relevant datum. The reason for this similarity is obvious: we are dealing here with an externality that is, essentially, a public good.

[19] Thus, for example, holding all other variables constant, to keep j's utility constant we must have $0 = du^j = u^j_z dz + u^j_{i*} dx_{i*j}$ from which the result (17) follows directly.

[20] Specifically, if the derivative exists, we have $\omega_{i*} = \partial u^1/\partial r_{i*}$, the marginal utility of individual 1 (the person whose utility is being maximized) of a unit increase in the quantity of labor available.

return briefly to the Kuhn-Tucker conditions (3)–(4). Their interpretation is now straight forward. Using ω_{i*} as the shadow price of labor, we find from (15) that (3°) and (3ᶜ) call for prices to be proportionate to marginal utilities; similarly, (4°) and (4ᶜ) indicate that these same prices should be proportionate to the ratios of marginal costs (products), all measured in terms of labor if we wish.

Note also that (8) calls for a tax on smoke *emissions*, not on either inputs or outputs directly. Inputs and outputs that generate smoke are, of course, subject to tax, but only in proportion to the smoke they produce. Common sense confirms the logic of this rule. After all, one wants to motivate the firm to reduce the emissions it generates when it produces a given output or uses a given quantity of an input, and a tax on outputs or inputs that is independent of the pollution generated by them is certainly not the way to go about this.[21]

Observe, finally, that from standard Kuhn-Tucker theory we know that

$$\omega_i\left(r_i - \sum_j x_{ij} + \sum_k y_{ik}\right) = 0 \qquad (i = 1, \ldots, n).$$

Consequently, because by (8) our solution calls for $p_i = \omega_i$, we have

Proposition Five. The prices p_i that can sustain a Pareto optimum will be nonzero only for items used up completely in the corresponding optimal solution, that is,

$$p_{i'} > 0 \quad \text{implies} \quad \sum_j x_{i'j} = r_{i'} + \sum_k y_{i'k}.$$

Looked at the other way, any item not utilized fully in an optimal solution must be assigned a zero price:

$$\sum_j x_{i''j} < r_{i''} + \sum_k y_{i''k} \quad \text{implies} \quad p_{i''} = 0.$$

5. THE DEPLETABLE EXTERNALITIES MODEL

This completes our discussion of the undepletable (public) externalities case. Fortunately, the models for the depletable and the mixed cases that remain to be examined require only relatively minor modifications of the model of the preceding sections so that our discussion of these cases can be considerably shorter.

[21] Compare Charles R. Plott, "Externalities and Corrective Taxes," *Economica* N.S. XXXIII (February, 1966), 84–7.

The distinguishing characteristic of the depletable externalities case is the reduction in the amount of the external product that remains for everyone else whenever some individual or firm increases its consumption of that item.[22] Two changes are now required in our model. First, instead of a single variable $z = \sum s_k$ representing total emissions, we now have for each individual j a variable z_j and for each firm k a variable z_k representing the quantity of z utilized by him (it). Now it is z_j and not z that enters utility function $u^j(\cdot)$, and z_k is the variable that now enters the production function, $f^k(\cdot)$. As the second basic change in our model, we must now add the constraint

$$\sum z_j + \sum z_k \leq \sum s_k, \tag{19}$$

representing feasible distributions of the external output. Thus, our model consists of maximand (1) and constraints (2) with the substitution of z_j and z_k for z as just described, and, in addition, the new constraint (19). We obtain, using the new Lagrange multiplier ρ for (19), the following Lagrangian form for Pareto optimality:

$$L = \sum \lambda_j[u^j(\cdot) - u^{*j}] - \sum \mu_k f^k(\cdot) + \sum_i \omega_i \left(r_i - \sum_j x_{ij} + \sum_k y_{ik} \right)$$
$$+ \rho(\sum s_k - \sum z_j - \sum z_k).$$

$$\text{all } x_{ij} \geq 0, \qquad s_k \geq 0, \qquad z_j \geq 0, \qquad z_k \geq 0,$$

y_{ik} unrestricted (with the exceptions noted earlier).

Our Kuhn-Tucker conditions continue to include (3°)–(4°) as before. However, because an increase in an external output no longer necessarily affects any particular individual's utility relationship or any particular firm's production constraint, (5°) changes drastically and is replaced by the considerably simpler relationship (20°) in Table 4–2. In addition, we now have two more pairs of Kuhn-Tucker conditions (21°) and (22°) in Table 4–2 corresponding to the variables z_j and z_k.

Once again, these necessary conditions for optimality must be related to the corresponding requirements for market equilibrium as founded on the behavior of the consumer and the firm. Upon individual j we now impose, in addition to his other costs that he wishes to minimize, a price (tax) p_j per unit of the externality he consumes giving him the Lagrangian

---

[22] In the depletable externalities case, it is easier to think in terms of a beneficial rather than a detrimental externality. The obvious way of looking at the matter is to consider the externality as a physical output generated unintentionally by its producers. Other members of the economy then compete against one another for a share of the resulting stockpile. It is harder to think of a plausible parable for an external product whose possession everyone wants to avoid.

TABLE 4–2

KUHN-TUCKER CONDITIONS: DEPLETABLE EXTERNALITIES

Variable	Pareto Optimality	Market Equilibrium	Price
s_k	$-\mu_k f_s^k + \rho \leq 0$ (20°) $s_k(-\mu_k f_s^k + \rho) = 0$	$-\beta_k f_s^k - t_k \leq 0$ (20ᵉ) $s_k(-\beta_k t_s^k - t_k) = 0$	
z_j	$\lambda_j u_z^j - \rho \leq 0$ (21°) $z_j(\lambda_j u_z^j - \rho) = 0$	$-\alpha_j u_z^j + p_j \geq 0$ (21ᵉ) $z_j(-\alpha_j u_z^j + p_j) = 0$	$\rho = -t_k$ $= p_j$ $= p_k$
z_k	$-\mu_k f_z^k - \rho \leq 0$ (22°) $z_k(-\mu_k f_z^k - \rho) = 0$	$-\beta_k f_z^k - p_k \leq 0$ (22ᵉ) $z_k(-\beta_k f_z^k - p_k) = 0$	

$$\sum p_i x_{ij} + p_j z_j + \alpha_j[u^{*j} - u^j(\cdot)] \tag{23}$$

with the same nonnegativity conditions as before.

Similarly, the firm k is now subjected to a price (tax) p_k per unit of the externality it consumes and a tax (price) t_k per unit produced, so that the requirements for profit maximization for the firm can now be determined from the Lagrangian

$$\sum p_i y_{ik} - p_k z_k - t_k s_k - \beta_k f^k(\cdot) \tag{24}$$

with the same nonnegativity requirements as above. Differentiating (23) and (24) in turn with respect to x_{ij} and y_{ik}, we obtain essentially[23] (3ᵉ)–(4ᵉ) of Table 4–1. However, differentiating with respect to s_k, z_j, and z_k, we obtain the new conditions (20ᵉ), (21ᵉ), and (22ᵉ) in Table 4–2.

As before, it is clear on inspection that there is one, and only one, set of prices (taxes) that transforms the market-equilibrium conditions (20ᵉ)–(22ᵉ) plus the constraints (2) and the corresponding complementary slackness conditions into the Pareto-optimality conditions that include (20°)–(22°). These are

$$-t_k = p_k = p_j = \rho. \tag{25}$$

---

[23] We do not obtain the tax terms in those expressions because, in the model with which we are now dealing, there is now no damage (benefit) effect on the individual corresponding to the *total* output of the externality and there is therefore no occasion to tax (compensate) for such effects.

But this solution simply amounts to the setting of a uniform price, ρ, on the production and the consumption of the externality, where ρ, the dual value corresponding to the externality, is, as usual, interpretable as its shadow price [that is, as its marginal utility to individual 1, the person whose utility was chosen (arbitrarily) for maximization in our Pareto-optimality calculation]. The producer of this beneficial externality receives a price of ρ dollars for every unit he supplies, and the firm or the individual pays ρ dollars for every unit he (it) consumes. That is exactly the role an ordinary competitive price would play. Thus we have:

Proposition Six.   With the assumed convexity conditions, a competitive economy with a depletable externality will achieve a Pareto optimum through the market mechanism if, and only if, it imposes on the production *and* consumption of that externality a price equal to its marginal social (= private) benefit.

6.   THE INTERMEDIATE CASES [24]

The literature recognizes clearly that there are types of outputs intermediate between the pure public and pure private goods, and, from the usual range of illustrations, including public health, education, housing, quality of neighborhoods, and the performing arts, it is clear that these encompass some of the activities that are generally considered to be critical for the "quality of life." Yet there is some ambiguity in the connotation of the term *intermediate* that may be unavoidable, because the object is to collect a mixed bag of activities that simply do not fall into either of the polar pure categories. Unfortunately, model building cannot tolerate such vague concepts, and we are, therefore, forced to adopt more explicit definitions. As was noted in the preceding chapter, we will, in fact, use two alternative concepts whose analysis, however, turns out to be very similar:

a.   *The mixed externalities* that can be taken to yield *both* undepletable and depletable benefits or costs;

b.   *The eventually depletable (congestible) cases* in which there can be "excess capacity" in the externality for particular levels of usage, but where, at some level, capacity becomes fully utilized or, alternatively, congestion gradually begins to set in.

Examples of both of these have already been given in Section 5 of the previous chapter, and in any case, they are familiar enough. Happily, we will

[24] This section, in part, draws upon the illuminating article by S. E. Holtermann, "Externalities and Public Goods," *Economica*, also cited in the preceding chapter.

see that a few simple tricks permit us to use the preceding constructs with some minor modification to describe these two intermediate cases.

7. THE MIXED CASE

Formalization of the first of these models is simply a matter of combining the depletable and the undepletable externalities models. Now, the utility of individual j will depend *both* on his consumption of the depletable externality, z_j (for example, the amount of on-the-job training he himself receives) and the total amount of the undepletable externality, call it z^*. In particular cases we may have $z^* = \sum z_j$ (for example, crime rates may be a function of the total amount of training received by all individuals in the community). Thus individual j's utility function now becomes

$$u^j(x_{ij}, \ldots, x_{nj}, z_j, z^*)$$

and, similarly, the production function for firm k now contains the two variables, z_k and z^*. Corresponding to s_k, the externality output of firm k, we obtain, instead of the conditions (5°) and (5ᵉ) for the undepletable case in Table 4–1, or the pure depletable conditions (20°) and (20ᵉ) in Table 4–2, the mixed conditions (26°) and (26ᵉ) in Table 4–3.

These, together with (3°)–(4°) and (3ᵉ)–(4ᵉ) from Table 4–1 and (21°)–(22°) and (21ᵉ)–(22ᵉ) from Table 4–2 constitute the pertinent conditions for the mixed case. There is no need to repeat the derivations, because they are essentially identical to those in the two pure models.

In a sense, this mixed case is the most general we have considered so far, with the two pure models being special cases of the model for the mixed externalities. That is, the undepletable case is described by the mixed model with all the z_j and z_k equal to zero, and so on. Conversely, the depletable case arises when z^* equals zero. The optimal price and tax policy for the mixed model is, correspondingly, an amalgam of the Pareto-optimal policies for the other two cases; that is,

Proposition Seven. The Pareto-optimal price-tax policy for a mixed externality in a competitive economy in which all the appropriate convexity conditions hold is a price plus a tax (subsidy) on the outputs of the externality. The price is equal to ρ, the marginal private cost (utility) of the depletable output; thus, ρ per unit is received by the producers of the depletable externality and is also charged to all of those who receive its benefits. The unit subsidy (tax) to the producer of the externality is equal to the marginal social benefit (damage) yielded by the undepletable portion of the externality, and there is no corresponding charge (compensation) to the beneficiaries (victims).

TABLE 4-3

KUHN-TUCKER CONDITIONS CORRESPONDING TO THE MIXED CASE

Variable	Pareto Optimality	Market Equilibrium	Price and Tax
$s_{\bar{k}}$	$(26o)$ $\begin{aligned} -\mu_{\bar{k}}\bar{f}^{\bar{k}}_s + \rho + \sum \lambda_j u^j_z - \sum \mu_k f^k_z &\leq 0 \\ s_{\bar{k}}(-\mu_{\bar{k}}\bar{f}^{\bar{k}}_s + \rho + \sum \lambda_j u^j_z - \sum \mu_k f^k_z) &= 0 \end{aligned}$	$(26c)$ $\begin{aligned} -\beta_{\bar{k}}\bar{f}^{\bar{k}}_s + p_s - t_s &\leq 0 \\ s_{\bar{k}}(-\beta_{\bar{k}}\bar{f}^{\bar{k}}_s + p_s - t_s) &= 0 \end{aligned}$	$\begin{aligned} p_s &= \rho \\ t_s &= -\sum \lambda_j u^j_z \\ &\quad + \sum \mu_k f^k_z \end{aligned}$

8. EVENTUALLY DEPLETABLE EXTERNALITIES

a. **The Case of Zero Marginal Congestion Costs Until Capacity.** We turn next to the eventually depletable case. The simplest variety is that in which there is a fixed capacity with no change in anyone's total cost or utility as capacity is approached. So long as utilization is at a level below capacity, we have, effectively, an undepletable externality. However, once capacity is reached, congestion sets in and the externality takes the depletable form.[25] Here we obtain the appropriate construct by a trivial reinterpretation of the depletable externalities model. We need merely take note of the inequality in constraint (19) (that is, $\sum z_j + \sum z_k \leq \sum s_k$) specifying the availability of the externality. So long as the externality is not fully utilized, (19) remains a strict inequality (whose associated dual variable, ρ, must then take the value zero). Congestion occurs when capacity is utilized fully so that (19) becomes an equation. Obviously, the corresponding model is then the same as that for the depletable case. The price-tax conditions thus coincide with those of the undepletable model for usage at less than capacity (price $\rho = 0$ to users), but a positive price, ρ, to both producers and consumers of the externality becomes appropriate when capacity is reached (the depletable case).

b. **The Case of Gradual Congestion.** More common in practice is the case where congestion occurs gradually; additional consumers of the externality impose congestion costs on existing consumers with the level of congestion varying directly with the number of consumers. If there is a well-defined capacity we still retain the total availability constraint (19). But now we define a slack variable, z^*, to represent the quantity of "unutilized" externality, so that

$$\sum z_j + \sum z_k + z^* = \sum s_k.$$

Then this slack variable itself will enter the utility and cost functions directly. That is, the quantity of unused externality itself affects the welfare of the economy. Our model is now formally equivalent to the earlier construct for mixed case.[26]

---

[25] A good with properties of this type is a theater or stadium with a fixed number of seats. The cost of using a seat may be zero when there are empty seats available, but it becomes positive at capacity when the use of a seat by one person prevents another spectator from viewing the performance. An analogous externality would be our case of the garden in Chapter 3, if there were a fixed number of places from which to view the flowers.

[26] Where there is gradual congestion but no well defined capacity figure, we may replace the slack variable, z^*, with a total utilization variable $z^{**} = \sum z_j + \sum z_k$. That is, in this case we must take total "consumption" of the external effect as our measure of congestion, with its attendant utility and cost consequences.

9. IMPLICATIONS OF THE MODELS

We are now in a position to draw a number of important conclusions about pricing and optimality in the presence of externalities, including several that were anticipated in the preceding chapter.

a. Our optimality and market equilibrium analyses jointly call for a unique set of (relative) prices to consumers for each and every product and each and every resource. After normalization by (9), each price becomes equal to the value of the Lagrangian multiplier for the corresponding constraint [that is, the shadow price (marginal utility to individual 1) of the corresponding item] so that $p_i = \omega_i$. Consequently, prices to competitive suppliers of those goods that yield no externalities should equal their (private) marginal resources costs, with each resource, i evaluated at its shadow price, ω_i.

b. For a producer whose activities generate an externality, however, we see from (8) that net revenue per unit (price minus tax or plus subsidy) should *not* simply be equal to its marginal resources cost. Rather, (8) indicates that unit receipts should also reflect both the marginal (dis)utility of the externalities to consumers, $\sum \lambda_j \dfrac{\partial u^j}{\partial z}$, and the marginal resources cost (benefits) imposed on firms, $\sum \mu_k \dfrac{\partial f^k}{\partial z}$. It follows that the optimal unit revenues of the externality-generating output equals its private marginal cost plus (minus) the value of the benefits (damage) imposed by the externalities. This is, of course, the standard Pigouvian result. In a competitive economy, it calls for a tax (subsidy) per unit on the externality-generating commodity equal to its marginal external damage (benefit).

c. We come next to results of the preceding chapter that are less well known. The first relates to the issue of compensation to the victims (beneficiaries) of the externalities. As already noted, there is disagreement on this subject in the literature, with some writers calling for compensation and others actually seeming to propose a tax upon the victims, on the ground that this will be required for optimal resource allocation. But (8) is unambiguous on that point. It indicates that the price of any consumer good that generates no externality should equal its (private) marginal cost. For with $t^j = t^k = 0$ by (8) (except for lump sum payments) we have for i^*, any input (negative output) actually used in firm k, and i any output of firm k, $p_i = \beta_k f^k_i$, $p_{i*} = \beta_k f^k_{i*}$ [by (4ᶜ)] so that eliminating β_k between these two equations we have at once [by the analog of (17)]

$$p_i = p_{i*} f^k_{i*}/f^k_{i*} = p_{i*}\partial \bar{y}_{i*k}/\partial y_{ik} \quad \text{where} \quad \bar{y}_{i*k} = |y_{i*k}|.$$

That is, the optimal price of i is the cost of the quantity of input i^* necessary to produce a unit addition in i, all other inputs and outputs held constant. In brief, it is the marginal *private* cost[27] of i. This means that if, for example, marginal smoke damage to the production of two firms of different types, k and k^*, is quite different (that is, if $\mu_k \partial f^k / \partial z \neq \mu_{k^*} \partial f^{k^*} / \partial z$), there will be no compensation to offset the differential effects on the optimal prices of the two outputs. Laundry and phonograph records will both sell at their private marginal costs though one cost is more heavily affected by smoke than the other. Thus, our results imply that, *in the case of an undepletable (public) externality, optimal resource allocation calls for pricing that involves zero taxation and zero compensation to those affected by the externalities* (but non-zero taxation of their generators). Laundry purchasers will then not be able to buy laundry at a price below the high marginal cost resulting from the presence of smoke, because there is no compensation.

   d.   Where the externality is depletable, however, the situation is quite different. We see from Table 4–2 that *compensation* in the form of a (negative or positive) price, ρ, should be paid by (to) the individual (firm) affected by the externality. *Optimal resource allocation in the presence of a depletable external benefit requires the payment of a price by those affected by it equal to its marginal rate of substitution with the* numeraire *commodity. If the beneficiary is a firm, this price is equal to the marginal cost saving the externality permits.*[28]

   e.   Moreover, for the depletable case, ρ can be treated as the price charged by the supplier of s. Thus, table 2 tells us that for each unit of s he provides, the supplier should receive a compensation payment, ρ. This price should be equal to the marginal cost of producing s.[29]

   f.   The results (d) and (e) imply that, *for Pareto-optimal resource use, we should price a depletable externality like any joint product that is sold competitively with the prices of the joint products together equaling marginal cost.*

The difference in pricing of the depletable and the undepletable externalities results, of course, from the fact that the consumption of a unit of a depletable product has a nonzero opportunity cost, but the opportunity cost of the consumption of a unit of an undepletable commodity by another individual or firm is, by definition, zero. Consequently, any nonzero price on its

---

[27] The reader may be disturbed at the notion of expressing marginal private cost in terms of the single input, i^*, rather than the full set of inputs used by the firm. However, in equilibrium the ratio of input price to marginal physical product will be the same for all of the firm's inputs. Hence, it will cost exactly the same whether the firm expands an output by a very small amount by using more of one input, i^*, or more of some other input, i^{**}, or *any* combination of these inputs.

[28] This follows from (21ᶜ) and (22ᶜ) after eliminating Lagrange multipliers, α_i and β_k from these relationships in the manner of the preceding paragraph c.

[29] This follows from (20ᶜ) after elimination of β_k in the manner of paragraph c.

consumption (either compensation, or taxation à la Coase) would prevent the attainment of a Pareto optimum.

For the depletable externalities, it is indeed true that the source of the problem is simply failure to price properly the external service (disservice). Were one to charge a competitive price for the externally supplied service, no resource misallocation need result.

Generally, the problem in these cases in practice is the difficulty for private enterprise of charging a price (the high administrative cost of exclusion and/or of price collection). In such cases, it may also be uneconomical for the government to impose and collect such prices. And where such pricing *is* worthwhile on balance, it can often be left to the private sector, where entrepreneurs will be happy to collect the revenues, barring some institutional impediment to their doing so.

g. In the case of the (generally more important) undepletable externalities, it is clear that no *one* price can achieve an optimum. What is required is two different prices:

(a) a zero price for the consumption of the externality, and

(b) a nonzero price to the producer of the externality to compensate him for the cost if it is an external benefit, or to make him pay the damage for an external cost.

Clearly, no normal market price can play this double role, and in such cases it is simply incorrect to assert that the externality results from failure to charge an appropriate price for the resources of society.

h. The Pigouvian tax or subsidy then turns out to be a flexible device that can provide either the single "price" required for optimal resource allocation in the case of the depletable externalities or the "double price" needed for the undepletable externalities. It can constitute the double price required in the latter case by taxing (subsidizing) those who generate the externality with the proceeds of the tax (positive or negative) going into the public treasury and not into compensation of those affected. In the case of the depletable externality, it can, at least in principle, replicate the single (or ordinary) price required for optimality by taxing those who benefit from the use of the externality and then paying the proceeds of the tax as a subsidy to those who supply it.

i. Turning to the mixed cases, we see that where an activity produces an externality that can be considered to have both depletable elements, z_j and z_k, and an undepletable element, z^*, the appropriate pricing (tax) structure will require elements of the pricing appropriate for the depletable case and the tax or subsidy for the undepletable cases. Users should then pay a price $p_s = p$ for each unit of the depletable externality that accrues to them *but nothing for the undepletable externality* no matter how it affects them. On the other hand, suppliers of the externality should receive an amount per unit equal to $(p_s + t_s)$ where t_s is given by (8); that is, they should be compensated (taxed) at a rate p_s for each unit of the externality they supply for private use, and *in addition*, they should be taxed (subsidized) for the social consequences of their public externality. Thus, in this case we also have the asymmetry of optimal pricing for suppliers and victims of externalities that characterizes the pure undepletable externalities case.

Similarly, a price, ρ, should be charged to those who contribute to congestion. If, however, marginal congestion costs will not be positive in an optimal solution, the solution becomes identical with that of the pure undepletable case and a zero congestion charge is appropriate.

chapter *5*

On Optimal Pricing of Exhaustible Resources[1]

As some growing scarcities have begun to alarm the public, the pricing of exhaustible resources has claimed increased attention. Thus, it seems appropriate to consider the issue here even though it represents something of a digression from the main line of our discussion. Here, again, optimality of pricing is defined in terms of resource allocation, but in this case the central issue is allocation among time periods rather than output categories. The results we will describe are all based largely on standard propositions of capital theory going back to the work of Irving Fisher and Bohm-Bawerk.

Yet when applied to exhaustible resources, some of our conclusions may be slightly surprising. For example, our instincts are likely to suggest that items in danger of depletion should tend to rise in price with the passage of time. We will see, however, that this is by no means generally true, and

---

[1] There is a considerable theoretical literature in this area, particularly on the subject of fisheries. The classic paper on the subject is Harold Hotelling's "The Economics of Exhaustible Resources," *Journal of Political Economy* XXXIX (April, 1931), 137–75. For excellent discussions of the broader subject and a bibliography, see Vernon L. Smith, "Economics of Production from Natural Resources," *American Economic Review*, LVIII (June, 1968), 409–31; O. R. Burt and R. G. Cummings, "Production and Investment in Natural Resource Industries," *American Economic Review* LX (September, 1970), 576–90; R. L. Gordon, "A Reinterpretation of the Pure Theory of Exhaustion," *Journal of Political Economy*, LXXV (June, 1967), 274–86. See also F. M. Peterson, "*The Theory of Exhaustible Natural Resources: A Classical Variational Approach*," (unpublished dissertation, Princeton University, 1972). Much of the published discussion concerns two issues that we will not examine in this chapter: the common-property characteristics of resources, such as fish, and the dynamics of resource depletion in which the time path of fishing activity is dependent on the size of the remaining fish population, and vice versa.

that, in some cases, optimality requires prices that decline, not only in discounted present value, but in current terms as well. Moreover, we will find that, although an optimal policy may call for prevention of the depletion of certain types of exhaustible resources, in other cases we should encourage their current utilization; obviously, this will be true of an item whose early use makes it possible to preserve some other resource whose returns to the future are larger.

Clearly, in dealing with the allocation of resources over time, the issue of intergenerational equity arises unavoidably. Most of the discussion of this chapter avoids direct consideration of this problem that the careful work of some of the most distinguished writers in the field has failed to resolve. Rather, we deal with the matter by the extension of the Pareto criterion to the interests of individuals living in different time periods, taking as our object the maximization of the welfare of some arbitrarily selected member of an arbitrarily selected generation, with no loss in utility to any other individuals in his or any other generation.

1.   THREE PROTOTYPE CASES

A little consideration of the matter suggests that the depletable resource case really encompasses several heterogeneous phenomena. As a standard of reference, we begin with the case that we call *pure resource depletion* (although it is one that is probably not even approximated in reality). Suppose that a fixed stock of a useful and perfectly divisible material (which we will call *glob*) is available at one single location and that it is certain that there are no undiscovered deposits of glob. Thus, there is no way of augmenting its supply and no prospect that it will increase of its own account. In addition, we take glob to incur no cost of storage and not to deteriorate. We assume, finally, that the marginal cost of acquisition, transportation, and utilization of glob does not change as its stock decreases. The pile in which it is kept simply grows smaller, like a stack of lumber in a lumberyard. If it is used at a steady rate, one simply runs out of it and that is the end of the story.

The second prototype we may call the *autonomous regeneration case*. This is a somewhat oversimplified representation of the depletion of a living species that is in danger of extinction by hunting, fishing, cutting, and so on. The essence of this case is that the available quantity of the resource will grow at a rate dependent on the quantity *not used up* at that moment. The exponential growth case (with which we will deal) is that in which growth is *proportionate* to the existing stock of the resource.[2]

---

[2] The model assumes away a variety of complications that are considered in the literature, such as the possibility of overpopulation of the species and the resulting fall in

We may describe our third prototype as the case of *rising supply costs*. Here the available stock of the resource in question may or may not be exhausted completely in the foreseeable future. The critical characteristic of this case is that the marginal cost of obtaining the item increases as its cheaper sources are used up.[3] The obvious examples of this case are the depletion of scarce mineral resources and the depletion of energy sources (the "fuel crisis"). The latter is clearly an example in which resources will not be exhausted in the pertinent future. We may use up our petroleum reserves, but then we can turn to nuclear or solar energy at a higher cost.

These three prototypes: pure depletion, autonomous regeneration, and the case of increasing costs perhaps do not represent the full range of phenomena falling under the heading "resource depletion."[4] However, they all capture important aspects of resource depletion problems, and their analysis will certainly serve to illustrate some of the relevant relationships.

2. THE BASIC MODEL

In most of our models in this chapter we will assume that there are three items to be consumed and whose consumption is to be allocated over time: our depletable resource, a second (storable) good whose production requires labor, and leisure (labor). Only labor is taken to be a productive input with our depletable resource serving only as a consumers' good. To keep the number of variables finite, we will also assume that there is a finite horizon and, hence, a finite future population. Because those finite numbers can be as large as we wish, and particularly because we can take the horizon to be well *beyond* the time at which scientists predict the demise of human life (or even the universe, if one wishes), this premise is not really very restrictive. Accordingly,[5] let

---

the growth rate. This does not, however, seem highly pertinent for a species threatened with extinction, the case with which we are concerned here.

[3] This is essentially the Ricardian case, in which cheaper sources are taken to be utilized before the more expensive ones. Note that sometimes there is little choice in the matter. One may have to mine coal that lies near the surface before it is possible economically to get to the deeper deposits. Of course, this "Ricardian" case is not properly to be attributed to Ricardo who admittedly did not discover the "Ricardian" rent theory. There is also a series of writings, including Volume III of *Capital*, in which it is argued that those natural resources whose utilization is less expensive are not necessarily used first.

Note also that rising costs, in the sense used here, need not always involve costs that increase monotonically with the passage of time because autonomous improvements in technology may offset the rise in expenses that would otherwise occur.

[4] Obviously, combinations of these cases are encountered in practice. For example, the marginal cost of fishing increases as the stock of fish grows smaller, making this a case of both the autonomous regeneration and the rising cost prototypes.

[5] In our discussion, we will not concern ourselves with individual producers and their outputs so that there is no need for a separate set of variables distinguishing output

x_{jt} = the quantity of the depletable resource consumed by person j in period t, where $(j = 1, 2, \ldots, m)$, $(t = 1, 2, \ldots, h)$

a_t = the unconsumed quantity of the resource at the end of t

a_0 = the initial stock of the depletable resource

k = rate of growth of the resource

q_{jt} = the quantity of the second good consumed by j during t

q_t = the total output of commodity Q in period t

b_t = the unconsumed quantity of Q remaining at the end of t

r_{jt} = the quantity of leisure consumed by j during t

r = the total labor time available per period

$f(q_t)$ = the labor time required to produce q_t

$u^j(x_{j1}, \ldots, x_{jh}, q_{j1}, \ldots, q_{jh}, r_{j1}, \ldots, r_{jh})$ = j's utility function.

This set of utility functions includes not only individuals alive at the time the calculation is carried out but also all members of generations yet unborn whose interests must be considered symmetrically with those of our contemporaries in a full analysis of Pareto optimality.

3. THE AUTONOMOUS REGENERATION CASE

We begin by considering not the pure depletion case but that of autonomous regeneration, because the regeneration case is in fact easier to understand. Pure depletion is best examined as a special case of autonomous regeneration: that in which the regeneration rate is zero.[6] Moreover, it is convenient to begin with the regeneration prototype, because that is the case in which Pareto optimality may most clearly call for prices that fall with the passage of time.

The basic device we will utilize to represent the automatic replenishing of our resource is simple. With a_t left over at the end of period t, we assume it will grow at rate k and thus add $(1 + k)a_t$ to the amount available during period $t + 1$.

Our problem, then, is to

$$\text{maximize } u^1(\cdot) \tag{1}$$

subject to

---

from consumption. To avoid a proliferation of subscripts, we use different letters to represent different outputs (inputs).

[6] Smith also treats pure depletion as a special case of autonomous regeneration, ("*Economics of Production from Natural Resources*,") p. 412.

$u^i(\cdot) \geq u^{*j}$ (constant) [for all individuals, $(j \neq 2, \ldots, m)$ in current and all future generations] (2)

$$\left. \begin{array}{l} \sum_j x_{jt} + a_t \leq (1 + k)a_{t-1} \\[2mm] \sum_j q_{jt} + b_t \leq q_t + b_{t-1} \\[2mm] f(q_t) + \sum_j r_{jt} \leq r, \end{array} \right\} (j = 1, \ldots, m)(t = 1, \ldots, h)$$

$$\begin{array}{r} (3) \\[2mm] (4) \\[2mm] (5) \end{array}$$

the initial values of a_t and b_t given and all variable values required to be nonnegative. Here constraint (4) implies that storage of q can be carried out without cost and without either increase or loss in the quantity of the commodity that has been put into inventory.

The preceding relationships immediately yield the Lagrangian[7]

$$L = \sum_j \lambda_j[u^i(\cdot) - u^{*j}] + \sum_t \alpha_t \left[(1 + k)a_{t-1} - \sum_j x_{jt} - a_t\right]$$
$$+ \sum_t \beta_t \left[q_t + b_{t-1} - \sum_j q_{jt} - b_t\right] + \sum_t \nu_t[r - f(q_t) - \sum_j r_{jt}], \quad (6)$$

where the λ_j, ν_t, α_t and β_t are Lagrange multipliers whose values are required to be nonnegative. We obtain from (6) the Kuhn-Tucker conditions

$$\begin{array}{lll} \lambda_j u^i_{xt} - \alpha_t \leq 0 & x_{jt}(\lambda_j u^i_{xt} - \alpha_t) = 0 & (7) \\[2mm] \lambda_j u^i_{qt} - \beta_t \leq 0 & q_{jt}(\lambda_j u^i_{qt} - \beta_t) = 0 & \left. \right\} (t = 1, \ldots, h) \quad (8) \\[2mm] \lambda_j u^i_{rt} - \nu_t \leq 0 & r_{jt}(\lambda_j u^i_{rt} - \nu_t) = 0 & (9) \\[2mm] (1 + k)\alpha_{t+1} - \alpha_t \leq 0 & a_t[(1 + k)\alpha_{t+1} - \alpha_t] = 0 & (10) \\[2mm] \beta_{t+1} - \beta_t \leq 0 & b_t(\beta_{t+1} - \beta_t) = 0 & \left. \right\} (t = 1, \ldots, h-1) \quad (11) \\[2mm] \beta_t - \nu_t f'(q_t) \leq 0 & q_t[\beta_t - \nu f'(q_t)] = 0 & (t = 1, \ldots, h) \quad (12) \end{array}$$

where we write u^i_{xt} to represent $\partial u^i/\partial x_{jt}$, and so on. First, simply as a manifestation of the horizon premise that, in effect, assumes that the end of the world occurs after period h, we prove

Proposition One. If $u^j_{xh} > 0$ for any[8] individual j for whom $\lambda_j > 0$,

---

[7] Here again, to put the Lagrangian into more conventional form we may set $\lambda_1 = 1$, $u^{*1} = 0$, though given the appropriate convexity assumptions there is no need for these restrictions.

[8] That is, roughly speaking, for any individual who "counts" in the social welfare function made up of the weighted sum of utilities $\sum \lambda_j u^j$. Obviously individual one is such a person if we take $\lambda_1 = 1$, in accord with the comment in the previous footnote. These weights must, of course, be those derived from the maximization problem as the u^{*j} values are varied.

then $a_h = 0$, that is, all stocks of our depletable commodity will be used up by the end of period h.

For because there is no α_{h+1} in our maximand, for $t = h$, (10) yields $\alpha_h a_h = 0$. But by (7), $\alpha_h > 0$ so that necessarily $a_h = 0$, as was to be shown. Thus in our model the resource in question will be consumed *and*, eventually, completely exhausted.[9]

To come now to the essential issue, assume that prices for our goods for each period are somehow assigned. We will examine now what values of these prices are necessary to sustain a Pareto-optimal consumption plan in accord with the Kuhn-Tucker requirements (7)–(12). Let p_{xt} represent the price of x in period t, *discounted to the initial period*, and so on. We will presently specify the units in which the prices can be measured. However, because for the moment we are concerned only with relative prices of a given commodity at different dates, that is not immediately relevant. Now if j is a utility maximizer, he will make his consumption decisions both among commodities and among time periods so that the relevant marginal rate of substitution between any two items that he actually uses is always equal to the corresponding price ratio. We thus have for any individual j who during t consumes some of the item in question that

$$c_j p_{xt} = u^j{}_{xt}, \qquad c_j p_{qt} = u^j{}_{qt}, \qquad c_j p_{rt} = u^j{}_{rt}. \qquad (c_j \text{ some constant}) \quad (13)$$

Now if person j consumes some of our depletable resource in two consecutive periods t and $t + 1$, then, if his choice is to be consistent with the requirements of intertemporal Pareto optimality, we must have by (13), (7), and (10)

$$\frac{p_{xt}}{p_{xt+1}} = \frac{u^j{}_{xt}}{u^j{}_{xt+1}} = \frac{\alpha_t}{\alpha_{t+1}} = (1 + k) > 1. \quad (14)$$

This gives us

Proposition Two. The present values of the prices that will sustain a Pareto-optimal choice pattern by individuals for a self-reproducible resource must *decline* with the passage of time over periods when the item is consumed. These present values will decline at precisely the same rate as the resource reproduces itself.

This paradox has a simple explanation. The reduced future price is just a bonus for postponed consumption of the item. For in every period that consumption is postponed, the corresponding supply will increase by itself in the proportion $(1 + k)$. As standard capital theory tells us, optimal pricing

---

[9] This proposition need not be taken to suggest that the assumption of a finite horizon is an unacceptable oversimplification. After all, h can be very long—longer than the expected duration of human life.

in such a case must put a premium on the postponement of the utilization of the resource and that is precisely what our result (14) calls for.

Thus we should perhaps not be so surprised that discounted prices decline with time, because we are used to prices in the distant future being discounted more heavily than prices that are closer to us. However, in our simple model, the same relationship can easily be shown to hold for prices expressed in some appropriate current terms, specifically, in terms of the quantity of q in period t for which the resource will exchange at time t.

For by (13), (8), and (11) we derive at once for any two consecutive periods in which stocks of q are not consumed completely but [so that $b_t > 0$ and hence (11) becomes an equality]

$$p_{qt}/p_{qt+1} = \beta_t/\beta_{t+1} = 1 \tag{15}$$

so that by (14)

$$\frac{p_{xt}/p_{qt}}{p_{xt+1}/p_{qt+1}} = \frac{p_{xt}}{p_{xt+1}} = (1 + k). \tag{16}$$

Moreover, assuming that the production function and the range in variation of outputs as determined by the maximization process are such that the marginal product of labor is approximately constant over the same two periods, the same is true if we measure the price of our resource in wage units of period t, because by (13), (9), (11), and (12)

$$p_{rt}/p_{rt+1} = v_t/v_{t+1} = \frac{\beta_t/f'(q_t)}{\beta_{t+1}/f'(q_{t+1})} \cong 1.$$

Thus we have

Proposition Three. Even measured in current terms in the simple economy described by (1)–(5), the optimal price of the depletable resource may decline and perhaps decline steadily in any sequence of periods in which the resource is consumed.[10]

Moreover, so far, discounting makes little difference to this result, because our model has up to now largely ruled out opportunity costs in terms of roundabout (time-using) methods of production.[11] That is, there is no way in our construct for the "other commodity," Q, to be produced more effectively by the use of time-consuming processes. To show the importance of

[10] The argument assumes there is at least one person who consumes the resource in any two such consecutive periods. However, for the proposition to hold in the interval from t to $t + 2$ it is sufficient for our purpose if j consumes some X in both t and $t + 1$, while some other person, j', consumes some of X in both $t + 1$ and $t + 2$.

[11] There is one way in which the opportunity cost of time does enter: people can reduce their current consumption of X by using more of Q instead. This will give more time for growth to the portion of X whose consumption has been postponed.

this consideration, we now modify our production relationships to introduce roundaboutness in the simplest possible manner.[12] We will assume that Q is something like unfelled lumber (trees). Once the labor is expended to plant the trees, people can, if they wish, leave the trees to grow further, say at a constant rate g.[13]

In that case constraint (4) must be replaced by

$$\sum_j q_{jt} + b_t \leq q_t + (1 + g)b_{t-1}, \tag{4*}$$

in obvious analogy with (3). Kuhn-Tucker condition (11) is then replaced by

$$(1 + g)\beta_{t+1} - \beta_t \leq 0 \qquad b_t[(1 + g)\beta_{t+1} - \beta_t] = 0, \tag{11*}$$

and, finally, assuming stocks of commodity Q are not exhausted completely in period t, so that $b_t > 0$, (15) becomes

$$p_{qt}/p_{qt+1} = (1 + g). \tag{15*}$$

It is now easy to show that undiscounted current prices of X measured in terms of Q need no longer fall with the passage of time, for by (14) and (15*), (16) is immediately changed into

$$\frac{p_{xt}/p_{qt}}{p_{xt+1}/p_{qt+1}} = \frac{1 + k}{1 + g} < 1 \text{ if } g > k. \tag{16*}$$

In effect, then, with time contributing to the productivity of labor in other substitutable outputs, we obtain a discount factor, $1/1 + g$, for prices are measured in terms of Q, and if g is sufficiently great it can produce the rising *current* prices that intuition may lead us to expect for exhaustible resources. But note that the *discounted* price of our self-replenishing resource must continue to fall at the rate indicated by (14), for, even in our modified model, (14) continues to be a necessary condition for Pareto optimality. Thus we have

---

[12] It is noteworthy that in our model the superior productivity of time-consuming methods of production will now be seen to suffice to introduce a positive discount rate; in its absence there will be no discounting as shown by comparison of (14) and (16), apparently regardless of the nature of the utility functions (that is, whether or not consumers have a subjective preference for present over future consumption). Actually this is more a matter of appearance than of substance. We have, in effect, assumed a diminishing marginal rate of substitution between consumption in two different periods. By (4) we have implicitly assumed that there is a *fixed* technological rate of transformation between q_t and q_{t+1}; that is, the former can be transformed into the latter by storage with neither loss nor gain. In equilibrium, the consumers' marginal rates of substitution must be adjusted and equated to that marginal rate of transformation.

[13] This relationship can, of course, be incorporated directly into the production function.

Proposition Four. The prices that will sustain a Pareto optimum for a resource that regenerates itself at rate $k > 0$ will always fall with the passage of time when expressed in discounted present value. However, if expressed in terms of some commodity that grows (or for which productivity increases) at a rate in excess of k, the current price of the resource will rise with time.

Once again, these conclusions are not difficult to explain intuitively. Our new relationship of current prices, as given by (15*), reflects the possibility that although postponement of consumption of X is productive, postponement of the consumption of Q will be more productive still. Consequently, in this case society will come out ahead of the game if it lives initially on its stock of X that multiplies itself slowly, thereby leaving its stock of Q to grow, unconsumed, until later periods. Thus, despite the fact that our model permits no *direct* technical substitution in the production of X and Q, it does permit indirect substitution that is equally effective in imparting a high opportunity cost to postponed consumption of our depletable resource, X.

We can also show

Proposition Five. If X and Q are perfect substitutes in consumption, but Q grows more rapidly than X, then, if it is optimal for any person to consume commodity Q during some period, t, it will never be optimal for anyone to consume X in any period after t.

In other words, when they are perfect substitutes, it will always be optimal to consume at an earlier date the commodity for which waiting contributes less to future output.

Proof (by *reductio ad absurdum*): Assume the contrary (that is, assume $q_{jt} > 0$, $x_{j't+1} > 0$, for some individuals j, j'. Then by (7) and (8) and the premise that X and Q are perfect substitutes

$$\alpha_t \geq \lambda_j u^i_{xt} = \lambda_j u^i_{qt} = \beta_t, \qquad \alpha_{t+1} = \lambda_{j'} u^{i'}_{xt+1} = \lambda_{j'} u^{i'}_{qt+1} \leq \beta_{t+1}. \qquad (17)$$

But because X is, by assumption, not producible, if $x_{j't+1} > 0$ some of it must have been left over from the previous period, that is, we must have $a_t > 0$. Thus (10) becomes an equality and so by (10), (17), and (11*)

$$\alpha_{t+1}(1 + k) = \alpha_t \geq \beta_t \geq \beta_{t+1}(1 + g)$$

so that with $g > k$,

$$\alpha_{t+1} > \beta_{t+1}. \qquad (18)$$

Now, because $x_{j't+1} > 0$, the second relation in (17) holds so that

$$\alpha_{t+1} \leq \beta_{t+1}$$

contradicting (18).

Thus, we have proved that if $q_{jt} > 0$ for any j, we cannot have $x_{jt+1} > 0$ for any j', and a direct extension of the argument shows the same result for any future period beyond $t + 1$. Q.E.D.

Proposition Five tells us, in effect, that if investment in Q is more productive than in X, it will pay the community to consume all of its stock of X before beginning to consume any of Q. For we have seen, in Proposition One, that the stock of X should be used up entirely at a time no later than the horizon period. But Proposition Five indicates that no X should ever be consumed *after* the consumption of Q begins. Hence, society's stock of X must be exhausted no later than the date at which consumption of Q begins.

3. THE PURE DEPLETION PROTOTYPE

As has already been noted, the pure depletion analysis is a special case of autonomous regeneration in which the autonomous growth rate, k, equals zero. We obtain our solution at once, for (14) becomes simply

$$p_1 = p_2 = \cdots = p_n. \tag{19}$$

That is, the solution calls for prices whose discounted present value remains completely unchanged over the period during which the stock of the commodity is exhausted. There is a simple explanation of this result that we obtain with the aid of a reformulation of our model. If we consider a plan formulated initially for the entire h periods, we see that there really are not h independent constraints. In fact, there is only one effective constraint circumscribing the entire decision process:

$$x_1 + x_2 + \cdots + x_h \leq \alpha_0.$$

That is, the total quantity of the resource, glob, used over the entire period cannot exceed the initial stock. Because there is only one constraint, there will be only one corresponding shadow price, that for the depletable resource, and, hence, the optimal price of glob will also remain unchanged as indicated by the constancy of this dual value.

In terms of current values, however, the optimal price of glob may rise with time, if price is measured in terms of a commodity, Q, whose output is increased by roundabout processes (that is, for which $g > 0$). For the reasons noted earlier, if p_t^* is the current price of X in terms of Q in period t, we will have

$$\frac{p_t^*}{(1 + g)^t} = p_t = p_{t+1} = \frac{p^*_{t+1}}{(1 + g)^{t+1}} \quad \text{so that} \quad \frac{p_t^*}{p^*_{t+1}} = \frac{1}{1 + g}.$$

Current prices of glob will then, indeed, be rising.

Obviously, the current *money* price of glob *must* be rising so long as the discount rate is positive, for otherwise in terms of present values these prices would be falling, in violation of (19). In sum, we have

Proposition Six.   Pareto optimality requires a constant discounted price for an item whose supply is fixed and whose supply cost does not rise as it is used up. This means that the annual rate of increase in its current price must equal the interest rate used in the discounting process.

4.   THE CASE OF RISING COSTS

We come, finally, to the case so important in practice, in which depletion of our resource manifests itself through rising production costs. Our model will continue to include the labor resource in terms of which costs can be expressed. Rising labor cost will then be interpreted as a rising labor input requirement per unit of output of our resource, as the cumulative consumption of the resource grows.[14] Under the appropriate convexity conditions, Pareto optimality therefore calls for us to maximize for all arbitrarily assigned set of weights, λ_j, the analog of our previous objective function

$$\sum_j \lambda_j [u^j(x_{j1}, \ldots, x_{jh}, r_{j1}, \ldots, r_{jh}) - u^{*j}] \tag{20}$$

subject to

$$\sum_j x_{jt} \leq x_t$$

$$\sum_j r_{jt} \leq r_t$$

$$w_t = x_1 + x_2 + \cdots + x_{t-1}$$

$$f(x_t, w_t) + r_t \leq R_t \qquad (t = 1, \ldots, h)$$

where

  x_{jt} is the quantity of resource consumed by individual j in period t,
  x_t is the total output of the processed resource in period t,
  w_t is the cumulative past consumption of the resource (leaving out
      consumption before the initial period as a "sunk" element),
  r_{jt} is unused labor (leisure) of individual j in period t,
$f(x_t, w_t)$ is the total labor cost of processing the resource in period t, and
  R_t is total labor resource available in t.

---

[14] We can easily continue to include in the calculation the consumption of other commodities. However, it is readily verified that their inclusions do not affect any of the Kuhn-Tucker conditions used to derive our conclusions; they merely increase the number of necessary maximum conditions, but these additional conditions are not used in our argument.

We assume

$$f_{xt} > 0 \qquad f_{wt} > 0 \quad \text{and} \quad f_{xwt} > 0, \tag{21}$$

where f_{xt} represents $\partial f/\partial x_t$, f_{xwt} represents $\partial^2 f/\partial x_t \partial w_t$, and so on. That is, we take the marginal cost of X to be positive, and both the unit and marginal cost of processing to be increased by resource depletion.

Our Lagrangian is

$$\sum_j \lambda_j [u^j(\cdot) - u^{*j}] + \sum_t v_t [R_t - f(x_t, w_t) - r_t] + \sum_t \alpha_t \left(x_t - \sum_j x_{jt} \right)$$
$$+ \sum_t \beta_t \left(r_t - \sum_j r_{jt} \right) + \sum_t \gamma_t \left(w_t - \sum_{s=1}^{t-1} x_s \right)$$

We obtain as Kuhn-Tucker conditions for all $x_{jt} > 0$, $r_{jt} > 0$ (so that necessarily $x_t > 0$, $r_t > 0$, $w_t > 0$)

$$\lambda_j u^j_{xt} - \alpha_t = 0 \tag{22}$$

$$\lambda_j u^j_{rt} - \beta_t = 0 \tag{23}$$

$$-v_t f_{xt} + \alpha_t - \sum_{s=t+1}^{h} \gamma_s = 0 \tag{24}$$

$$-v_t + \beta_t = 0 \tag{25}$$

$$-v_t f_{wt} + \gamma_t = 0. \tag{26}$$

Eliminating α_t, β_t, and γ_t by substitution of (24), (25), and (26) into (22) and (23) we have

$$\left.\begin{array}{l} \lambda_j u^j_{xt} = v_t f_{xt} + \sum_{s=t+1}^{h} v_s f_{ws} \\[2mm] \lambda_j u^j_{rt} = v_t. \end{array}\right\} (t = 1, \ldots, h) \qquad \begin{array}{l}(27)\\[4mm](28)\end{array}$$

Hence, substituting for v_t and v_s from (28) into (27) and dividing through by λ_j we obtain

$$u^j_{xt} = f_{xt} u^j_{rt} + \sum_{s=t+1}^{h} f_{ws} u^j_{rs} \tag{29}$$

or

$$u^j_{xt}/u^j_{rt} = f_{xt} + \sum_{s=t+1}^{h} f_{ws} u^j_{rs}/u^j_{rt}.$$

If prices p_{xs}, and p_{rs} are somehow assigned to x and r in period s, for the usual reasons, we may assume that the utility maximizing individual who consumes some of each of these items will select quantities such that their relative price equals the marginal rate of substitution. Thus (29) becomes

$$p_{xt}/p_{rt} = f_{xt} + \sum_{s=t+1}^{h} f_{ws}u^j_{rs}/u^j_{rt}. \tag{30}$$

Equation (30), which for convenience can be rewritten as

$$p_{xt} = p_{rt}f_{xt} + p_{rt}\sum_{s=t+1}^{h} f_{ws}u^j_{rs}/u^j_{rt}, \tag{31}$$

is the relationship we are seeking. It tells us

Proposition Seven. Pareto optimality requires that the price of an item whose supply cost increases as it is used up be made up of two components: the marginal input cost of the item (that is, its marginal private cost), $p_{rt}f_{xt}$, plus an expression that represents, in terms of inputs, the cost that current utilization imposes on future consumers of the commodity.

The interpretation of this last term in (31) is not difficult to justify. Because, by definition, $\partial w_s/\partial x_t = 1$ for $s > t$, it follows that

$$f_{ws} = \frac{\partial f}{\partial w_s}\frac{\partial w_s}{\partial x_t} = \frac{\partial f (R_s, W_s)}{\partial x_t}$$

represents the incremental labor cost in period s resulting from a unit increase in x_t. Therefore, because u^j_{rs}/u^j_{rt} is the *MRS* of labor in s and t, we see that $p_{rt}f_{ws}u^j_{rs}/u^j_{rt}$ represents the marginal cost that x_t imposes on production in period s measured in terms of labor of period t.

Two significant conclusions can be drawn from pricing equation (31):

1.   Because by definition $w_{t+1} \geq w_t$, then by (21), $f_{xt+1} \geq f_{xt}$. Hence, there is at least one component in (31), the expression for the Pareto-optimal discounted price of our resource, that is monotonically nondecreasing over time. In other words, this is the only one of our three cases in which it is at least possible for the time path of Pareto-optimal *discounted* prices for the depletable resource to follow the rising pattern that we might have expected in advance, though even here we cannot be certain of it. Much depends on the time path of the price of labor and the behavior of the summed terms in (31) as the horizon date approaches and the number of these remaining terms consequently declines.

2.   Our second conclusion from (31) is that current consumption in this case imposes an increased production cost on future generations so that the optimal price of the resource must exceed its current marginal resources cost. Strictly speaking, this cost is not an externality; it is rather a case where a certain quantity of resources is available to a group of individuals, so that the more that is consumed by one of them, the less there is left for the others.

What is involved, therefore, is not really an externality but rather a redistribution of the available stock of resources.[15]

It is nevertheless appropriate for us to ask whether the market is likely to misallocate such resources by pricing them improperly. The answer here is that, generally, it need *not* do so. Suppose there were a single proprietor-supplier of the depletable item and that his lifetime were expected to extend beyond horizon period h. If he were to follow the dictates of his own interests he would then surely price in accord with (30), making consumers pay for all the costs that are incurred in supplying goods to them. Just as monopolization can internalize an externality that extends within an industry, a single ownership that lasts through the full set of relevant periods can lead to the setting of a price that eliminates the adverse consequences of the intertemporal interdependencies in our model.

But we know that if this is true for a single owner, it may also hold for the entire community. That is, an ideal futures market for our scarce resource can lead to current prices that reflect fully the social costs of consumption of the item. The market may be able to achieve this even if the rise in costs is introduced through a switch in technology and a concomitant change in the source of the output (input) in question. If exhaustion of our petroleum reserves simply hastens the day when we will have to make use of solar energy which, we may assume, will be very costly to process, the price of oil will rise as the date of substitution approaches, because of its rising opportunity cost; in a competitive market, this will be reflected as a higher current price. Of course, to the extent that markets are imperfect, that our telescopic faculty really is defective, or that interest rates differ from the appropriate social discount rate, the allocation produced by the market will depart from an intertemporal Pareto optimum.

[15] It may also be interpreted as a user cost—a case where wear and tear resulting from usage of an item reduces its efficiency in future use—again, not something we would normally call an externality. We are grateful to F. M. Peterson for this observation and for saving us from several errors in the following paragraphs.

chapter 6

Market Imperfections
and the Number
of Participants

In Chapter 4 we derived our results for optimal taxes and payments from a competitive model in which individuals and firms both behave as price-takers. In this framework, prices *and* our prescribed fees are parameters for individual decision-makers; they take them as given and simply respond so as to maximize utility or profit.

In this chapter, we consider some of the complications that market imperfections introduce into the analysis. More specifically, we will examine the implications of two sources of such imperfections. First, a firm that generates externalities (smoke emissions) may not sell its output in a competitive market. For example, we will consider how a profit-maximizing monopolist will respond to the Pigouvian taxes prescribed in Chapter 4. We will show that an emissions tax rate that is appropriate for the pure competitor will not, in general, induce behavior that is consistent with optimality in the second-best world inhabited by a monopolist.

We then consider a second source of imperfection: the presence of polluters who are not "fee-takers." There can be situations involving few polluters, the manipulation of whose activity levels can influence the *unit* tax paid on waste emissions. In such cases, we will see that producers (and perhaps also consumers) of externalities will have an incentive to adjust their behavior so as to influence not only their tax bills, but also the tax *rate* they pay per unit of pollution. As for the monopolist, this necessitates some modifications in the prescription for an optimal fee. In fact, we will find one case to which the Coase result calling for a tax on victims is applicable.

Finally, we offer a proposition that relates, not only to the number of producers of an externality, but also to the number of consumers or victims. This establishes a strong presumption that increasing marginal costs will characterize many sorts of externality-generating activities (particularly those involving congestion).

1. EXTERNALITIES PRODUCED BY A MONOPOLIST

We found in Chapter 4 that a unit fee on the polluting activities of competitive firms equal to the costs at the margin that they impose on other economic units is, in general, required to sustain a Pareto-optimal pattern of resource use. However, Buchanan has shown that the levying of such a fee on a monopolist will not usually lead to optimality, and, under certain circumstances, can even reduce the level of welfare.[1] The problem is that the Pigouvian tax on the output of the polluter may be too much of a good thing. Such a tax normally will reduce the outputs of the industry below their previous levels. However, a monopolist will already have restricted his outputs below their optimal levels, and the additional contraction in output induced by the tax may, on balance, be detrimental to society. The point is that a polluting monopolist subjects society to two sorts of costs: the external costs associated with the pollution and a cost resulting from the restriction of output. Our Pigouvian tax, while reducing the pollution costs, at the same time increases the welfare loss resulting from excessively low levels of production, so that the *net* effect on social welfare is uncertain.

2. A PARTIAL ANALYSIS

We can obtain some further insights into this problem with the aid of a simple diagram. In Figure 6–1, let DD' represent the industry demand curve confronting the monopolist, with DMR being the corresponding marginal-revenue curve. We assume that the monopolist can produce at constant cost (PMC = private marginal cost) but that his production activities impose costs on others. In particular, in the absence of any fees, the monopolist's (private) cost-minimizing technique of production generates pollution costs per unit equal to AB so that the SMC (social marginal cost) curve indicates the true cost to society of each unit of output. To maximize profits, the monopolist would produce OQ_m.

Suppose next that we subject the monopolist to a pollution tax, a fee

[1] J. M. Buchanan, "External Diseconomies, Corrective Taxes, and Market Structure," *American Economic Review* LIX (March, 1969), 174–77.

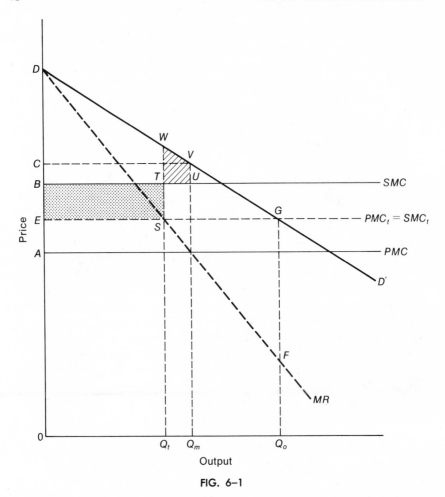

FIG. 6–1

per unit of waste emissions. This will provide an incentive to him to alter his production process in a way that yields lower emissions per unit of output. In Figure 6–1, this would have two effects: it would raise the *PMC* curve and, over some range, would tend to lower[2] *SMC*. This second effect results from the choice of what from *society's standpoint* is a lower-cost method of production (taking into account the costs of pollution). The minimum social cost of production will be reached when the pollution costs are wholly internalized so that $PMC_t = SMC_t$ (where the subscript t refers to costs in the presence of a Pigouvian tax). At this point, the firm's selection of a production

---

[2] Buchanan's analysis assumes a fixed external cost per unit of output that is independent of the method of production.

process will be based upon a set of input prices (including a price of waste emissions) that reflect true social opportunity costs.

In Figure 6–1, we see that the optimal output is OQ_o, which is produced at the least social cost. To achieve this optimum, we would require *two* policy actions: a Pigouvian tax on waste emissions in order to reduce SMC to SMC_t *and* a subsidy per unit of output equal to GF (the difference between marginal cost and marginal revenue at the optimal level of output). For, because we have two types of distortion, full correction generally requires two policy instruments.

An environmental protection agency, however, will not typically have either the authority or the inclination to offer subsidies to monopolists. Suppose, more realistically, that it is empowered only to tax waste emissions. What would be the effect on social welfare of a standard Pigouvian tax on pollution? We see in Figure 6–1 that this would result in a reduction in output from OQ_m to OQ_t. At this output, the tax would generate a cost saving to society indicated by the shaded rectangle $EBTS$. On the other hand, it would be accompanied by a welfare loss represented by the trapezoid $UVWT$; this is the loss in consumers' surplus resulting from the contraction in output to OQ_t. The net effect on social welfare obviously depends on the relative size of these two areas, leaving the environmental authority with (the usual) difficult problem of estimation of surpluses for its policy alternatives.

3. MONOPOLY AND EXTERNALITIES IN A GENERAL EQUILIBRIUM SETTING

This section is intended to pursue further the complexities besetting the analysis of optimal taxation for externalities generated by a monopolist and to suggest a formal approach to the matter which, unfortunately, we have not succeeded in carrying very far. The conceptual difficulties that arise in this case are readily illustrated with the aid of a standard diagram (Figure 6–2) showing the production frontier PP' for the monopolist's output, y_m, and the aggregated output, y_c, of all other industries, which are assumed to be competitive.

We assume also that the monopolist is the only generator of externalities, and (for concreteness) that these externalities are detrimental. We also posit that there is a well defined and well behaved social welfare function so that, A, the point of tangency between the possibility locus and one of the isowelfare curves is the *optimum optimorum*.

We may note that, if the externality-generating industry had been competitive, a standard proposition, which will be reaffirmed in Chapter 7, indicates that its output would have been excessive. But that does not mean that the competitive market equilibrium point would then be a point, such as B,

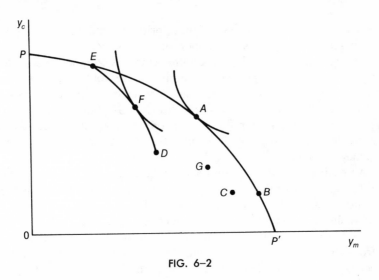

FIG. 6-2

that lies *on* the possibility frontier somewhere to the right of the optimal point, A. Rather, because externalities produce output vectors that are *inefficient* as well as nonoptimal,[3] the competitive equilibrium is represented by a

[3] By efficiency we mean that the output of any one product is as large as it can be without any loss in the output of any other commodity. To illustrate the argument with a simple model, assume we have only one resource, labor, and that the resource requirement functions are $r_1 = c^1(y_1,s_1)$ and $r_2 = c^2(y_2,s_1)$ for industries 1 and 2 that compose the entire economy. Here, s_1 is the externality generated by industry 1 that affects the resources cost of industry 2. Then, by definition, efficiency requires that we, say,

$$\text{maximize } y_1 \text{ (the output of industry 1)}$$
$$\text{subject to } y_2 \geq y_2^*$$
$$c^1(y_1,s_1) + c^2(y_2,s_1) \leq r.$$

This yields the Lagrangian

$$L = y_1 + \lambda_a(y_2 - y_2^*) + \lambda_b[r - c^1(\cdot) - c^2(\cdot)].$$

Then, assuming $y_1 > 0$, $y_2 > 0$, $s > 0$, we obtain the first-order conditions

$$1 - \lambda_b c_1^1 = 0 \qquad \lambda_a - \lambda_b c_2^2 = 0, \qquad \lambda_b(-c_s^1 - c_s^2) = 0.$$

By the first of these conditions, $\lambda_b \neq 0$ so that efficiency requires

$$c_s^1 = -c_s^2, \tag{1}$$

meaning that the externality (say, smoke emissions) should be carried to the point where its marginal resource saving to the generator is equal to its marginal resource cost to the victim.

In the corresponding profit-maximization model, the firm's objective function is $p_1 y_1 - p_3 c^1(\cdot)$, where p_1 is the equilibrium price of output 1, and p_3 is the equilibrium price of labor. Direct differentiation with respect to s_1 shows readily that, in the absence of a Pigouvian point, such as C, that lies *inside* the production frontier and to the right of the optimal point.

Now the polluting monopolist will presumably produce a smaller output than that of the competitive industry but the monopolist, too, will violate the efficiency conditions, by the argument of the preceding footnote. Hence, in the world in which the externality is produced by a monopolist, the free-market solution will be represented by a point, such as G or D, that lies inside the possibility frontier to the left of competitive equilibrium point, C. However, there is no way one can determine in general whether the monopoly equilibrium point will lie to the right or the left of optimal point, A.

Suppose, now, that a Pigouvian tax equal to actual marginal social damage is levied on the monopolist and that the monopolist considers its value a parameter that is fixed and beyond his control. This will reduce his output further. But, as is easy to see, it will also lead him to eliminate the inefficiency in his (society's) production activities. For this purpose we need only consider emissions disposal as an input to his production process. A standard result of monopoly theory shows that, when the profit-maximizing monopolist pays the social cost of his inputs, he will always use them in efficient proportions (that is, his decisions will be consistent with the attainment of a point that lies on the production-possibility frontier to the left of the optimal point). It follows that the Pigouvian tax rate, t_p, will have moved the monopolist to a point, such as E, that lies on the possibility frontier, but to the left of the free market point (say, point D). The locus EFD will trace out the free-market (monopoly) equilibrium points corresponding to intermediate tax rates t, where $0 \leq t \leq t_p$.

We see that the Pigouvian tax rate has both advantageous and disadvantageous consequences: it eliminates inefficiency but yields too small an output of the monopolist's commodity, which, despite the externality, may conceivably already be too small even in the absence of a tax.

In the diagram there is an optimal *intermediate* tax rate (a positive tax rate less than the Pigouvian rate) corresponding to point F at which the locus of free-market equilibrium points EFD is tangent to an isowelfare locus. At that point, society will have achieved an optimal compromise between productive inefficiency and resource misallocation (monopolistic output restriction). However, we have only been able to conjecture that such an intermediate tax rate will usually be required for the achievement of the second-

---

tax, if $p_3 > 0$ the polluter will emit up to the point at which $c_s^1 = 0$. That is, because it costs him nothing, he will emit smoke up to the point where his marginal private gain from additional emissions is zero. (This holds, incidentally, whether the industry is or is not competitive. In a monopoly, of course, p_1 is no longer fixed, but that does not affect the result.) Thus, if the externality is not entirely inframarginal, so that $c_s^2 \neq 0$, the market equilibrium must violate the necessary condition for efficiency (1). Essentially, the same argument will hold in a more disaggregated model.

best optimum.[4] For it obviously depends on the social welfare function. If the community's desire for the good produced by the monopoly is sufficient, so that the absolute value of the slope of the isowelfare loci is very great, end

[4] A formal model of the second-best taxation in the presence of externalities produced by a monopoly is not difficult to formulate, but we have not succeeded in deriving from it an intelligible expression for the optimal tax. Such a model differs from the standard analysis of Pareto optimality in one fundamental respect—it must include among its constraints a number of relationships describing the behavior of the monopolistic and competitive sectors of the economy. The monopolistic behavior constraints are, in a sense, the heart of the matter, for it is they that prevent the achievement of the true optimum.

An illustrative model will indicate the nature of the constraints. Consider an economy with one consumer and three commodities: y_1 which is produced by the monopoly and generates an externality, s; good y_2 which is produced by the competitive sector; and labor (negative leisure), $y_3 \leq 0$. The monopolist seeks to maximize $p_1(y_{11})y_{11} + p_3 y_{31} - t_s s_1$ subject to its production function constraint

$$f^1(y_{11}, y_{31}, s_1) \leq 0, \tag{2}$$

which (assuming all variables take nonzero values) yields the first-order conditions

$$\left.\begin{array}{r} dp_1 y_{11}/dy_{11} - \alpha f_1^1 = 0 \\ p_3 - \alpha f_3^1 = 0 \\ -t_s - \alpha f_s^1 = 0. \end{array}\right\} \tag{3}$$

Similarly, the competitive sector obviously must satisfy the first-order conditions

$$\left.\begin{array}{r} f^2(y_{22}, y_{32}, s_1) \leq 0 \\ p_2 - \beta f_2^2 = 0 \\ p_3 - \beta f_3^2 = 0 \end{array}\right\} \tag{4}$$

while our consumer's behavior satisfies

$$\left.\begin{array}{r} p_1 x_1 + p_2 x_2 \leq p_3(y_{31} + y_{32}) \\ p_1/p_3 = u_1/u_3 \\ p_2/p_3 = u_2/u_3, \end{array}\right\} \tag{5}$$

where u_i is the marginal utility of i.

Thus, quasi-Pareto optimality requires maximization of

$$u(x_1, x_2, x_3, s_1)$$

subject to

$$x_1 \leq y_1$$
$$x_2 \leq y_2$$
$$y_{31} + y_{32} + x_3 \leq y_3^* = \text{available quantity of labor-leisure,}$$

plus the constraints given by (2)–(5) and the appropriate nonnegativity conditions.

For those who get some illumination by counting variables and constraints, it may be comforting to note that we have 13 constraints and the 14 variables y_{11}, y_{22}, y_{31}, y_{32}, x_1, x_2, x_3, s_1, p_1, p_2, p_3, t_s, α, and β.

We can, of course, get rid of one of the prices by normalization (perhaps using Walras's law to argue that one of the constraints is dependent on the others). Thus, if the remaining constraints were independent equations, we would be left with one degree of freedom, permitting us to select an optimal value of t_s, which is the object of the exercise.

Unfortunately, our attempts to work with this model have only produced results suggesting the wide variety of considerations that must be taken into account in determining the optimal value of the tax variable. It may be useful to attempt to apply some of the fixed point D of arc EFD may in fact be the second-best optimum, and a zero tax rate will be called for. Similarly, if the relative valuation of the monopolist's product is sufficiently small, point E may be the quasi-optimum, and a Pigouvian tax rate will be appropriate.

Accordingly, it is not difficult to show that the tax level necessary to sustain a second-best optimum depends on price elasticities of demands of the affected commodities, and not just on the marginal social damage of the externality, as in the competitive case. The more inelastic the demand, the smaller, apparently, is the change in output resulting from a given change in the tax. This seems to suggest that, other things being equal, we should adopt a higher emission tax where the product demand is more price inelastic. As is widely recognized, this role of elasticity is typical of many second-best problems of pricing and resource utilization. In sum, we find that the task of the environmental authority, with its objective of optimization of some sort, becomes a good deal more complicated in the presence of monopoly industries.

4. MONOPOLISTIC OFFSETS TO EXTERNAL EFFECTS

There is one line of argument that suggests that monopolization can sometimes reduce the need for tax measures in the control of externalities. Should a monopoly take over both the firms that generate some externalities and those that are affected by them, the externalities would be internalized and, therefore, what (in this respect) is good for society would then be good for the monopoly. For example, an electricity-laundry combine that took control of both these activities might soon enough recognize the costs to the laundry of the smoke generated by electricity production, and it would be motivated to deal with the smoke in the most economical manner available.

Although the argument is valid, it seems to us that its relevance is rather limited. Some of the most serious externalities that now beset society affect private individuals far more than they do firms. There is presumably no way in which we as individuals can merge with or be acquired by a monopoly firm, so that the health effects of the pollutants we breathe become a relevant entry in the account books of the polluting firm. Moreover, even where

---

point algorithms that have recently been designed by Scarf, Hansen, Kuhn, and MacKinnon for the solution of general equilibrium systems. See, for example, J. B. Shoven and J. Whalley, "A General Equilibrium Calculation of the Effects of Differential Taxation of Income from Capital in the U.S.," *Journal of Public Economy*, I, No. 3/4 (November, 1972), 281–321; H. W. Kuhn and J. MacKinnon, "The Sandwich Method for Finding Fixed Points," (forthcoming); J. MacKinnon, "Urban General Equilibrium Models and Simplicial Search Algorithms," (unpublished manuscript); and H. E. Scarf, with the collaboration of T. Hansen, *The Computation of Economic Equilibria*, (New Haven, Connecticut: Yale University Press, 1973).

the polluter and his victim are both firms, their fields of operation are often so diverse that their merger is simply not practical. Conglomerates made up of oil refineries or electricity generating plants *and* laundries do not seem very common in practice.

5. POLLUTION BY MANIPULATORS OF THE TAX RATE [5]

Even where a polluting activity is not carried out by a monopolist, the analysis may have to take account of a small-numbers problem if only one or a very few sources of substantial emissions are to be found in a particular geographic area. There are many communities whose air and water quality is effectively determined by the activities of one or several producers and smaller cities that are enveloped by the smoke emitted by one factory's chimneys.

Although voluntary negotiation is no more to be expected here than in the large-numbers case, another analytic complication for the Pigouvian approach does arise that our discussion up to this point has assumed away. The polluting firms may recognize that their behavior can affect the rate at which their emissions are taxed. Just as a monopolist or an oligopolist can profit by adjusting his output to obtain a more profitable price, he may be able to benefit by modifying his emissions to obtain a more favorable tax *rate*. And in both cases the result will generally violate the requirements for Pareto optimality unless special corrective measures are undertaken.

6. PRELIMINARY: TWO INTERPRETATIONS OF INTERIM PIGOUVIAN TAX RATES

Before getting down to a more formal discussion of the issue, we must note an ambiguity in the definition of the Pigouvian tax prescription for a situation that is, at least initially, *not* Pareto-optimal. Suppose that, in an optimal solution, five thousand gallons of a given effluent will be emitted into a stream and that the marginal damage at that point is five cents per gallon. Today, however, suppose four times that much is being poured into the waterway and that the corresponding marginal social damage is ten cents per gallon. What, then, is the appropriate Pigouvian tax rate on effluents for *today:* the optimal social damage level (that is, five cents), or the current

[5] The discussion of the next three sections is based entirely on the analysis of Earl A. Thompson and Ronald Batchelder, "On Taxation and the Control of Externalities: Comment," *American Economic Review* (forthcoming).

marginal social damage (ten cents per gallon)? The literature is ambiguous on this point and, indeed, Coase and others have questioned whether the second of these two possibilities, a tax rate that varies over time with the current marginal damage rate, would actually converge to an optimum. Elsewhere, one of the authors of this book has argued that it would converge if the usual stability and convexity assumptions for a competitive equilibrium also hold in the presence of externalities.[6] It can, indeed, be argued that this is true by definition: if the market equilibrium is unique and (with the appropriate tax-subsidy rates) is also Pareto-optimal, then the assumption of stability means that the economy must approach the optimum, with current tax rates converging to optimal tax rates as marginal damages approach their optimal levels. After all, in this sense, the tax rates are perfectly analogous to competitive prices that converge along with marginal products and marginal rates of substitution to their optimal values.

The distinction between the two Pigouvian solutions is critical for the discussion of this section. If we define the Pigouvian prescription to call for the calculation and imposition of an optimal tax rate from the beginning, leaving it invariant come hell or high water, then it will obviously constitute no invitation to the isolated firm to modify its emissions in order to influence that tax rate.

However, if the tax rate is adjusted (iteratively) to the magnitude of current marginal damage, the single polluter may find it in his interests to take into account the effects of his decisions on the tax rate he pays. He may find it profitable to emit more or less than he otherwise would in order to improve his tax position.

Certainly, the analogy with flexibility of competitive pricing makes it worth considering the case of the current Pigouvian tax that is adjustable with current damage costs. We may remark, however, that there is little justification for the view that this iterative approach is somehow the more "practical" of the two (that is, that it is simpler to approach the optimal tax rates step by step rather than trying to construct a detailed model of the entire economy and calculating the optimal tax rate from the start). In our view, as we will note again in a later chapter, neither of these procedures seems to lend itself well to implementation. The fixed tax rate does not, because we are still very far from being able to construct from empirical information the requisite general equilibrium model in the detail needed for numerical evaluations of all the many pertinent tax rates. But the iterative method is hardly more promising, because the calculation of detailed and periodic revisions of estimates of marginal social damage for all significant externalities problems is an undertaking we do not know how to carry out.

[6] See W. J. Baumol, "On Taxation and the Control of Externalities," *American Economic Review*, LXII (June, 1972), 307–22.

7. A SINGLE-POLLUTER MODEL

To investigate the behavior of the polluter (or of his victim, if one or the other of them is a single-decision unit), we utilize the Kuhn-Tucker relationships corresponding to the emissions variable in our undepletable externalities model of Chapter 4. It will be recalled (Table 1 of Chapter 4) that relationship $(5°)$ constitutes the relevant necessary condition for Pareto optimality. For $s_k > 0$ (that is, positive emissions by our one emitting firm), $(5°)$ thus becomes, after some obvious modification of notation,

$$-\mu_k f_s^k + \sum \lambda_j \mu_z^j - \sum_{\bar{k} \neq k} \mu_{\bar{k}} f_z^{\bar{k}} \equiv -\mu_k f_s^k - D = 0. \tag{5°}$$

Here we take firm k to be the polluter, and all other firms $\bar{k} \neq k$ to suffer some pollution damage (that may, in some cases, be zero). Thus, the first term in $(5°)$ represents the marginal cost to the emitting firm, k, of a reduction in emissions, and (after multiplication by -1) the other two terms, which we now write for simplicity as D, represent the marginal social damage to individuals, j, and to other firms, k^*, as was shown in Chapter 4. The optimal pricing policy in the large-numbers case, as described in (8) of Chapter 4, called for a tax rate on emissions equal to the marginal social damage. Specifically, we have

$$t = -\sum \lambda_j u_z^j + \sum \mu_{\bar{k}} f_z^{\bar{k}} = D. \tag{6}$$

Let us now examine the profit calculation of the emitting firm, k, when such a tax is imposed. Its Lagrangian profit function becomes (where y_{ik} is its quantity of output or input i)

$$L = \sum p_i y_{ik} - \beta_k f^k(y_{1k}, \ldots, y_{nk}, s_k) - s_k D$$

in which the last term represents the emissions tax payment. The first-order maximum condition corresponding to the variable s_k now becomes, writing D_s for $\partial D / \partial s_k$,

$$\frac{\partial L}{\partial s_k} = -\beta_k f_s^k - D - s_k D_s = 0. \tag{7}$$

Comparing the condition for profit maximization (7) with the corresponding optimality requirement $(5°)$, we see that the two are no longer identical. Only if D_s is zero will the two equations be the same.[7] But if there is only a single emitter of smoke, we can no longer assume that this element will be zero,

---

[7] It will be remembered that, then, as was shown in Chapter 4, $\beta_k = \mu_k$. On this, see (8b) in Chapter 4.

because the level of its emission can affect the marginal cost of smoke to others. Thus, suppose an increase in pollution leads others to move away from the vicinity of the source and thereby reduces the marginal damage of its emission. Then D_s will be negative, so that at the point at which $-\beta_k f_s^k - D = 0$, as Pareto-optimality condition (5°) requires, $\partial L/\partial s_k$ will still be positive, that is, the polluting firm will benefit by increasing its smoke emissions. The reason, of course, is that by doing so, it will drive some of those who suffer from the smoke away from the source and hence reduce the number of individuals subject to smoke damage, with the firm's tax rate declining correspondingly. In that event, optimality requires a tax rate higher than that given by the Pigouvian prescription. The additional tax is necessary to discourage the excess smoke emissions that would otherwise become profitable.

Thompson and Batchelder point out that this analysis is symmetrical in the sense that the Pigouvian rule works no better where there are many polluters but only a single victim, a case of some theoretical interest though it is probably of rather limited importance in practice. If the one victim is a firm, for example, it will benefit by transferring a proportion of its operations in excess of the optimum to the geographic area where there is pollution damage. The single laundry will move an excessive proportion of its activities near its plant that suffers from pollution, knowing that thereby the marginal smoke damage and, hence, the tax rate will be increased. It does this as a means to force an uneconomically large amount of investment in pollution control on the emitters.

In this case Coase does turn out to be right, after all. A tax on the victims is necessary to prevent resource misallocation. The tax must be sufficiently high to discourage excessive absorption of damage by the single victim, something he will undertake as a means to beat the tax game by forcing emitters to be cleaner than is socially desirable.

8. WHY MARGINAL CONGESTION COSTS MUST GENERALLY BE INCREASING

So far, we have considered almost exclusively the role of the number of generators of an externality. We come now to a significant policy issue in which the number of persons consuming the externality also has an important bearing on the matter. It has been observed that the social costs of externalities seem to increase more rapidly than the density of the population involved. A case in point is that of congestion, where damage appears to rise disproportionately to the number of individuals causing the crowding. What has not generally been recognized is that the very logic of congestion costs makes it implausible that they will increase only linearly with the size of the relevant population.

Let

n be the size of the population creating and consuming the congestion (for example, the number of cars on a stretch of highway);

$c(n)$ be the congestion cost per capita of this population (for example, the number of minutes lost per vehicle in traversing the stretch of highway).

Evidence on congestion problems suggests that, after some point at which congestion begins to set in,

$$c'(n) > 0.$$

That is, per unit congestion costs will be increased by an increase in numbers. But *total* social cost to *all* persons affected must be

$$f(n) = nc(n).$$

The result follows immediately, for we must have

$$f'(n) = c(n) + nc'(n),$$

so that the elasticity of congestion cost with respect to n is

$$\frac{n}{f(n)} f'(n) = \frac{nc(n)}{nc(n)} + \frac{n^2 c'(n)}{nc(n)} = 1 + \frac{nc'(n)}{c(n)} > 1.$$

Hence, the social cost of congestion *must* increase more than proportionately with the number of individuals involved unless $c'(n) \leq 0$. In practice, of course, observation indicates that once congestion begins to set in, both $c'(n)$ and $c''(n)$ are positive and substantial in magnitude so that the preceding result will be strengthened correspondingly.[8]

Clearly, the preceding observation does not apply only to congestion problems. It is equally relevant to any case involving reciprocal externalities.

---

[8] Numerous studies of highway congestion indicate the striking rapidity with which traffic speed is reduced by additional vehicles once congestion has set in.

chapter 7

Are Competitive Outputs with Detrimental Externalities Necessarily Excessive?

In this chapter we examine the direction of the bias produced by externalities. Is it true, as often asserted, that when an activity generates external benefits, its competitive equilibrium level will always be below its optimum, and that where an activity imposes external costs, its equilibrium level must be excessive? [1]

This is a proposition that underlies much of the policy advice given by economists on externalities issues: allocate more resources to goods that yield beneficial externalities and reduce their allocation to those that generate detrimental externalities. But suppose that advice is not always correct— what do such exceptions imply about the economist's advisory role?

As a matter of pure theory this problem is not as serious as the one discussed in the next chapter, for the difficulty we are considering here does

---

[1] The literature on this issue includes J. M. Buchanan and M. Z. Kafoglis, "A Note on Public Goods Supply," *American Economic Review* LIII (June, 1963), 403–14; W. J. Baumol, "External Economies and Second-Order Optimality Conditions," *American Economic Review* LIV (June, 1964), 358–72; A. Williams, "The Optimal Provision of Public Goods in a System of Local Government," *Journal of Political Economy* LXXIV (February, 1966), 18–33; W. C. Brainard and F. T. Dolbear, Jr., "The Possibility of Oversupply of Local 'Public' Goods: A Critical Note," *Journal of Political Economy* LXXV (February, 1967), 86–90; A. Williams, "The Possibility of Oversupply of Public Goods: A Rejoinder," *Journal of Political Economy*, LXXV (February, 1967), 91–92; P. E. Vincent, "Reciprocal Externalities and Optimal Input and Output Levels," *American Economic Review* LIX (December, 1969), 976–84; M. Olson, Jr. and R. Zeckhauser, "The Efficient Production of External Economies," *American Economic Review* LX (June, 1970), 512–17; Peter A. Diamond and James A. Mirrlees, "Aggregate Production with Consumption Externalities," *Quarterly Journal of Economics* LXXXVII (February, 1973), 1–24.

not undermine the Pigouvian tax-subsidy solution. So long as the appropriate convexity conditions hold and the economy is competitive, one need merely impose the appropriate tax rates and the market equilibrium must occur at a Pareto optimum, wherever it may lie in relation to the equilibrium that would hold in the absence of Pigouvian taxes.

In practice, however, as will be emphasized in Part II, we do not know how to find or perhaps even to approximate optimal tax rates and so considerably coarser policy measures must be utilized. Usually these rely heavily on the conventional wisdom that constitutes the subject of this chapter: the acceptance of the view that one should expand outputs that yield beneficial externalities, and conversely.

We will find that there can, indeed, be cases in which the equilibrium output of a competitive industry that yields external benefits exceeds its optimal level and the reverse may be true in the case of damaging externalities. But, contrary to what has been implied in a number of recent writings (including a note by one of the present authors)[2], we will show that this cannot occur where there is a single activity that generates one externality and the usual convexity premises hold. That is, if there is one externality-producing activity and if convexity holds throughout, the conventional wisdom on this subject is strictly accurate: the competitive output of a good that generates external benefits will always be less than any of its Pareto-optimal values, and that of an output that yields detrimental externalities must always exceed such an optimum.

This result is rather more surprising than it may at first appear, for the obvious implication of an externality about the direction of change that is socially desirable is only *local* (that is, it tells us only about the best direction for a *small* move from the competitive equilibrium). Yet comparison between the competitive equilibrium and a social optimum is a *global* issue. We will see that the assumptions that have just been listed are sufficient to permit us to leap from the local to the global conclusion.

Although this result seems to be comforting to those who use theory as a basis for advice to policy makers, it is a weak reed on which to rely in practice. For, as will be shown, the theorem can break down if *any one* of the following four conditions holds:

a. the initial position is not a point of perfect competitive equilibrium;

b. there is more than one activity in the economy that yields an externality, or where different activities yield different externalities;

[2] See Baumol, "External Economies and Second-Order Optimality Conditions," *American Economic Review*. Different errors in a recent attempt to prove my original contention were pointed out to me by Robert Dorfman and by members of my seminar at the Stockholm School of Economics in January, 1973. I am, of course, deeply grateful to them for keeping me from falling into traps of my own devising. W.J.B.

c. there exists any activity such as recycling or purification that can abate the externality;

d. the standard concavity-convexity conditions are violated somewhere in the economy.

Because *none* of these conditions is in fact satisfied in reality, we end up with relatively little confidence in the applicability of the global proposition that was just described. Moreover, as we will show in the next chapter, the presence of externalities contributes to the likelihood that the concavity-convexity assumptions constituting the second-order optimality conditions will not be satisfied. To put the matter starkly but not inaccurately, the more significant an externality, the more likely it is that the convexity assumptions will break down, thereby reducing the confidence we can have in the rules about the relation between the competitive equilibrium and the social optima that are described in this chapter. Add to this the likelihood that violation of the convexity conditions will be accompanied by a multiplicity of local maxima, and it is clear that this can complicate enormously the problems of policy design; in particular, it can undermine a price-tax program designed to induce optimal resource usage.

1. MARGINAL EXTERNALITIES AND THE DIRECTION OF MISALLOCATION

Before turning to the relatively new materials beginning in Section 3 we must, as a basis for comparison, review what may be considered the fundamental policy proposition of the theory of externalities:

Proposition One. If $y_1^c = \sum y_{1k}^c$ is the competitive level of the only activity that generates externalities,[3] or if the activity levels of all other items that generate externalities are held constant, then

a. If y_1 generates social damage, a small decrease in y_1 from y_1^c (that is, a marginal transfer of resources from y_1 to other activities) will increase social welfare;

b. If y_1 yields marginal social *benefits*, a small transfer of resources from other activities to y_1 will increase social welfare.

The proposition may be considered self-evident. In competitive equilibrium, the marginal private benefit of an increase in any activity level is zero ($mpb_1 = mpb_2 = 0$). But for any other activity, 2, whose level is per-

---

[3] Commodity 1 can, of course, be a composite of all externality-generating activities, some of which may be detrimental while others may be beneficial. A few moment's consideration confirms that no change in argument is required by this generalization.

mitted to vary because it produces no externalities by hypotheses, we have $mpb_2 = msb_2$ (marginal social benefit of 2). For activity 1, say, in the detrimental externalities case, $msb_1 < mpb_1$. Hence, in competitive equilibrium we must have $msb_1 < msb_2$, and it follows that a transfer of resources from 1 to 2 will be socially beneficial. That is, essentially, all there is to the matter.

2. A MORE EXPLICIT ANALYSIS

A proof taking explicit cognizance of the pertinent general-equilibrium relationships is somewhat tedious and not really more rigorous. Nevertheless, we provide it now, first, because, so far as we are aware, it is not available elsewhere, and, second, because it is needed for our analysis at a critical point later in the chapter.

In deriving our result, we return to our undepletable externalities model of Chapter 4. We again use the notation

x_{ij} = the level of consumption of commodity i by individual j

y_{ik} = quantity of output (input equals negative output) i produced (used) by firm k

r_i = the available quantity of resource i

s_k = the output of pollutant by firm k

$z = \sum s_k$ = total pollution output

$u^j(x_{1j}, \ldots, x_{nj}, z)$ = individual j's utility function

$f^k(y_{1k}, \ldots, y_{nk}, z)$ = firm k's production relationship

$s_k = g^k(y_{1k}, \ldots, y_{wk})$ = firm k's emissions function,

where the $y_{1k}, \ldots, y_{wk}$ are those activities that either generate externalities or can be used to suppress them (for example, labor used in recycling). We will refer to $y_{1k}, \ldots, y_{wk}$ as the activities *directly affecting* the magnitude of the externality.

Then the production constraints for a Pareto-optimality calculation are:

$$
\left.
\begin{aligned}
f^k(\cdot) &\leq 0 & \text{(all } k) \\
\sum_j x_{ij} &\leq r_i + \sum_k y_{ik} & \text{(all } i) \\
z &= \sum g^k(\cdot)
\end{aligned}
\right\}
\tag{1}
$$

and the nonnegativity conditions listed in Chapter 4.

To derive Proposition One, we will posit a small change, dy_{1k}, in the activity levels y_{1k}, holding constant the levels of all other activities that affect externalities directly; that is, we set

$$dy_{2k} = \cdots = dy_{wk} = 0. \tag{2}$$

We will then undertake an adjustment in all other activity levels that renders this change feasible (that is, we will find a set of dx_{ij}, dy_{ik}, dz values that, given the dy_{1k}, will satisfy our constraints). These adjustments in the values of the other variables that are required for feasibility will be obtained by total differentiation of our constraint relationships. We will then substitute these feasible changes in the values of the variables into an appropriate objective function to see whether its value increases or decreases. In this process we will also make use of the information derived from the assumption of competitive equilibrium to relate the state of affairs on the production side with that on the consumption side of the equilibrium. This, in outline, is the logic of the argument.

To derive our proposition, we must assume that our constraints (1) hold as equalities throughout or that the two sides of any such relationship differ by a constant that drops out in differentiation. This may seem to evade the issues that led to the utilization of inequalities in our model. However, in the analysis of Proposition One, this premise is required by the logic of the issue, because it is equivalent to the assertion that the level of employment and of direct waste of resources is held constant throughout. These *must* be held constant in this analysis, because we are concerned here with the effects of *reallocation* of resources as contrasted with changes in their level of employment.

To obtain values of the changes in activity levels consistent with the conditions our technological constraints impose on the reallocation (that is, requiring the postulated change in the externality-generating activity y_{1k} to be feasible), we differentiate each of the constraints (1) totally to obtain

$$df^k = \sum f_i^k \, dy_{ik} + f_z^k \, dz = 0 \quad \text{or} \quad \sum f_i^k \, dy_{ik} = -f_z^k \, dz \quad \text{(all } k) \tag{3}$$

$$\sum_j dx_{ij} = \sum_k dy_{ik} \quad \text{(all } i) \tag{4}$$

$$dz = \sum_k \sum_{i=1}^{w} g_i^k \, dy_{ik} = \sum_k g_1^k \, dy_{1k}, \tag{5}$$

because by (2) we have assumed $dy_{ik} = 0$, $(i = 2, \ldots, w)$.

We now want to determine how much the resulting changes are worth to the individuals who compose the community. For this purpose we evaluate the effects on each individual, j, in terms of the amount of some numeraire commodity, call it item n. We take n to be something like labor (leisure) that is used by every individual and every firm. Thus, a change, dx_{ij}, in the quantity of item i in j's possession would be evaluated as $(u_i^j/u_n^j)\,dx_{ij}$, where the expression inside the parentheses is the marginal rate of substitution between i and n. Hence, the total value of the output changes we are considering to the community as a whole is

$$dv = \sum_i \sum_j (u_i^j/u_n^j)\,dx_{ij} + \sum_j (u_z^j/u_n^j)\,dz. \qquad (6)$$

If $dv > 0$, we say that the change is a *"potential* Pareto improvement." [4]

We assume the system is in competitive equilibrium at prices p_i, with p_n, the price of the numerative commodity, equal to unity. Consequently, by the standard result [compare relations (3ᶜ)–(5ᶜ) of Chapter 4] we have for every individual and firm that uses (produces) some of i and n

$$p_i = u_i^j/u_n^j = f_i^k/f_n^k \qquad \text{(all } i, j, k). \qquad (7)$$

We obtain, through the following sequence of tedious but straightforward steps, a translation of dv into a form that is directly interpretable in terms of the externality. Using the simplified notation

$$T \equiv \sum_j (u_z^j/u_n^j)\,dz, \qquad (8)$$

we have, substituting from (7) into (6)

$$dv = \sum_i \sum_j p_i\,dx_{ij} + T \qquad (9)$$

$$= \sum_i p_i \sum_j dx_{ij} + T$$

$$= \sum_i p_i \sum_k dy_{ik} + T \qquad \text{[by (4)]}$$

---

[4] This is tantamount to a use of the Hicks-Kaldor criterion because we are, in effect, asking whether the gainers from the change would be willing to compensate the losers. If that compensation is actually paid, the change is obviously a Pareto improvement because someone gains and no one loses. In (6), dv may be interpreted as the maximal payments that the gainers would be willing to make rather than forego the change, minus the minimal amounts the losers must receive if they are not to suffer from the change. As is now generally recognized, the Hicks-Kaldor criterion evades the evaluation of income distribution by taking each individual's income and, hence, his ability to pay, as given. It should be recognized that, like the standard theorem on the gains from free trade, Proposition One need not hold if income redistributions are not ruled out and if arbitrary interpersonal evaluations are not prohibited. For if the elimination of an externality damages the well-being of even one individual and the welfare function weighs that individual's interests sufficiently, we are forced to reject the change, no matter how great the benefits it offers the remaining members of the community. See J. R. Hicks, "The Foundations of Welfare Economics," *Economic Journal* XLIX (December, 1939) pp. 696–712; Nicholas Kaldor, "A Note on Tariffs and the Terms of Trade," *Economica*, New Series VII (November, 1940) pp. 377–80; and for an evaluation, I. M. D. Little, *A Critique of Welfare Economics*, 2nd ed. (Oxford: Clarendon Press, 1957).

$$= \sum_i \sum_k p_i \, dy_{ik} + T$$

$$= \sum_i \sum_k (f_i^k/f_n^k) \, dy_{ik} + T \qquad \text{[by (7)],}$$

or recalling the expression (8) represented by T, then by (3)

$$dv = [- \sum_k (f_z^k/f_n^k) + \sum_j (u_z^j/u_n^j)] \, dz. \qquad (10)$$

This states that the net effect of the changes in question is simply the sum of the values of the resulting external effects to each affected firm, k, and each affected individual, j, all measured in terms of the numeraire commodity.[5]

Our result now follows directly from (5), because by our assumption that the y_{1k} produce the externality, we have $g_1^k > 0$. It also follows immediately, by permitting the appropriate $dy_{ik} \neq 0$, $(i = 2, \ldots, w)$, that if one were to have simultaneous increases in several activities, all of which directly increase (or all of which decrease) the magnitude of an externality, then Proposition One applies, with the obvious modifications, to this reallocation of resources to a number of activities directly affecting the externality.

Finally, note that we have proved with (10), in addition to Proposition One,

Proposition Two. Starting from a position of competitive equilibrium, the net effects of a marginal increase in exactly one of the outputs that affect externality levels directly *and any adjustments in other activity levels* necessary to meet the requirements of productive feasibility, will be evaluated by the affected firms and individuals, in terms of a numeraire commodity, at the net value of the external effects alone.

Proposition Two consequently confirms that a competitive equilibrium involving an externality but no corrective taxes or subsidies can never be Pareto-optimal, and shows that a small increase in the level of an activity that yields external benefits can always be introduced in a way that constitutes a *Pareto improvement*,[6] and that the same is true for a marginal decrease in the level of an activity that yields a detrimental externality.

---

[5] It will be recalled from the discussion of Section 4 of Chapter 4 that the expression inside the brackets in (10) is equivalent to the expression for the external damage $\sum_j \lambda_j u_z^i - \sum_k \mu_k f_z^k$ that is used in (5°) of Chapter 4 and from which the Pigouvian tax rate is determined.

[6] That is, the changes will make some persons better off without harming anyone, *provided* the initial gainers compensate the losers. As usual, a Pareto improvement will occur if a change satisfies the Hicks-Kaldor criterion *and* compensation is paid.

3. WHICH WAY TOWARD THE OPTIMUM? INEFFICIENCY AND RESOURCE REALLOCATION

Having gone this far, one is immediately tempted to go one step further. The literature is full of assertions that at least suggest the following proposition:

Proposition Three. If output $y_1 = \sum y_{1k}$ is the only activity that generates net social benefits, then Pareto optimality[7] requires an output of y_1 larger than that which would occur in competitive equilibrium, and the reverse holds if y_1 generates social damage. That is, if $(y_1^c, \ldots, y_n^c)$ and $(y_1^o, \ldots, y_n^o)$ are competitive and Pareto-optimal output vectors, respectively, then $y_1^c < y_1^o$ if y_1 produces external benefits and $y_1^c > y_1^o$ if y_1 yields external damage.

The difference between this and the Proposition One is that the former deals with *marginal* changes from the competitive equilibrium that yield increases in welfare, but the present proposition makes a much stronger assertion about the direction of the (*possibly large*) change needed to attain optimality when *all* activity levels are changed to their optimal values. That is, Proposition One relates to *ceteris paribus*[8] marginal changes that yield (presumably small) Pareto improvements; Proposition Three refers to large changes in which society moves all the way to an optimum and in which *all* other variable values are adjusted appropriately. As already indicated, the proposition of the preceding section is true, but this one is not always valid. However, as we will show in the next two sections, Proposition Three *is* valid if the appropriate convexity conditions hold and there is only one externality-yielding activity.

Before attempting to show the validity of Proposition Three under the convexity assumption, we must comment on a significant matter of interpretation. Though Proposition Three refers to levels of the externality-generating activities themselves, it seems frequently to have been interpreted

---

[7] Strictly speaking, we may not include all Pareto-optimal points in our calculation, but only those that constitute *potential* Pareto improvements over the initial point, in the Hicks-Kaldor sense indicated by expression (6).

[8] That is, other activities that affect externalities directly are held constant in Proposition One, though, obviously, feasibility does require a change in some other activity levels from which the resources are transferred in order to make possible the postulated marginal change.

to refer to the allocation of society's *resources* among them. But, as we will now see, these two propositions are *not* equivalent to one another; the latter states that excessive quantities of resources will be allocated by the market to an activity that generates detrimental externalities, but our formal Proposition Three asserts that the level of such an activity will be excessive.[9] For if the efficiency conditions are not satisfied, an increase in the level of x_1 will not necessarily require an increase in the quantity of resources allocated to activity x_1.

Buchanan and Kafoglis[10] demonstrate that *if efficiency is not assumed,* the assertion that refers to resource allocation is clearly false. Unlike the activity-level analysis of the next few sections, no formal argument is needed to show this. Instead, we need only consider a simple counterexample. Imagine a community in which police protection against crime is not provided by the state; rather, it takes the form of the employment of private policemen by individuals and organizations who can afford it. Assume that each additional policeman hired reduces the overall crime rate and thus contributes an external benefit. In these circumstances, optimality may well require more police protection, but it need *not* call for the hiring of more policemen. For, if a centralized department of police can protect the general public more efficiently than an uncoordinated set of policemen, then optimality may require more protection but a smaller allocation of resources for the purpose.

It is easy to provide other examples of this phenomenon, some of them quite significant. Consider the possibility of the substitution of relatively inexpensive public health measures, such as the spraying of the breeding grounds of disease-carrying insects as a substitute for individual inoculation against a communicable disease. Whenever individualistic decision making leads to inefficiency in the supply of an external benefit, it is clear that, even if optimality calls for an increase in the supply of the benefit, it does not follow that an expansion in the quantities of resources devoted to its production need be required.[11] Interpreted in terms of resource use, where production is not efficient, the standard allegation about the direction of resource misallocation produced by externalities is obviously false: despite its external benefits, the competitive allocation of inputs to police protection may exceed the optimal level.

---

[9] Olsen and Zeckhauser, "Efficient Production of External Economies," *American Economic Review*, seem to have been the first to point out the difference between the two assertions, and to discuss the difference systematically.

[10] "A Note on Public Goods Supply," *American Economic Review*.

[11] For more formal counterexamples, see Buchanan and Kafoglis. Careful analytic discussion of these examples can be found in Vincent "Reciprocal Externalities and Optimal Input and Output Levels," *American Economic Review* and in Olsen and Zeckhauser, "Efficient Production of External Economies," *American Economic Review*.

4. DIRECTION TOWARD THE OPTIMUM IN THE CONVEX CASE: GRAPHIC VERSION OF THE ARGUMENT

We will now provide a somewhat heuristic, graphic argument showing that under appropriate convexity assumptions, Proposition Three relating to the levels of externality-generating activities must be valid. A more formal analysis is offered in the following section.

In our graphic discussion, the variables have been aggregated highly so that we end up with the three variables, x_1, x_2 (representing the total consumption of all other goods), and x_3 (representing the consumption of resources, say of labor, in the form of leisure). In Figure 7–1a, the three-dimensional region $ORST$ represents our production-possibility set,[12] Y, corresponding to the constraints (2). The figure also depicts what we may refer to as an isowelfare locus given by setting $dv = 0$ (that is, v = constant) in our social valuation relationship (6). The figure shows the intersection of the upper boundary of the production-possibility set with one of the family of isowelfare loci. The projection of several such intersection loci on the x_1x_2 plane is shown in Figure 7–1b. Such a locus plus its interior constitutes a set, W_c, (Figure 7–1a) of points socially preferable or indifferent to points on its

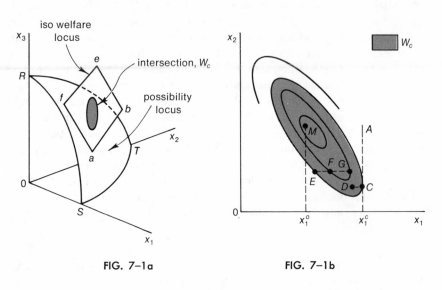

FIG. 7–1a   FIG. 7–1b

boundary. Now, by assumption, neither x_2 nor x_3 generates any externalities. Hence, starting from a competitive equilibrium point, if we hold $x_1 = y_1$

---

[12] We assume in this section that every net output is consumed totally, so that for each i we have $x_i = y_i$.

constant but increase x_2 (with whatever change in x_3 is required), we will have $dz = 0$ (no change in the externality level) so that by (10), social welfare will neither rise nor fall. That is, the marginal shift in resources (say, to produce more x_2 and less leisure) will not cause any change in social utility because, in competitive equilibrium, the marginal private yields of resources in the two activities will be equal, and, for these two activities, marginal private and marginal social yields will also be equal.

Now, the increase in x_2 (holding x_1 constant) represents a vertical move in the x_1x_2 plane.[13] It follows that any competitive equilibrium must occur at a point on an isowelfare curve at which that curve is vertical (that is, a point such as C in Figure 7–1b). Thus, the curve must have a vertical tangent, $x_1^c CA$, at the competitive equilibrium point C. Because the shaded set of points, w_c, preferred to or indifferent to C is convex, it must lie entirely to the left of $x_1^c CA$ or it must lie entirely to the right of that vertical line segment.

Our result now follows at once. For, say, if x_1 yields a detrimental externality, by Proposition One some small decrease in x_1, say the leftward move from C to D, must move us into the shaded region of points preferred to or indifferent to C. Hence, by the convexity property, *all* points in the shaded region must lie to the left of C. But the points in the shaded region represent all possible reallocations that are potential Pareto improvements over the competitive equilibrium point C. Hence, any point that represents a Pareto improvement over C must lie in this region, including the Pareto-optimal points, in which opportunities for Pareto improvement have been exhausted. In particular, if there is a point, M, that represents a maximal Pareto improvement over C [Δv, as indicated by (6), maximal], then M must lie in this shaded region.

5. DIRECTION TOWARD THE OPTIMUM IN ACTIVITY SPACE: CONVEX CASE

We will now formalize the graphic argument of the preceding section, showing that Proposition Three, taken as a statement about the relation between competitive and optimal *output* levels, is valid if the appropriate convexity conditions hold.

Among the premises is the assumption that the production set, call it Y [that is, the set described by constraints (1)], is convex. We take this set to lie in the n-dimensional space of all possible levels of the n production activities. Assuming that the competitive process and the initial incomes yield

---

[13] This is the point in the argument at which our premise that we begin from a competitive equilibrium plays its crucial role.

a unique distribution of every output combination represented by a point in that space,[14] let us utilize the function v, defined implicitly by (6), to measure the improvement in social welfare. In particular, let $\Delta v(x, x^b)$ represent the sum of the maximal payments that the members of the economy who gain in the process are willing to offer rather than forego the change from x^b (the vector representing the initial or base position) to some other point, x, minus the minimal payments necessary to compensate those who lose from the change, all calculated in terms of a numeraire commodity.

Accordingly, we can use the

Definitions. x^a is potentially Pareto-preferred to x^b if

$$\Delta v(x^a, x^b) > 0, \tag{11a}$$

and x^a and x^b are potentially Pareto-indifferent if

$$\Delta v(x^a, x^b) = 0. \tag{11b}$$

Now let x represent the vector $(x_{11}, \ldots, x_{nm})$ and x^a and x^b be any two such vectors with some particular values of the x_{ij}. It seems natural to assume that the function v is strictly quasi-concave in x space in the sense that if x^a is potentially preferred to or indifferent to x^b (that is, if $\Delta v(x^a, x^b) \geq 0$, then for any intermediate point, $x^r = \alpha x^a + (1 - \alpha)x^b$, where $0 < \alpha < 1$, we must have $\Delta v(x^r, x^b) > 0$.

Now, let c designate a competitive solution point, at which the variables take the values x_{ij}^c, and let v^c be the corresponding value of our social maximand, v. Define V_c to be the set of all values of x such that $\Delta v(x, x^c) \geq 0$, which may be described, somewhat inaccurately, as the set of all solutions socially preferred or indifferent to the competitive solution, x^c. Then the set $W_c = Y \cap V_c$ will also be convex, where W_c can be characterized as the set of all *feasible* solutions preferred to or indifferent to x^c. We assume that W_c is not empty and that it contains some interior points.[15]

---

[14] That is, every point $y = (y_1, \ldots, y_n)$ in n-dimensional output space is associated with a unique point $x = (x_{11}, \ldots, x_{nm})$ in the $n \times m$ dimensional consumption space representing distributions of the n commodities among the m consumers.

[15] In fact, W_c need not inevitably have some interior points. If the production set, Y, includes only one process with absolutely fixed proportions it is represented by a ray with no interior points and so there must be no interior point in $W_b = Y \cap V_b$. However, as Figure 7–1a indicates, if the Y and V_c have the shapes usually assumed of them in neoclassical analysis, then interior points of W_c must exist. For the production possibility set is bounded from above by surface RST, which is concave to the origin, and V_c is bounded from below by the surface $abef$, which is convex to the origin. If the competitive solution is not optimal, as must be the case when externalities are present, then W_c, the shaded intersection of these two sets, will not be empty and will have an interior that is not empty.

We will now show that our equilibrium point, c, must lie in the set of the boundary points of the convex set, W_c. For, by our externalities assumption, the competitive equilibrium point, c, is not Pareto-optimal. Hence, with o designating a potentially-preferred point we must have $v^o > v^c$. Thus, if c were not on the boundary of W_c, then W_c must contain a line segment ock^* whose end points are o and k^*, with c an interior point of that line segment. Because k^* lies in W_c, we must by definition have $v^{k^*} \geq v^c$. But because c is in the interior of this line segment, the strict quasi concavity of v requires either $v^c > v^{k^*}$ or $v^c > v^o$, which produces a contradiction. We have proved:

lemma. The competitive equilibrium point, c, must lie on the boundary of W_c.

Next, consider the hyperplane, call it $y_1 = y_1^c$, that is obtained by fixing y_1 at y_1^c, the competitive value of the externality-generating activity, leaving the values of all other variables unrestricted. We will show now that this is a supporting hyperplane of W_c. Obviously, it includes the boundary point c of W_c. Moreover, the hyperplane $y_1 = y_1^c$ can include no interior point of W_c, for suppose, on the contrary, that there is such a point, call it p. Then by the convexity of W_c, the line segment pc must lie entirely within W_c and within the hyperplane $y_1 = y_1^c$. Then, any point q on pc arbitrarily close to c must be potentially preferred to c by the strict quasi-concavity of the function v. But it is impossible for q to be potentially preferred to c because the move from c to q involves $\Delta y_1 = 0$ and so, presumably,[16] all $\Delta y_{1k} = 0$, so that in the limit, by (5), this move yields $dz = 0$ and hence, by (10), $dv = 0$. Thus, the assumption that the hyperplane $y_1 = y_1^c$ contains p, an interior point of W_c, leads to a contradiction.

In sum, because the hyperplane includes a boundary point, c, of W_c and none of the interior points of W_c (which we have assumed to exist), it must be a supporting hyperplane for the convex set W_c.

Proposition Three now follows at once from Proposition One. For W_c, the points socially preferred to or indifferent to c, have now all been shown to lie in one of the halfspaces bounded by the supporting hyperplane $y_1 = y_1^c$. Taking, for example, the beneficial externalities case, because a small increase in the value of y_1 must increase social welfare as measured by v, by Proposition One, it follows that *no* decrease in the value of y_1 can ever increase the value of v (that is, any Pareto-optimal point that is potentially superior to the competitive equilibrium must involve a $y_1^o > y_1^c$). Obviously, the corresponding argument holds for the detrimental externalities case.

---

[16] We require a zero change in *each* y_{1k} and not just in their sum, y_1, because otherwise a decrease in the activity level of a lightly polluting plant and an equal increase in that of a heavily polluting plant would raise emissions despite the absence of any change in *total* y_1. As will be proved in the next section, if we permit independent changes in the individual y_{1k}, Proposition Three can be violated.

6. INVALIDITY OF PROPOSITION THREE WHERE SEVERAL ACTIVITIES YIELD EXTERNALITIES

It is trivial to show by simple counterexample that, if Proposition Three is amended to permit two activities to yield an externality (or to permit two different types of externalities directly affected by several activity levels), then the resulting proposition is no longer valid. That is, we simply are not entitled to say in advance whether an optimal level of an activity that yields a detrimental externality is or is not smaller than its competitive value.[17] Moreover, we will show by concrete illustration (a) that the problem is a very real one, and not a mere theoretical curiosity, and (b) that the choice of those externality-yielding activities that should not be reduced is apt to be a complex matter requiring considerable information and the demanding calculations that are generally called for by interdependencies.

To prove that the theorem is invalid, we utilize a simple linear programming model in which the social welfare function is taken to be known and to be such that its components that are purely private benefits (ignoring externalities) are maximized in the competitive equilibrium.

Using the same notation as before, let there be two outputs, x_1, and x_2, each of which yields some of the externality, z, and one resource of which the available quantity is r. Then the social welfare function is

$$w = a_{01}x_1 + a_{02}x_2 - a_{03}z, \tag{12}$$

which is to be maximized subject to the two production conditions

$$a_{11}x_1 + a_{12}x_2 \leq r \quad \text{(the resource constraint)} \tag{13}$$

and

$$a_{21}x_1 + a_{22}x_2 = z, \quad \text{(the externality output function)} \tag{14}$$

where all parameter values, a_{ij}, are assumed positive and all values of the variables are nonnegative.

Under pure competition, we assume that (14) and the last term in (12) will play no role in the market equilibrium. Instead, the equilibrium will

$$\text{maximize } a_{01}x_1 + a_{02}x_2 \tag{15}$$

subject to (13), which has the solution

[17] This suggests that one of the things that may go wrong in moving from the local Proposition One to its global counterpart, Proposition Three, is that, in the latter, other externality-generating activities cannot generally be held constant. Optimality may *require* all such activity levels to change and the resulting interaction can lead to consequences that follow no simple rule of thumb.

$$x_1^c = 0, \qquad x_2^c = r/a_{12} > 0 \tag{16}$$

if and only if

$$a_{01}/a_{11} < a_{02}/a_{12}. \tag{17}$$

However, social optimality requires maximization of (12) subject to (13) and (14). Direct comparison with the previous solution is facilitated by the elimination of z between (14) and (12), yielding the maximand

$$w = (a_{01} - a_{03}a_{21})x_1 + (a_{02} - a_{03}a_{22})x_2. \tag{18}$$

This is again to be maximized subject to the constraint (13). Assuming the first expression in parentheses is positive, this will have the solution

$$x_1^o = r/a_{11} > 0 \qquad x_2^o = 0 \tag{19}$$

if and only if

$$\frac{(a_{01} - a_{03}a_{21})}{a_{11}} > \frac{(a_{02} - a_{03}a_{22})}{a_{12}}. \tag{20}$$

For suitable values of the externality coefficients a_{03}, a_{21}, and a_{22}, (17) and (20) are clearly compatible. For example, setting $a_{01} = 1$, $a_{02} = 2.3$, $a_{03} = 0.2$, $a_{11} = 1$, $a_{12} = 1$, $a_{21} = 2$, $a_{22} = 10$ we have, in accord with (17),

$$1 = \frac{a_{01}}{a_{11}} < \frac{a_{02}}{a_{12}} = 2.3$$

but, as called for by (20),

$$0.6 = \frac{a_{01} - a_{03}a_{21}}{a_{11}} > \frac{a_{02} - a_{03}a_{22}}{a_{12}} = 0.3.$$

Thus, by (16) and (19), $x_1^c < x_1^o$, even though x_1 produces an externality, z, as shown by (14), and that externality is detrimental, as shown by (12), and even though all the convexity conditions required for maximization are satisfied, as is always true in a linear programming problem for which a solution exists.[18]

Thus we have proved that modified Proposition Three does not necessarily hold where more than one activity produces an externality, and the same sort of argument shows readily that the proposition breaks down where one activity produces an externality and another can be used to suppress it.

---

[18] It should be fairly clear that the linearity of this counterexample is in no way essential for the argument and that the only purpose of the linearity assumption is to provide a very simple case of the phenomenon.

A simple illustration, transportation by railroad and private automobile, will show intuitively why this is so and will suggest that the problem is very real and significant. It is well known that emissions of pollutants per passenger mile by railroads are much smaller than those of autos. It is clear then that Pareto optimality may call for a decrease in the use of automobiles from the competitive level and some offsetting increase in the use of rails, despite the fact that railroad transportation is a polluting activity. The world of reality is full of such cases in which we cannot eliminate pollution but instead have to consider substituting more of a slightly polluting activity for another that is highly damaging.[19]

A similar problem arises where there are several different types of emissions. For example, automobiles give off carbon monoxide, particulates, lead aerosols, hydrocarbons, and a number of other deleterious pollutants. But devices for the suppression of some of these emissions characteristically contribute to others.[20] If these pollutants are not equally harmful and their suppression is not equally costly, it is obvious that a Pareto-optimal solution may actually call for an increase in the emission of some pollutants that are themselves undesirable, but are less damaging than others.

These illustrative cases suggest the subtle and complex character of comprehensive policy analysis. As a further example, consider two emissions, z_1 and z_2, each of which does damage that is measurable in money terms. Suppose a pound of z_1 does twice as much damage as a pound of z_2. It does not follow that z_2 should be increased and z_1 diminished. If suppression of z_2 is ten times as costly per unit as that of z_1, then the reverse is more plausible, and suppression of both of them at a much greater cost cannot be ruled out a priori. A reexamination of the issue indicates that selection of the activity to be increased requires a delicate balancing of their relative (marginal) valuation by consumers, the relative marginal damage resulting from the emissions they produce, the relative costs of the activities, of suppression of their emissions, and of substitute and complementary activities and emissions.

As has been recognized by designers of emission control programs, whether for waterways or for automobiles, the interdependencies involved in such calculations easily get beyond the powers of unaided intuition or the simple sort of advice that seems to follow from Proposition Three.

---

[19] An example will also indicate why Proposition Three can be violated by an activity that abates the effects of an externality. It is conceivable that an optimal change in the competitive output of electricity requires both the production of more smoke suppression equipment *and* the generation of more electricity.

[20] For example, it is reported that a number of scientists have expressed concern over the sulphates and "sulphuric acid mists" yielded by the catalysts planned for installation on automobiles as a means to reduce the emissions of hydrocarbons and carbon monoxide. See V. K. McElheny, "Environmental Agency Is Divided over Car Pollution Control Issue," *The New York Times*, October 15, 1973, p. 40.

7. VIOLATIONS OF PROPOSITION THREE RESULTING FROM NONCONVEXITY

Next, we turn briefly to the sort of case in which (a modified) Proposition Three may not hold even where only a single activity produces a single pollutant. It involves a situation that will be discussed more carefully in the next chapter: a case of multiple local maxima resulting from the violation of the usual convexity-concavity assumptions. The nature of the problem in this case is almost self-evident. Where there are several maxima, even if the rule proposed by Proposition Three can be relied upon to move the economy toward a local optimum, it may very well propel it away from the global optimum.

Leaving the details for the following chapter, the problem can be illustrated with the box diagram in Figure 7–2. The activity of an electricity pro-

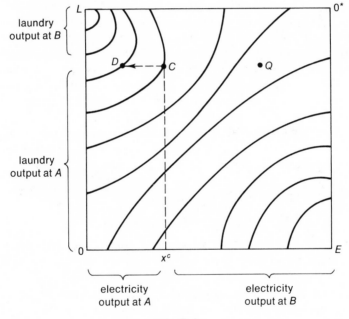

FIG. 7–2

ducer generates smoke; it operates near a laundry industry and the results are economically inefficient. We assume that there are two possible locations, A and B, in which industry can operate, so that laundry and electricity output can be separated either by moving the former to A and the latter to B or vice versa. In our diagram, the abscissa and ordinate of any point, such as C, show the quantities of electricity and laundry produced at location A. Assuming that whatever is not processed here will be turned out at the other location, the outputs of electricity and laundry at B are indicated analogously, taking point O^* rather than O as our origin. If smoke damage is sufficiently costly, there will be (at least) two possible arrangements that are desirable and so constitute local optima: a) locating all (or most) of the laundries elsewhere without the electricity producers reducing their smoke output at A (point E in the diagram), or b) placing the electricity producers at B while the laundries remain in operation at A (point L). Accordingly, the isowelfare loci in the diagram are at their highest near points E and L, and are relatively low at points in the diagram, such as Q, representing simultaneous operation of both industries at A.

Suppose now that C is the competitive equilibrium point at which marginal private yields are zero. Then, as Proposition One tells us, and as we would expect, society will benefit from a *small* decrease in the output of the electricity industry at A, the generator of the external disservice; that is, the move from C toward D moves society to a higher indifference curve. We cannot tell from the diagram whether point E or L is the global maximum, but suppose it is point E. Then the optimal output of electricity produced at A will in fact be greater than the market equilibrium output, Ox^c. This is precisely what we wanted to show: where the social optimum is not unique and other things (the laundry output's location) are *not* held equal, the competitive equilibrium output of an item that generates an external disservice may, in fact, be less than its optimal level.

How such a case can arise is also easy to understand; it is a relative of Coase's well-known example in which society benefits if electricity output at A is curtailed, but, say, because cheap generating power is available at A and not at B, it benefits even more if electricity output at A is increased and laundry activity is simultaneously moved elsewhere.

8. INVALIDITY OF PROPOSITION THREE IF THE INITIAL POINT IS NONCOMPETITIVE

It is now easy to indicate intuitively why Proposition Three, suitably amended, does not hold for an initial point that is not a competitive equilibrium.

Returning to Figure 7-1b, if our initial point is not a competitive equilibrium, it need not correspond to a vertical point on an isowelfare boundary, such as point C. Suppose, then, we begin at point E from which a small rightward move is socially beneficial (presumably there is a local beneficial externality). The diagram shows how the optimal point, M, can nevertheless lie to the left of E. Moreover, without detailed knowledge of the social welfare function and the social production set, information which is not usually available, there is no way of realizing that a small increase in x_1, say from point E to F, is beneficial, but that once we get to G and beyond, things begin to get worse. There is no iterative process whereby society can move in a sequence of steps always in a preferred direction.

For an illustration of this difficulty, we can simply recall a problem we posed in the preceding chapter. If we have a polluting monopolist, we cannot be sure whether social welfare will be increased or decreased by a reduction in his output below the profit-maximizing level. A fall in output will presumably reduce the social costs his waste emissions impose, but at the same time it will add to the welfare losses resulting from his failure to extend production to the point where marginal cost equals price. The net effect on social welfare depends upon the particular values of the variables in each case, and one simply cannot construct a dependable rule of thumb about the direction in which the firm should be induced to move to serve the interests of the community.

9. CONCLUSION: IMPLICATIONS FOR POLICY RECOMMENDATIONS

The upshot of all this seems fairly clear. Although the domain of validity of Proposition Three may be somewhat greater than some people had previously believed to be the case, it cannot be relied upon to hold in any class of cases that is really relevant for policy. That is, there seem to be few, if any, areas in which we can *depend* on the rule of thumb implied by that proposition. The world confronts us with many difficult and complex trade-off decisions, and there just seems to be no simple rule that permits us to cut through them.

chapter 8

Detrimental Externalities and Nonconvexities in the Production Set[1]

The preceding chapter showed that the conventional wisdom concerning the direction in which to modify output in the presence of externalities is likely, at least sometimes, to be misleading. The problem can arise whenever the relevant convexity conditions break down.

In this chapter, however, we will show that detrimental externalities of sufficient strength *will* produce a breakdown in the concavity-convexity conditions (the so-called second-order conditions) usually postulated for a social maximum, so that instead of a unique optimum, society may have the difficult task of choosing among a set, and, sometimes, a substantial set of discrete local maxima. Indeed, in a system otherwise characterized by constant returns everywhere (that is, a linear model), *any* detrimental externalities, however minor, can produce a nonconvexity. This problem is no mere theoretical curiosity. We will see that it produces some very real and difficult issues in the choice of policy.

Moreover, even in theory, prices and taxes cannot help with this matter. Prices and taxes (which, in general, influence the first-order maximum conditions) can affect the decisions of individuals and firms and thereby determine the location of the economy in relation to its production-possibility set. However, prices or taxes cannot change the shape of the possibility set itself to transform it from a nonconvex into a convex region, for that is essentially

[1] Our colleague, David F. Bradford, is a coauthor of this chapter, which draws heavily on W. Baumol and D. Bradford, "Detrimental Externalities and Non-Convexity of the Production Set," *Economica* XXXIX (May, 1972), 160–76.

a technological matter. Moreover, as we will see later in the chapter, in the presence of nonconvexities, these prices may also give the wrong signals —directing the economy away from the social optimum.

It is not our objective here to review in any detail the difficulties caused by nonconvexity. Some of these consequences have long been recognized and are widely known.[2] However, until the recent appearance of papers by Starrett, Portes, Kolm, and Baumol,[3] it was apparently not recognized that externalities themselves are a source of nonconvexity. These more recent writings suggest more than one connection between the two phenomena. However, one particularly straightforward relationship seems to have received little or no attention. With sufficiently strong interactive effects, nonconvexity follows from the simple fact that if *either* of two activities, one of which interferes with the other, is operated at zero level, no hindrance is suffered.[4] The goal of this chapter is to explore this phenomenon and to show how it is that sufficiently severe detrimental externalities and nonconvexity necessarily go together.

In the first three sections we show, with the aid both of illustrative examples and more general analysis, that detrimental externalities of sufficient magnitude must always produce nonconvexity in the production possibility set for two activities: one generating the externality and one affected by it. In the fourth section we show that the problem is reduced, but not generally eliminated, by the possibility of spatial separation of offender and offended. However, achievement of the "right" spatial separation turns out not always

[2] Pigou, for example, commented that ". . . if several arrangements are possible, all of which make the values of the marginal social net products equal, each of these arrangements does, indeed, imply what may be called a *relative maximum* for the [national] dividend; but only one of these maxima is the unequivocal, or absolute, maximum. . . . It is not necessary that all positions of relative maximum should represent larger dividends than all positions which are not maxima. On the contrary, a scheme of distribution approximating to that which yields the absolute maximum, but not itself fulfilling the condition of equal marginal yields, would probably imply a larger dividend than most of the schemes which do fulfill this condition and so constitute relative maxima of a minor character." *The Economics of Welfare*, London: Macmillan and Co., 1938 (4th ed.), p. 140.

[3] See D. A. Starrett, "Fundamental Nonconvexities in the Theory of Externalities," *Journal of Economic Theory*, 4, (April, 1972), 180–99; R. D. Portes, "The Search for Efficiency in the Presence of Externalities," in *Unfashionable Economics: Essays in Honor of Lord Balogh*, ed. Paul Streeten (London: Weidenfeld and Nicolson, 1970), pp. 348–61; S. C. Kolm, "Les Non-Convexites d'Externalité," CEPREMAP Rapport No. 11, mimeograph, 1971; and Baumol, "External Economies and Second-Order Optimality Conditions," *American Economic Review*.

[4] Note that this observation does not hold for externalities that Davis and Whinston (page 244) have termed "separable." Here, if industry 1's output affects the costs of industry 2, the latter's cost function would be of the form $f(x_2) + g(x_1)$. This implies that $g(x_1)$, the ill effects of industry 1 upon industry 2, would remain unaffected even if 2 were to go out of operation altogether! There is obviously no contradiction in such a premise, but it would seem to cast doubt upon the widespread applicability of the separable-externalities concept. See O. A. Davis and Andrew Whinston, "Externalities, Welfare, and the Theory of Games," *Journal of Political Economy* LXX (June, 1962), 241–62.

to be a simple matter. Section 5 contains some speculations about the way in which the number of local peaks in the production-possibility function grows with the number of interacting activities. In Section 6, we discuss the possibility of using Pigouvian taxes to sustain desirable behavior and, in a concluding seventh section, we review briefly the problems for social policy inherent in the sort of nonconvexity we have been analyzing.

An appendix contains a formal demonstration of the workability of Pigouvian taxes in this context. It is shown that, as long as individual production sets are convex, all socially efficient output vectors *can* be sustained as a sum of profit-maximizing output choices under taxes designed to equate marginal social and private costs.

1. A SIMPLE MODEL

Consider a two-output, one-input economy in which each output is produced by a single industry. To avoid compounding problems we shall assume that each industry has a convex technology in terms of its own inputs and outputs.[5] However, the presence of detrimental externalities means that increases in the output of one of the industries raise the other's costs of production, which is to say, the amount of input required to produce any given output. What we wish to show is that, if this detrimental externality is strong enough, then the social production set must be nonconvex.[6]

For consistency with the general analysis in the appendix, let us begin by carrying through this example following the practice of measuring inputs as negative outputs. As in the previous chapter, we consider an economy having three or more outputs that, for concreteness, we take to be leisure, electricity, and laundry. The shaded region of Figure 8–1a shows the production set (the set of attainable net output vectors) for the electricity industry, bounded by the ray OE. Figure 8–1b displays the production set for the laundry industry under two alternative assumptions about output in the electricity industry. The detrimental externality generated by electricity means that, for a given input of labor to laundry, less laundering will be

---

[5] Thus, if r_k is the quantity of input to industry k and y_k is its output, and if (r_k^*, y_k^*) and (r_k^{**}, y_k^{**}) are two feasible input-output combinations (holding constant inputs and outputs in other sectors), then $0 < \alpha < 1$ implies that $[\alpha r_k^* + (1 - \alpha) r_k^{**}, \alpha y_k^* + (1 - \alpha) y_k^{**}]$ is also a feasible input-output combination. Convexity of a production set is sometimes referred to as *generalized nonincreasing returns*, which means that a convex technology cannot exhibit increasing returns to scale and that it obeys the laws of diminishing marginal rates of substitution among factors and among outputs, and diminishing marginal productivity of outputs by factors.

[6] In the notation of footnote 1, the social production set is the set of all vectors $(r_1 + r_2, y_1, y_2)$, such that (r_1, y_1) and (r_2, y_2) are *simultaneously* feasible for their respective industries.

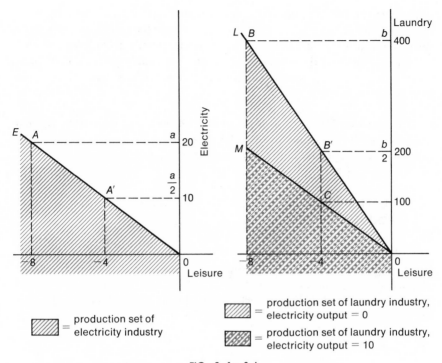

FIG. 8–1a & b

produced when electricity output is positive than when it is zero. Thus, in Figure 8–1b, OM, the ray serving as the laundry production frontier when some positive level of electricity is produced must lie below OL, the laundry frontier when no electricity is produced. To make things easy to follow, we have assumed constant returns to scale for each of the industries taken alone; hence the straight-line boundaries. We will now show that in this linear model any detrimental externality, however weak, can undermine the convexity conditions.

Consider two social production vectors on frontiers OE and OL, vector A on OE (-8 leisure, 20 electricity, 0 laundry) and vector B on OL (-8 leisure, 0 electricity, 400 laundry). Obviously both of these are technically feasible, as are (by constant returns to scale) the vectors A': (-4, 10, 0) and B': (-4, 0, 200), which are, respectively, half way to the origin from A and B. However, the vector $V = (-8, 10, 200)$, which is a convex combination of A and B because $V = A' + B' = 1/2\ A + 1/2\ B$, is *not* feasible technically. If we wish to give up 8 units of leisure altogether and insist on 10 units of electricity, requiring four of these units of leisure, the most we can obtain is 100 units of laundry (point C). More generally, if L is the amount of leisure devoted to the two outputs and *a* and *b* represent the respective outputs of electricity and laundry, if L is devoted exclusively to the one or the other, then the assignment of $1/2 L$ to each output must necessarily provide less than $b/2$ of laundry output if there is any detrimental externality present. Point B' is never attainable under these conditions and nonconvexity *must* follow. Thus we have

Proposition One. In a linear model, *any* detrimental externality that occurs only when there are nonzero levels of each of two activities must produce a nonconvexity in the social possibility set.

2. AN ALTERNATIVE VERSION OF THE NONCONVEXITY ARGUMENT

Another way of looking at the matter may be helpful to the intuition. Figure 8-2 depicts an ordinary production-possibility frontier RAR' in the absence of externalities. Dropping our earlier assumption of a constant marginal rate of transformation between outputs, we take this curve to bound the convex feasible region $ORAR'$. Let us, for expository convenience, intro-

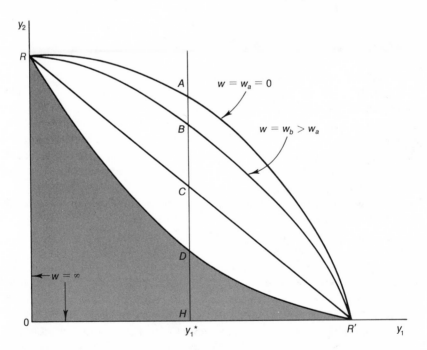

FIG. 8-2

duce a parameter w measuring the strength of the externality. In terms of our example, w can be taken to measure the mean addition to the resources cost of cleaning a given batch of laundry that occurs when an added unit of electricity output causes smoke to increase. By definition, then, along RAR', which corresponds to the absence of external effects, the value of w (call it w_a) is zero.

Consider what happens to the production-possibility locus as the value of w is increased. We will show that the position of the end points R and R' will be totally unaffected, but all other points on the locus will be shifted downward. Point R, where electricity production is zero, will be unaffected by a rise in the value of w; whatever the social cost of smoke, at that point there will be no increase in damage because, by assumption, there is no smoke produced in the absence of any electricity output. Similarly, the location of R', where laundry output is zero, is invariant with w, because at that point no resources are devoted to laundry production, and hence there can be no increase in the resources cost of laundry output. There simply is no laundry to be damaged so that the electricity industry can smoke away without causing any harm to the only other output in our model.

However, consider some intermediate level of electricity output, say y_1^*. Here an increase in w means that with a given amount of electricity and a given quantity of resources, a smaller quantity of clean laundry can be produced than before. Consequently, point A must shift downward to some lower point, B, and the entire possibility locus becomes something like RBR'. With further increases in the value of w, point A will be shifted lower still. If, at some value of w, it is pulled below line segment RCR', the possibility set becomes a nonconvex region, such as shaded region $ORDR'$.

This must certainly happen if the individual industries exhibit constant returns to scale, as in our example of the previous section,[7] so that the production possibility frontier is a line segment like RCR'. For then *any* downward shift in point C, with points R and R' stationary, must yield a nonconvexity. Thus, in the nonlinear case, a detrimental externality will produce a nonconvexity if it is sufficiently strong to offset the influence of the diminishing marginal rate of transformation between the outputs in question.

Even in the nonlinear case, if the external damage is sufficiently serious[8]

---

[7] Figure 8–2 can be connected directly to the interrelated individual production sets of Figure 8–1a and 8–1b. Points R and R', respectively, represent the social output vectors $(-8, 0, 400)$, that is, point B in Figure 8–1a, and $(-8, 20, 0)$, that is, point A in Figure 8–1a. With constant returns to scale and a single input, the production frontier, in the absence of externalities, must be the line segment RCR'. However, with electricity output at $y_1^* = 10$ in Figure 8–2, the most laundry we can obtain in the presence of the externality is $HD = 100$, not $HC = 200$.

[8] Of course, even if A lies below C, the resulting nonconvexity need not lie in the interior of curve RAR'. For example, the frontier may cut the vertical axis at some point R^* that lies below R, with a perfectly well behaved segment of the frontier connecting R^* and R'. This case certainly seems implausible.

(that is, for sufficiently high values of w), A *must* lie below C. For if the marginal smoke output is so great and so noxious that no quantity of resources can get laundry as clean as it would be in the absence of smoke, then A must fall all the way to the horizontal axis (point H). That is, in the limit, the possibility locus then must consist simply of the axis segments ROR'.

The simplicity of the preceding argument may belie its generality and rigor.[9] The point is that, with any pair of commodities at least one of which interferes with the production of the other, there will be no such interference if one or the other is not produced. On the other hand, if the interference is sufficiently great, the maximal output of the activity suffering the external damage will approach zero for *any* nonzero level of output of the other and a nonconvexity in the feasible set is unavoidable.

Note that this argument holds for such a pair of commodities no matter how many goods the economy produces; so that if there is a nonconvexity in the production set for *any* pair of commodities, the full n-dimensional production set in the n-commodity economy is also necessarily nonconvex.

Thus, we have

Proposition Two. If it is sufficiently strong, a detrimental externality that arises only when the level of each of two activities is nonzero must produce a nonconvexity in the social production set.

3. A FURTHER ILLUSTRATION

Some readers may prefer to deal with a concrete algebraic example explicitly relating a measure of the degree of detrimental externality to the "wrong" curvature of a production-possibility frontier of the type displayed in Figure 8–2. We therefore offer a case in which the separate production sets of the two industries are strictly convex. Let y_e be the output of electricity and y_t the output of laundry services, r_e and r_t be the amounts of labor (negative leisure) used by them, and suppose

$$r_e = y_e^2/2 \tag{1}$$
$$r_t = y_t^2/2 + wy_ey_t.$$

Thus each industry separately is subject to strictly diminishing returns to scale in terms of its own input. The coefficient w now measures the strength of the effect of electricity output on laundry costs; the effect is detrimental if $w > 0$. If a total of r units of labor is available for the two activities, we can

---

[9] For further discussion of the preceding argument as well as an ingenious examination of a great variety of other connections between externalities and nonconvexity, see Kolm, "Les Non-Convexites d'Externalité," CEPREMAP.

write the implicit equation for the laundry-electricity possibility frontier as

$$r = y_e^2/2 + wy_ey_t + y_t^2/2, \tag{2}$$

$$y_e \geqq 0, \qquad y_t \geqq 0.$$

We can deal with any such differentiable possibility locus in an obvious manner, calculating its second derivative and showing generally that when the externality parameter, w, becomes sufficiently large, that derivative must take positive values. The present illustration, however, permits us to show this result more directly. If $w = 0$ (no externality), (2) describes a quarter circle in a (y_e, y_t) coordinate system. This boundary obviously has the "right" curvature. For small positive w, the boundary continues to be concave to the origin. However, when $w = 1$, (2) becomes the equation of a straight line $[(y_e + y_t)^2 = 2r]$, and, for larger values of w, nonconvexity of the production set occurs.

In the preceding example, the boundary between convexity and non-convexity happens to involve a value of w, that is, $w = 1$, that is independent of the magnitudes of the outputs and that can, perhaps, be considered fairly large. More generally, however, the appearance of the nonconvexity will depend both on the magnitude of the externality parameters and on the values of y_e and y_t. For example, suppose in the preceding illustration, we leave the electricity-cost function unchanged but make the laundry resource requirement function

$$r_t = y_t + wy_ey_t.$$

Then the production-possibility locus is given by

$$r = r_e + r_t = y_e^2/2 + wy_ey_t + y_t.$$

A straightforward but tedious calculation of the second derivative[10] shows that the production set will be convex if and only if

$$2w^2y_t + wy_e < 1.$$

Clearly, for w or y_e or y_t sufficiently large, this requirement will not be satisfied. In this illustrative example, the maximum feasible values of y_t occur in the vicinity of $y_e = 0$. Here we have $y_t = r$ the total quantity of resource available, and it is not difficult to imagine values of w and r that will violate the preceding convexity requirement. If r is very large, say on the order of thousands or millions of units, even a very small value of the externality

---

[10] See Appendix A, which also presents a more general version of the arguments for the three-output production possibility locus using the differential calculus.

parameter, w, will violate the second-order conditions. For example, if $r =$ 10,000, then any $w > 0.01$ will have this effect.

4. SPATIAL SEPARATION AS A PALLIATIVE[11]

A lower bound to the degree of nonconvexity in the social production set arising from detrimental externalities is provided by the possibility of separating the generators and their victims geographically, for instance, by moving the laundries from the vicinity of the electricity producers or vice versa. This is illustrated by the following example:

Assume once more that we have two outputs, this time call them 1 and 2, and that these can be produced at either of two locations, a and b, with respective output levels, y_{1a}, y_{2a}, y_{1b}, and y_{2b}. To begin with, we take all substitution relationships in the absence of externalities to be perfectly linear. Let us assume that, were there no externalities, it would pay to produce both

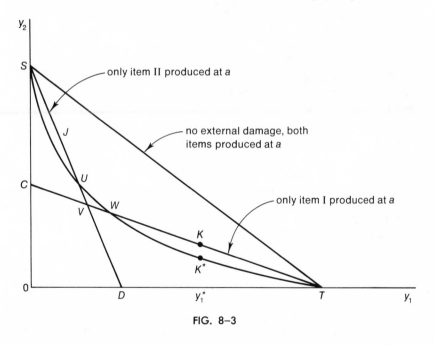

FIG. 8–3

items at the same location, say A. In Figure 8–3, line segment *ST* represents the production-possibility locus for our two items when external damage is

[11] For a very careful analysis of the location issue, see T. C. Koopmans and M. Beckmann, "Assignment Problems and the Location of Economic Activities," *Econometrica* XXV (January, 1957), 53–76.

zero and both are manufactured at the more economical location, A. SD represents the more restricted set of output levels[12] that remains possible if y_2 were still produced at A but the production of y_1 were moved to B. Because B is assumed to be a less suitable site, all of SD must lie below ST, with the exception of endpoint S, which corresponds to production of y_2 alone, which, by hypothesis, still occurs at A. Similarly, line segment CT represents the production possibilities when manufacture of y_2 is moved to B and that of y_1 takes place at A.

Now suppose that externalities generated by the production of y_1 at A grow serious, so that the locus corresponding to manufacture of both items at A shifts from the line segment ST to the convex locus $SUWT$ by the process described in the discussion of Figure 8-2. Then, if society wishes to produce, say, quantity y_1^* of item 1, it can only obtain $y_1^*K^*$ of y_2 if both goods continue to be produced at A. However, by separating the two production processes, shifting the manufacture of item 2 to site B, the community can increase its output of commodity 2 to y_1^*K.

Obviously then, if we take into account the possibility of spatial separation of output processes, the production-possibility locus becomes $SJUWKT$. In no event can externalities force this locus to retreat closer to the origin than SVT. However, even here, the feasible region $OSVT$ cannot be convex, because the boundary point V must lie below the line ST. Figures 8-4a and 8-4b generalize the argument of Figure 8-3 to the case of non-

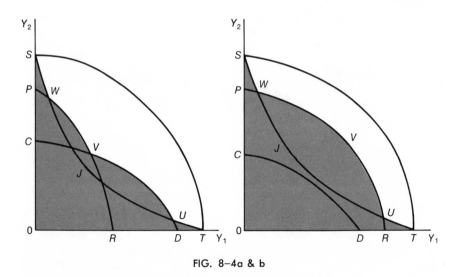

FIG. 8–4a & b

linear substitution relationships in which it is no longer necessarily true that one location, *A*, is the best place for both outputs. Once again, *ST* is the possibility locus in the absence of externalities. The two possibility curves corresponding to the two ways of separating the two outputs geographically are *PR* and *CD*. These two curves need no longer have even a point in common with *ST* because along *ST* some of one or both items may now be produced at *B* as well as at *A*. Nor, as Figure 8–4b shows, need *PR* and *CD* intersect. They will limit the extent to which externalities can pull the possibility locus toward the origin, but they cannot prevent the appearance of a nonconvexity in the feasible region, as Figures 8–4a and 8–4b indicate. For suppose externalities transform the locus *ST*, along which the activities are not separated, into the curve *SJT*. The true possibility locus will now be *SWVUT*, yielding a feasible region *OSWVUT* (shaded areas) that is nonconvex.

In sum, these figures illustrate

Proposition Three. Sufficiently severe externalities make locational specialization economical. Separation limits the magnitudes of the nonconvexities resulting from externalities but does not prevent them.

The figures also bring out a disconcerting possibility.

Proposition Four. The location pattern that will be optimal socially may vary with the proportions among the various outputs that is desired by the community.

Thus, in Figure 8–4a, with fairly strong externalities the production possibility function is *SWVUT*. For output combinations along segment *WV*, all of y_2 is produced at *A*, all y_1 at *B*. Along segment *VU*, the specialization is reversed. The danger of an incorrect choice by planners in this context appears clear, particularly because in this area it may be very difficult and costly to undo an incorrect decision or one that was appropriate at the time it was made but no longer is.

5. THE TWO-LOCATION CASE: AN ALTERNATIVE GRAPHING

A somewhat different graphic representation of the two-location case from that in the preceding section may help to show how nonconvexities arise when geographic separation is possible, and will tie the discussion back to a topic discussed at the end of the previous chapter (Figure 7–5 of Chapter 7).

Suppose, once more, that there are two locations, *A* and *B*, and that it is proposed to establish at one or both of these two places two activities, at least one of which yields externalities detrimental to the other. We also still suppose that these are the only activities (other than leisure) under consideration, with y_{1a} and y_{1b} representing the quantities of the first item produced at the two locations, and y_{2a} and y_{2b}, the corresponding outputs of the other. To avoid any problems about variation in total outputs resulting from the differing effects of externalities when geographic patterns vary, let us assume that the investment plan calls for a fixed proportion between the *total* outputs of the two commodities, $(y_{1a} + y_{1b})/(y_{2a} + y_{2b})$. This leaves us, essentially with two degrees of freedom: $v_1 = y_{1a}/(y_{1a} + y_{1b})$, and $v_2 = y_{2a}/(y_{2a} + y_{2b})$, the respective proportions of the two outputs produced at location A.

This formulation permits us to utilize a box diagram to describe the effect of the externalities (Figure 8–5a). Along the two axes, we represent the values of v_1 and v_2, where clearly $0 \leq v_1 \leq 1$ and $0 \leq v_2 \leq 1$. Point E in the diagram with coordinates (1, 1) represents the case where both outputs are concentrated at location A and, similarly, the origin is the case where all activity takes place at B. The two other corners, C and D, are the arrangements under which the two activities are completely separated.

Now, if the externality were completely negligible or innocuous, a plausible social welfare function might very well have an interior maximum, as shown by the isoproduct curves in Figure 8–5a at point K. For example, having laundries next to electricity-generating plants will save on transmission costs, and having some of each type of plant at each location will avoid congestion costs and, perhaps, reduce the transportation costs of serving local customers. Depending on the geographic features of the two locations, the optimal scale of activity at the two locations will vary. In Figure 8–5a, the optimal solution point K involves the location of about two-thirds of each activity at A.

Now consider the opposite case, in which the emissions of one activity substantially reduce the efficiency of the other. In that case, when the emission cost becomes sufficiently great, total output will be maximized by separating the two activities completely. There will now be (at least) two local maxima. One of them will be point C, with all of output 2 located at A and all of item 1 production at B. The other local maximum will be D, where the locations are simply reversed. Figure 8–5b illustrates the isoprofit curves in such a case. Here O and E are both local minima, and the arrows indicate directions of increasing welfare. It is clear also that there can be intermediate cases when the social cost of the externality is more moderate, with the result that there exists some interior local maximum M, as well as the two corner maxima, C and D (Figure 8–5c).

The important point is that these sorts of relationships arise whenever one activity interferes with the efficiency of another, so that their separation can increase the efficiency of resource utilization. In any such case, a multiplicity of maxima is in the nature of things. It is plausible that the social wel-

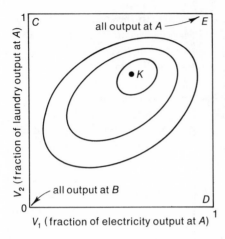

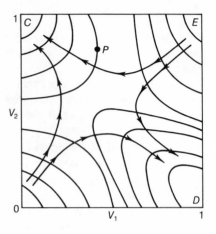

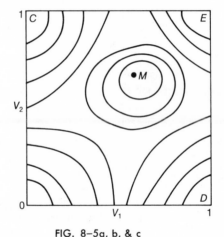

FIG. 8–5a, b, & c

fare function will exhibit at least two local maximal values of (y_{1a}, y_{1b}, y_{2a}, y_{2b}) occurring at (y_{1a}^*, 0, 0, y_{2b}^*) and (0, y_{1b}^*, y_{2a}^*, 0), (that is, at the solution points in which the two activities are carried on at different locations).

To return briefly to the subject matter of the preceding chapter, the diagrams indicate once again that, in the presence of a multiplicity of local maxima resulting from nonconvexity of the possibility set, the market-determined output of an activity that generates detrimental externalities may be *below* its optimal level, contrary to the impression that seems to be so widely held. For suppose (Figure 8–5b) that the social optimum is point D (all of y_1 produced at A, all of y_2 at B). With electricity output at A yielding harmful externalities, point P is a possible competitive equilibrium point. For with the indifference curve at P vertical, a small shift in laundry output will not change social welfare, but a small shift in electricity output from location A to B will increase social welfare (MSC of electricity greater than MPC—marginal private cost). Yet the socially optimal proportion of total output of electricity to be produced at A, as indicated by point D, is greater than it is at P, as was to be shown. The point, of course, is the well-known observation that, with a multiplicity of local maxima, a route that takes one uphill may, in fact, lead away from the highest point in the graph.

6. GENERALIZATION TO *n* ACTIVITIES

The arguments of the preceding sections have dealt with a world in which (including leisure) there are only three "activities." However, as was already indicated, generalization of the argument to a world of n activities is immediate.[13] In a world of n outputs, convexity can be guaranteed only if *each* of the partial possibility loci representing substitution between a pair of commodities is concave. Any single exception, like that in Figure 8–2, means that at least two local maxima become possible. Thus, the analysis holds whether the economy encompasses two outputs or n.

There is, however, one aspect of the matter that does require explicit analysis in terms of n commodities. One may well ask whether and to what extent the number of local maxima is likely to grow as the number of activities in an economy increases. Here we can offer only a few observations about some polar cases, none of them rigorous. They suggest, however, that in at least some cases the number of local maxima may grow *very* rapidly with the number of activities involved.

First, however, we deal with a case in which a proliferation of activities does not necessarily increase the number of local maxima.

Polar case a: if one activity imposes external costs on m other activities, even if the detrimental effects are very great, no more than two local maxima need result;[14] and

[13] Our discussion has also confined itself only to *detrimental* externalities. In principle, the presence of external benefits can also produce a multiplicity of local maxima, but here it is not so clear that the problem is likely to be serious. On this see Baumol, "External Economies and Second-Order Optimality Conditions," pp. 366–67.

[14] This does not preclude the possibility that there will be more than two maxima if the relevant functions violate the appropriate concavity-convexity conditions in the absence of externalities. Even where the maximum would otherwise be unique, externalities that are of intermediate strength may lead to three (or more) local maxima, characteristically two corner maxima produced by the externalities, and one interior maximum, a vestige of the unique maximum that would occur in the absence of externalities. An illustration occurs in Figure 8–5c. Complications such as these and the possibility of irregularities in the relevant hypersurfaces probably limit the profitability of a more rigorous discussion of the subject of this section.

Polar case b: a similar result holds when *n* activities each impose external benefits on one other activity. These results are suggested by Figure 8–6a, in which the smoke from electricity production is taken to increase

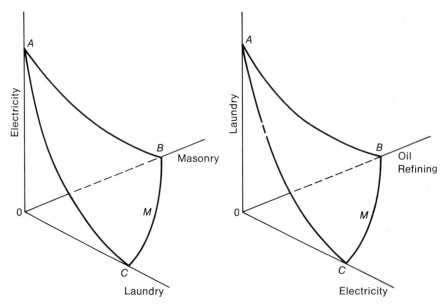

FIG. 8–6a & b

laundry cost and make it more expensive to produce deterioration-resistant masonry. The production locus will then tend toward the form indicated (surface *ABC*). Because laundry and masonry activity impose no adverse external effects upon one another, their production-possibility locus can be assumed to have the normal shape (concave to the origin) illustrated by curve *CB*. However, for the reasons indicated in the discussion of Figure 8–2, if smoke damage is sufficiently serious, the other two partial loci will have shapes like those of *AC* and *AB*. We may then expect two local maxima, one at *A* and perhaps another at a point such as *M*. The interpretation of Figure 8–6b is exactly the same and we merely pause to draw the reader's attention to the remarkable similarity of the diagram for the two-victim, one-polluter case with that for one victim and two polluters.

Next, we come to cases involving more complex patterns of interdependence and show that here the number of local maxima may indeed increase rapidly with the number of activities involved. We have

Polar case c: if each of *n* activities produces and suffers from very strong *mutually* detrimental externalities and spatial separation is not possible, some *n* local optima can be expected.

The reason is that, in the limit, as external damage becomes sufficiently great, it will be optimal (indeed, it will only be possible) to carry on just one of the n activities because the externalities resulting from any one activity effectively prevents the operation of any other. Clearly, there are exactly n possible choices of the activity to be continued. But each such solution, $y_i > 0$, all $y_{i'} = 0$ for $i \neq i'$ is a local maximum in the sense that it yields an output whose value is greater than is possible if we attempt to set some $y_{i'} \neq 0$ when $y_i > 0$. Hence, we do indeed have n local maxima, $y_i > 0$, $y_{i'} = 0$ $i \neq i'$, $i = 1, \ldots, n$.

If matters are not quite so serious, so that only a smaller number, k, of activities need be discontinued, it may be conjectured, somewhat surprisingly, that the number of local maxima actually will increase to the order of magnitude of the number of combinations of n activities chosen k at a time.

Finally, we deal with the possibility of spatial separation that, rather out of line with its role in our earlier discussion as a bound to the degree of nonconvexity, seems to increase the growth in number of maxima with the number of activities involved. We have

Polar case d: if there are n activities, each of which produces and suffers from externalities, and there are just n discrete locations into which they can be separated, then, if the externalities are sufficiently severe, we can expect at least $n!$ local maxima. Note that we have n candidates for the first location and, for each such choice, there remain $n - 1$ candidates for the second location, then $n - 2$ candidates for the third, and so on; this implies that there are altogether $n!$ different ways of achieving the desired isolation.

In practice, in some respects, this probably exaggerates the number of possibilities; in other ways, it understates them. There really is no fixed finite number of discrete locations, and so one will normally have more than n geographic areas in which to locate n activities. If that is the right way of looking at the matter, it is clear that the number of local maxima (that is, the number of ways of isolating each activity) will exceed $n!$ On the other hand, airborne pollution is known to travel over enormous distances. In that sense, we may have no hiding place from one another's emissions. We may then find ourselves back at the one-location case with its smaller number of local maxima but its higher levels of social damage.

7. CONVEXITY IN SOCIAL AND INDIVIDUAL FIRMS' POSSIBILITY SETS

In one respect the externality-induced nonconvexity poses a less-serious problem for social control than one might expect, for, as all of our examples indicate (see, notably, Figure 8–1)

Proposition Five. Nonconvexities in the social production-possibility set arising from detrimental externalities are entirely compatible with convexity in the sets over which individual producers make their choices.

This has an important theoretical consequence,

Proposition Six. Despite the presence of nonconvexities in the social production-possibility set as a result of detrimental externalities, it is possible through the use of prices and taxes alone to induce any individual firm to choose any designated point on its production-possibility frontier. We can thus use these devices to sustain any designated point on the social possibility frontier, despite its "incorrect" curvature.

This may be contrasted, for example, with the case of nonconvexity due to increasing returns to the scale of individual producers' production. There, if every firm's average costs decline continually with scale over some substantial range, a competitive producer confronted by a fixed price will either turn out zero output or some large quantity of output. Output combinations calling for intermediate levels of production of the good in question cannot be attained with the aid of the price mechanism alone.[15] But the nonconvexities with which we are now concerned affect only the *social* possibility set, and so they are perfectly consistent with the possibility that a producer can be induced to turn out any intermediate quantity of output by an appropriate choice of prices.

The general principle may be illustrated with the example of Section 3, involving two producers using their input fully, with input cost functions (1). If a fixed total quantity of the input is used, *any* pair of output choices by the two producers will be on the production-possibility frontier. It need, then, only be demonstrated that any attainable (y_e, y_l) combination will be chosen by them at some specifiable set of prices. Let the prices p_e for electricity (y_e) and p_l for laundry (y_l) be chosen and let labor be given a price of unity. The profit functions of the two firms are then given, in accord with (1), by

$$\pi_e = p_e y_e - y_e^2/2 \tag{3}$$
$$\pi_l = p_l y_l - y_l^2/2 - w y_e y_l.$$

With the individual production sets being strictly convex in each firm's "own" decision variable, the profit functions are strictly concave in its own variables.

---

[15] Note, however, that intermediate output levels for the competitive industry are perfectly possible in these circumstances. In an industry producing two outputs, y_1 and y_2, if each firm's possibility set is nonconvex some firms will specialize in the production of y_1 and others will now produce only y_2. See Jerome Rothenberg, "Non-convexity, Aggregation and Pareto Optimality," *Journal of Political Economy* LXVIII (October, 1960), pp. 435–58, and see E. Malinvaud, *Lectures on Microeconomic Theory*, (Amsterdam: North-Holland Publishing Co., 1972) Chapter 7 for a more general discussion of nonconvexities in the large numbers case.

That is, the second derivatives of both profit functions are negative. Specifically,

$$\frac{\partial^2 \pi_e}{\partial y_e^2} = \frac{\partial^2 \pi_t}{\partial y_t^2} = -1.$$

Hence, the first-order conditions are sufficient, as well as necessary, for profit maximization by the individual firms. These first-order conditions are obtained directly by differentiation of (3) to yield

$$y_e = p_e \qquad (4)$$

$$wy_e + y_t = p_t.$$

Equations (4) are obviously invertible, which means that any desired pair of outputs (y_e, y_t) can be obtained as a solution to (4) for some combination of prices. Thus despite the fact that, as shown in Section 3, for $w > 1$, (that is, for externalities sufficiently strong), this set of functions yields a nonconvex social possibility set, there is a unique pair of prices that induces the firms to produce any efficient output vector (y_e^*, y_t^*) that is desired. This simple counterexample is in fact sufficient to prove our point here; that is, that nonconvexities in the social possibility set resulting from externalities *need not* result in nonconvexities in the private possibility sets and so may not prevent the price system from yielding any predetermined efficient vector of outputs.

Having dealt with the position of the firm in our world with a nonconvex social possibility region, we must next bring consumers into the picture. In Figure 8–7b, let *II'* be a social-indifference curve, so constructed that along it social welfare is constant and that its slope at any point equals the common slope of all consumers' indifference curves at the corresponding distribution of the two goods.[16] A social welfare maximum involving positive outputs of the two goods must be characterized by tangency of a social-indifference curve with the production-possibility frontier, as at point *T* in Figure 8–7b. As we have just suggested, so long as the only source of nonconvexity is the presence of detrimental externalities, such a point can be sustained as a tax-adjusted competitive equilibrium, in which producers are maximizing profits and individuals are maximizing their utilities in the small and in the large.

With this observation we are now in a position to offer some comments on the consequences of externality-induced nonconvexities for social welfare.

---

[16] See P. A. Samuelson, "Social Indifference Curves," *Quarterly Journal of Economics* LXX (February, 1956), 1–22 or W. J. Baumol, *Welfare Economics and the Theory of the State* (2nd ed.), (Cambridge, Mass.: Harvard University Press, 1965); Chapter 3, Section 9, and Appendix.

8.   WHO NEEDS CONVEXITY?

It has long been recognized that the absence of convexity creates problems for public policy.[17] However, aside from the fact that earlier writers
generally did not see that the externalities themselves tend to produce the
nonconvexities that are the source of the problem, they may not have recognized the full extent of the complexity that besets the policy problem here
both in theory and in practice.

Where the appropriate concavity-convexity assumptions are satisfied, it
will be recalled that everything works out nicely in the competitive equilibrium
case:

> **a.**   There will be a set of prices that determine an optimal budget line (hyper-
> plane). In the differentiable case with an interior maximum, this budget line
> will simultaneously be tangent to the production-possibility locus and to a
> community-indifference curve at the optimal point. More generally, the
> budget hyperplane will constitute a separating hyperplane for the possibility
> set and the preference set at that point.
> **b.**   At that optimal point and at those prices, all consumers and all producers
> will be in equilibrium.
> **c.**   The value of total output at the optimal prices will be maximized at the
> optimal point. That is, the budget line described in **a.** will be the highest of
> the family of parallel budget lines that has any point in common with the
> production-possibility set. It is this property, the fact that maximization of
> value of output coincides with maximization of social welfare, that permits
> us to infer the Pareto optimality of the competitive equilibrium.

With the nonconvexities introduced by externalities, the preceding
properties run into complications that increase, at least in principle, the
problem of formulating rules capable of leading the economy to an optimal
solution.

For simplicity in the following discussion we will assume that the
production-possibility curve is strictly convex, (that is, that the possibility
set has the simple smooth upper boundary RR' illustrated in Figure 8–7a).
The reader can consider for himself the additional complexities that arise
where this locus takes on a more irregular shape involving both concave and
convex ranges.

As we can see in Figure 8–7a, with such a possibility set, no interior
point on the possibility locus can be a point of maximum value at any positive
output prices. Let the set of parallel lines labelled $P_o, P_1, \ldots$ be members of
the family of price lines. Then it is clear that the point of tangency, T, between such a price line and the possibility locus must be a point of *minimum*
output value, given production efficiency, (that is, P_o must be the lowest price

---

[17] See, for example, the quotation from Pigou at the beginning of this chapter.

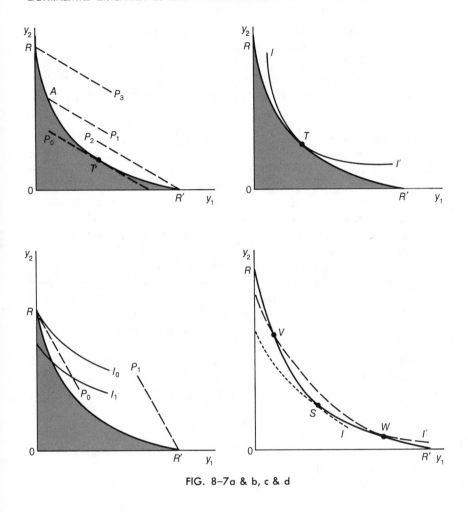

FIG. 8–7a & b, c & d

line along RR'). At any other interior point on RR', such as A, obviously the output value will not be a maximum either. Only at R and at R' will we have two local value maxima. Which of these is the global maximum depends on the prices in question.

However, in this case it is *not* true that the social optimum must lie at one of the corner points. Figure 8–7b shows a well behaved interior optimum at T, the point of tangency of the possibility locus RR' and the social-indifference curve II'. All that is required is that the curvature of the indifference curve be greater than that of the possibility locus. Here, then, the social-optimum point obviously *cannot* be a point of maximum output value, because it does not lie on the highest price line passing through the possibility set.

Moreover, even if the social optimum occurs at a corner (Point R in Figure 8–7c), this still need not be the global *value* maximum. Thus, we observe in Figure 8–7c that if we use the prices corresponding to price line P_o tangent to the community indifferent curve I_o at the social optimum, then it is price line P_1R' through point R' that gives the maximum value of output.

We conclude,

Proposition Seven. With nonconvexity of the possibility set, the social optimum may or may not lie at a corner, but if the possibility frontier is convex (to the origin) throughout, there will be a local point of maximum output *value* at every corner of the possibility frontier (and nowhere else). *In neither case need the social optimum and the value maximum coincide,* as they would in the case where the usual convexity assumptions hold.

As a final curiosity, in Figure 8–7d we see a point of tangency, S, which is a point of *minimum* social welfare and, yet, which, after the imposition of Pigouvian taxes,[18] is a possible point of competitive equilibrium! After all, we assume that individual consumer and producer relationships have the convexity properties required by the second-order conditions. But at S, the first-order conditions for consumer and producer equilibrium must be satisfied, as we have just seen. Hence S now becomes a competitive equilibrium point.[19]

Note also that even if the point of tangency is like T in Figure 8–7b, it may only represent a local maximum. Thus, in Figure 8–7d, point W is such a tangency point, but any position on RR' to the left of V is better than W. And this is possible even when the social-indifference curves are entirely well behaved.

9. CONCLUSION: THE POLICY RELEVANCE OF EXTERNALITY-INDUCED NONCONVEXITIES

In sum, we can no longer utilize the familiar proof of the optimality of competitive equilibrium that depends upon convexity in the set of attain-

---

[18] One must keep in mind that in the competitive equilibrium under discussion here, Pigouvian taxes and subsidies have been imposed in order to induce consumers and producers to make their decisions in accord with the correct marginal rates of substitution and transformation. This point is important because our discussion is intended to show that, even after proper corrective taxes have been imposed, the nonconvexities problems remain.

[19] Whether S will be a point of *stable* equilibrium is not entirely clear. It depends in part whether Pigouvian tax-subsidy levels are adjusted when the economy leaves point A. It is our conjecture that if these tax values are not changed, with a suitable set of adjustment relationships S need not be unstable, but if taxes are varied continuously so that they are always equal to marginal social damage then S will generally be unstable. Thus, with a sufficiently sensitive taxing scheme we should at least be able to prevent the economy from settling at a welfare minimum point, such as S.

able output combinations to show that the actual output point attained as an equilibrium, in this case with appropriate corrective taxes (that is, taxes forcing producers to take externalities into account), must maximize the value of output at efficiency prices that are also market-clearing. Now that other attainable points may be more valuable at current prices, the equilibrium need no longer be Pareto optimal. Prices no longer can be depended upon to give the right signals. They do not tell us whether we are at a welfare maximum or minimum, whether a maximum is local or global, or in which direction the economy should move to secure an increase in welfare.

In short, in a world in which detrimental externalities are sufficiently severe to cause nonconvexities, efficiency prices are robbed of much of their normative usefulness. Although it remains true that an equilibrium that maximizes the value of output over all feasible outputs is Pareto optimal (this is assured by the convexity of preferences), it is no longer true that the availability of outputs that are more valuable (at current equilibrium prices) means that the current output is not Pareto optimal. Thus, in Figure 8–7b, point *T* is obviously the optimal output, but the most valuable output combination must lie either at *R* or *R'*. Notice that this problem arises even where the more valuable outputs can be obtained by infinitesimal (marginal) adjustments. More generally, *even if we know the entire set of feasible output points, equilibrium prices tell us nothing about the Pareto optimality of current output or the direction in which to seek improvement.* Although tax instruments may still be of some help in guiding the economy, as later chapters will suggest, the choice of the equilibrium point at which it is desired to have the economy settle must somehow be made collectively, rather than by automatic market processes.

APPENDIX A

ANALYTIC REPRESENTATION: NONCONVEXITIES IN THE POSSIBILITY LOCUS WITH THREE ACTIVITIES

In Section 3, we presented a concrete illustration of a possibility locus to show explicitly how externalities can produce nonconvexities in such a case. This appendix generalizes the argument of Section 3 using some elementary differential calculus and derives explicitly the numerical results reported at the end of Section 3.

We again consider a three-activity economy that provides electricity (industry e), laundry (industry ℓ), and leisure (unused labor). We have well defined production functions for the two industries. From the two production functions, we deduce the shape of the production-possibility locus and see how it responds to changes in the coefficient of the externalities term. Both activities are taken to use the same resource, labor, as their only input. The greater the quantity of electricity generated, the more labor it takes the laundries to get a given wash to an acceptable level of cleanliness; that is all there is to the externality.

Proceeding first in general terms, we have as our resources-demand functions for the two industries

$$r_e = c^e(y_e) \qquad r_\ell = c^\ell(y_e, y_\ell) \tag{1}$$

where r_k = the quantity of input used by industry k and
y_k = the output of that industry.

Then, the equation of the production-possibility locus corresponding to the utilization of some fixed quantity, r, of the labor resource is clearly

$$r = c^e(y_e) + c^\ell(y_e, y_\ell). \tag{2}$$

From this, we derive immediately [letting c_e^e represent $dc^e(y_e)/dy_e$, and so on]

$$(c_e^e + c_e^\ell) \, dy_e + c_\ell^\ell \, dy_\ell = 0.$$

Because increased outputs presumably require increased quantities of inputs and because we are considering a detrimental externality, we must have

$$c_e^e > 0, \qquad c_e^\ell > 0, \qquad c_\ell^\ell > 0. \tag{3}$$

Consequently,

$$\frac{dy_\ell}{dy_e} = -\frac{c_e^e + c_e^\ell}{c_\ell^\ell} < 0. \tag{4}$$

We assume that there are diminishing private returns (increasing costs) to each output, so that

$$c_{ee}^e > 0 \qquad c_{\ell\ell}^\ell > 0. \tag{5}$$

From (4), we obtain directly

$$\begin{aligned}
\frac{d^2 y_\ell}{dy_e^2} &= -\left[\frac{\left(c_{ee}^e + c_{ee}^\ell + c_{e\ell}^\ell \frac{dy_\ell}{dy_e} \right) c_\ell^\ell - \left(c_{\ell e}^\ell + c_{\ell\ell}^\ell \frac{dy_\ell}{dy_e} \right)(c_e^e + c_e^\ell)}{(c_\ell^\ell)^2} \right. \\
&= \left. \frac{-(c_{ee}^e + c_{ee}^\ell)c_\ell^\ell + (c_{e\ell}^\ell + c_{\ell e}^\ell)(c_e^e + c_e^\ell) - c_{\ell\ell}^\ell \frac{(c_e^e + c_e^\ell)^2}{c_\ell^\ell}}{(c_\ell^\ell)^2} \right]. \tag{6}
\end{aligned}$$

If there were no externalities, so that $c_e^\ell = c_{e\ell}^\ell = c_{\ell e}^\ell = c_{ee}^\ell = 0$, then (6) would be unambiguously negative by (3) and (5) because its numerator would reduce simply to $-c_{ee}^e c_\ell^\ell - c_{\ell\ell}^\ell (c_e^e)^2 / c_\ell^\ell$. Thus, the production-possibility locus would have a negative slope by (4) and be concave by (6), as the second-order conditions require. However, with detrimental "cross-marginal" externalities (increasing marginal laundry cost with an incremental rise in smoky electricity output), we may expect $c_{e\ell}^{\ell} = c_{\ell e}^{\ell} > 0$, and the sign of (6) is no longer clear. The externality term $(c_{e\ell}^{\ell} + c_{\ell e}^{\ell})(c_e^e + c_e^{\ell})$ is positive. Hence, if it is sufficiently large relative to the other terms, it must give (6) a positive value, thus violating the concavity condition.

Specifically, utilizing the second illustrative example of Section 3, we have

$$r_e = c^e(y_e) = y_e^2/2 \text{ (electricity cost function) and}$$

$$r_\ell = c^\ell(y_e, y_\ell) = y_\ell + w y_e y_\ell \text{ (laundry cost function),}$$

so that by direct differentiation we obtain

$$c_e^e = y_e \qquad c_e^\ell = w y_\ell \qquad c_\ell^\ell = 1 + w y_e$$

$$c_{ee}^e = 1 \qquad c_{ee}^\ell = 0 \qquad c_{e\ell}^\ell = c_{\ell e}^\ell = w \qquad c_{\ell\ell}^\ell = 0.$$

Thus, substituting into (6) we obtain directly

$$\frac{d^2 y_\ell}{dy_e^2} = \frac{-(1 + w y_e) + (2w)(y_e + w y_\ell)}{(1 + w y_e)^2} = \frac{w y_e + 2 w^2 y_\ell - 1}{(1 + w y_e)^2},$$

which will clearly be negative if, and only if, $2 w^2 y_\ell + w y_e < 1$, as asserted in the text. That is, for w (or y_e or y_ℓ) sufficiently large, the production-possibility set cannot be convex.

APPENDIX B

A FORMAL MODEL OF EXTERNAL EFFECTS AND CORRECTIVE TAXES

BY DAVID F. BRADFORD

This appendix is intended to show that, when every individual producer's choice set is convex, *any* socially efficient net output vector can be sustained by profit-maximizing production with externality-offsetting taxes, as asserted in Section 7. For this purpose, we first offer a formalization of our definition of detrimental externalities of the sort discussed above. Armed with this definition, we show that social efficiency requires individual efficiency when external effects are all detrimental. A producer's net output vector (including negative entries for inputs) can be said to be "individually efficient" if no dominating net output vector is available to him without changing some other producer's net output choice. From this, we go on to derive our result about the sustainability of socially efficient output vectors.

Let $y^k = (y_{1k}, \ldots, y_{nk})$ be the net output vector of the kth producer, where negative entries represent net inputs. We assume that y^k is chosen from a *feasible set* Y^k. For the usual reasons,[20] we assume that Y^k always includes the origin and the negative orthant of Euclidian n-space (free disposal), and that Y^k has no elements other than the origin in the non-negative orthant (no outputs without inputs).

The size and shape of Y^k depend on the net output choices of *other producers*. Let Y stand for the matrix of net output choices of the m producers in the economy, whose $(i,k)^{\text{th}}$ element, y_{ik}, is the net output of commodity i by producer k. We shall represent the dependence of Y^k, the feasible set for k on the choices of other producers, as a functional relationship, mapping Y into subsets of n-space, and denote this relationship by $Y^k = Y^k(Y)$. Thus $Y^k(Y)$ is defined as the set $\{y^k | y^1, \ldots, y^{k-1}, y^{k+1}, \ldots, y^m\}$. We shall say that *these relationships embody detrimental external effects if for any two different producers, k and k'*

$$\lambda > 1 \Rightarrow Y^{k'}(\ldots \lambda y_{ik} \ldots) \subset Y^{k'}(Y),$$

where $(\ldots \lambda y_{ik} \ldots)$ denotes the matrix obtained from Y by replacing y_{ik} by λy_{ik}. This definition implies that every producer tends to hurt every (strictly, "at best doesn't help any") other producer by increasing the intensity of any of his own net outputs *or* net inputs. Obviously, a definition of beneficial external effects would be obtained by reversing the set-inclusion sign in this definition. The definition can also be made to apply specifically to a particular element, y_{ik}, so that variables can be taken to exhibit either detrimental or beneficial external effects. We confine our attention to relationships involving only detrimental externalities, which, by the definition, include the case of zero externality.

a. Requirements of Socially Efficient Production.
Under this definition, it follows trivially that socially efficient production (total net output of some one item maximized for any set of given totals of the other net outputs) requires efficiency on the part of every individual producer. For, if a producer has chosen an individually inefficient net output vector, he can alter his choice in a way that preserves his net output but reduces his net input usage. Because the external effect of the latter action in our case must, if anything, *enhance* the productive opportunities of the other producers, such a choice is clearly required by social efficiency.

Because, by assumption, the feasible set of each producer, considering only variations in the vector under his control, is convex, any point in that set that is efficient from the producer's point of view will be a profit-maximizing choice for some vector of prices. And since, as we have just shown, any socially efficient point will be composed of a sum of points efficient for each producer, it follows that any socially efficient net output vector can be sustained as a profit-maximizing point for all producers if the prices are appropriately adjusted for each producer by a set of taxes. It remains only

[20] See, for example, J. Quirk and R. Saposnik, *Introduction to General Equilibrium Theory and Welfare Economics* (New York: McGraw-Hill, 1968).

to show that the "appropriate" taxes are precisely equal to the marginal external damages arising from changes in output and input choices.[21]

For this demonstration, it will be convenient to assume that the feasible set of the kth producer is defined by the inequality $f^k(Y) \leq 0$, where f^k is a differentiable function. Recall that Y is a *matrix* of which the typical element, y_{ik}, specifies the net output (negative for inputs) of the ith commodity by the kth producer. Fixing net output vectors $y^{k'}$ for $k' \neq k$, $f^k(Y) = 0$ defines the "private production possibility frontier" constraining y^k, the net output vector choice of the kth producer. By assumption, the set of vectors y^k satisfying $f^k(Y) \leq 0$ in this case is convex.

If the rows of the matrix Y^* sum to a point on the social production possibility frontier, then it is a solution to the nonlinear programming problem

$$\text{maximize } \sum_{k=1}^{m} y_{1k} \text{ (maximize total output of commodity 1)}$$

subject to

$$\sum_{k=1}^{m} y_{ik}^* - \sum_{k=1}^{m} y_{ik} \leq 0 \ (i = 2, \ldots, n) \text{ (no reduction in any other output)}$$

$$f^k(Y) \leq 0 \quad (k = 1, \ldots, m).$$

By a simple extension of the Kuhn-Tucker theorem on optimization with inequality constraints, necessary conditions[22] for a solution to this problem are that there exist nonnegative multipliers $\lambda_2, \ldots, \lambda_n$, corresponding to the constraints requiring no reduction in availability of commodities other than commodity 1, and $\gamma_1, \ldots, \gamma_m$, corresponding to the individual production constraints, such that

$$1 - \sum_{k'=1}^{m} \gamma_{k'} f_{1k}^{k'} = 0 \quad (k = 1, \ldots, m)$$

$$\lambda_i - \sum_{k'=1}^{m} \gamma_{k'} f_{ik}^{k'} = 0 \quad (k = 1, \ldots, m)$$

$$(i = 2, \ldots, m).$$

(The notation $f_{ik}^{k'}$ stands for the partial derivative of $f^{k'}$ with respect to y_{ik}.) By the usual interpretation, λ_i equals the amount of commodity 1 (in effect here, the numeraire commodity) obtainable by a unit reduction in the amount of commodity i produced. The multiplier γ_k is the value (in commodity 1 terms) of the extra output that could be obtained if firm k's production constraint were relaxed by requiring $f^k(Y) \leq 1$ instead of $f^k(Y) \leq 0$.

---

[21] Note the formal similarity of the following argument to the basic analysis of Chapter 4.

[22] Strictly speaking, a certain "constraint qualification" must be satisfied at the solution values to assure the necessity of these conditions. The qualification concerns a possibility that we may take to be pathological in this context. See any textbook treatment of the Kuhn-Tucker theorem.

b. Requirements of Individual-Producer Equilibrium.
Consider next the profit-maximizing problem faced by producer k faced with
a vector $p = (p_1, \ldots, p_n)$ of prices *and* a vector $t^k = (t_{1k}, \ldots, t_{nk})$ of taxes:

$$\text{maximize} \sum_{i=1}^{m} (p_i - t_{ik})y_{ik},$$

$$\text{subject to } f^k(Y) \leq 0,$$

where all variables other than the "own" vector, y^k, are treated as exogenously
fixed in the constraint. By the Kuhn-Tucker theorem, if y^k is a solution, there
necessarily exists a nonnegative multiplier, δ_k, such that

$$p_i - t_{ik} - \delta_k f_{ik}^{k}(Y) = 0 \quad (i = 1, \ldots, n).$$

Furthermore, because the constraint set is convex, these conditions, together
with the constraint, are sufficient as well as necessary for a constrained
maximum. The multiplier δ_k indicates the profit that would be *lost* to the kth
producer if his production constraint were "tightened" by one unit.

c. Synthesis: Producer Equilibrium and Productive Efficiency.
Now we need only put the two problems together. If Y is a set of individual
producer vectors summing to a point on the social production possibility
frontier, use the Lagrange multipliers from the associated nonlinear programming problem and set

$$p_1 = 1, p_2 = \lambda_2, \ldots, p_n = \lambda_n$$

$$t_{ik} = \sum_{\substack{k' \neq k \\ k' = 1}}^{m} \gamma_{k'} f_{ik}^{k'} \quad (k = 1, \ldots, m)$$
$$(i = 1, \ldots, n)$$

Then the Kuhn-Tucker conditions for the social production possibility
frontier reduce immediately to

$$p_i - t_{ik} - \gamma_k f_{ik}^{k} = 0.$$

Thus, we see that y^k, a point that satisfies these social frontier requirements,
is associated with a set of prices and taxes at which y^k also satisfies the
necessary and sufficient conditions for a profit maximum for producer k, with
the multiplier δ_k of his problem equal to γ_k in the economy-wide problem.
    To interpret this result, note that for $k' \neq k$, $f_{ik}^{k'}$ is, in effect, the *con-
striction* in the k'^{th} production constraint per unit increase in the kth producer's net output of the ith good. Hence, $\sum_{k' \neq k} \gamma_{k'} f_{ik}^{k'}$ is the total external social
cost per unit increase in y_{ik}. Furthermore, because $\delta_{k'} = \gamma_{k'}$, the external
social cost will also exactly equal the marginal external profit loss per unit
increase in output of Y_i by firm k. That is, when the proper corrective taxes
are applied, the marginal tax on a firm that generates externalities will exactly
equal the marginal profit loss it imposes on other firms.

part 2

TOWARD
APPLICATION

chapter 9

Introduction
to Part 2

We have now completed our discussion of the basic theoretical framework. There is much to the theory of externalities that we have made no attempt to cover, for our central objective is the formulation of an analytic structure for the study of environmental policy.

At this point, we seem to have an illuminating, but somewhat destructive, set of results—one that creates severe difficulties for the application of theory to practical problem solving. In this part of the book, we decrease the level of abstraction of our discussion and seek to approach more closely the problems of application. Here too, we will encounter obstacles, though of a different kind from the theoretical complications of Part I. For example, we will find reason to suspect that many proposed environmental programs may well make the distribution of income more unequal.

Nevertheless, we will argue that these obstacles do not preclude the design of effective environmental programs; and, in spite of the difficulties encountered in Part I, that economic theory can be very helpful in the design of these programs.

In particular, Chapter 10 presents a proposal for a feasible tax-subsidy program. We suggest what we believe to be a practical and effective procedure for the protection of the environment: the use of pollution charges to implement a predetermined set of standards for environmental quality. Some degree of arbitrariness in the design of such standards is inevitable. And in agreeing to such a procedure, one gives up any attempt to reach any true social optimum. Yet this proposal, which is essentially a "satisficing" [1] approach to the problem, can be shown to offer some significant optimality properties. Aside from the administrative savings made possible by avoidance of central direction and direct controls, we will show that the proposed procedures, properly designed and implemented, can lead to the attainment of the selected standards and that in appropriate circumstances, they can do so at something approximating minimum cost to society.

Chapter 11 represents a further departure from the economist's usual policy recommendations; here, we suggest that direct controls can be a useful supplement to a system of charges for the continuing maintenance of acceptable environmental conditions. Their usefulness arises from the inflexibility of tax rates and the comparative ease with which certain types of direct controls can be instituted, policed, and removed. The problem is that the state of environmental quality at any time depends not only on the level of emissions but on such essentially stochastic influences as wind velocity and rainfall, which determine the rapidity of the dispersion of accumulated pollutants. As a result, we can expect occasional environmental crises that can, at best, be predicted only a short time before they occur. It would be too costly to society to keep tax rates sufficiently high to prevent such emergencies at all times. Instead, it may be less expensive in such cases to make temporary use of direct controls, despite their static inefficiency. The chapter ends with the description of a nonlinear programming model that illustrates the logic of the design of an optimal mixed program (that is, a program utilizing both fiscal methods and direct controls in a way that minimizes society's expected cost of achievement of its environmental targets).

Chapter 12 turns to a third instrument for the control of detrimental externalities: the use of subsidies as a reward for decreased damage by those who generate the externalities. First, we describe formally the conditions under which fees and subsidies are equivalent. Here we find that the equivalent subsidy is a very strange sort of construct, one that we are unlikely to encounter in practice. Next, we show that subsidies in the more conventional sense are, at least theoretically, a poor substitute for taxes. Although the two may be equally effective in reducing emissions by the individual firm, the subsidy encourages the entry of new firms (or plants) into the industry, whereas taxes encourage their exit. As a result, we can expect that a subsidy program will be less effective in discouraging pollution than a tax program with similar marginal rates. In particular, we find that, under pure competition, if emissions are uniquely determined by the industry's output level and rise monotonically with output, a subsidy program will necessarily backfire. Although the subsidy will produce a reduction in the emissions of each firm, it will lead to an entry of new firms that more than offsets it. Total emissions under a

[1] That is, there is no attempt to seek any sort of optimum. Rather, one seeks merely to find policies capable of meeting some preset standards and, so, of producing results considered acceptable or "satisfactory." The term *satisficing* was coined by Herbert Simon.

subsidy program will in this case *always* be greater than they would have been if no cleanup subsidy program had ever been instituted!

Chapter 13 discusses a practical issue that can be of considerable significance for environmental policy. Measures designed to improve the quality of life may, unfortunately, make it more difficult to deal with a second of the major issues of our time: the distribution of income. We will suggest, on theoretical grounds, that under a variety of circumstances the rich can be expected to value the benefits flowing from an environmental program more highly than the poor. Using the Samuelson and Tiebout models of public goods as polar constructs, we argue that programs offering similar observable benefits to everyone are likely to offer greater welfare gains to the affluent, and that even programs whose effects differ by income class cannot be presumed to favor the impecunious. Moreover, it is by no means clear that progression in the tax system means that the rich will bear a disproportionate share of the costs. For example, where waste-treatment plants are financed locally, a considerable share of the costs may well fall on the central cities with their heavy concentrations of the poor. In addition, a review of the available empirical evidence (which is, unfortunately, very limited in quantity and subject to all sorts of qualifications) certainly does not suggest that taxes on pollutants and other types of environmental damage are likely to be progressive. Given the types of activity that are prime candidates for such charges and the pattern of consumption by income class of the outputs from these activities, there is some reason to suspect the reverse.

Finally, in Chapter 14, we turn to the international side of environmental policy. Here we discuss two issues: the effects of measures for environmental protection on the balance of payments and the level of income of the country that imposes them; and the control of environmental damage that flows across the borders of the source country and affects welfare in neighboring states.

On the first of these issues, we contend that matters are not as cut and dried as intuitive judgment is likely to suggest. The analysis indicates that there are circumstances under which a country's balance of payments can be improved by its unilateral adoption of effective environmental policies, and that its domestic employment may also be stimulated in the process. The analysis specifies conditions under which this can occur, as well as circumstances under which such measures can, in fact, aggravate the country's short-run economic problems. Finally, we consider what the rest of the world can do about a country whose economic activity generates externalities that are harmful to people outside its borders. In such a case, the usual free-trade argument may no longer apply, and an appropriate set of tariffs against the offending products may serve as a partial substitute for Pigouvian taxes; we find that nonzero tariffs are generally required for international Pareto optimality, taking into account the interests of the externality-generating country as well as those of the rest of the world.

Efficiency Without Optimality: The Charges and Standards Approach[1]

The results arrived at in Chapter 8 may seem to constitute insuperable barriers to a rational environmental policy. The very presence of externalities is likely to produce a large number of local maxima among which, in practice, it seems impossible to choose with any degree of confidence; we may not even know in which direction to modify the level of an externality-generating activity if we want to move toward an optimum. It should be emphasized that these problems beset equally all attempts to achieve optimality by any of the means usually proposed—direct controls and centralized decision-making at one extreme and pricing schemes, such as the Pigouvian taxes and subsidies, at the other.

Nevertheless, we believe that it is possible to design policies for the control of externalities that are reasonably efficient. The approach that we will propose in this and the next chapter consists of the use of a set of standards that serve as targets for environmental quality coupled with fiscal measures and other complementary instruments used as means to attain these standards. The standards, while admittedly somewhat arbitrary, are, in principle, not unlike the growth or employment goals that have guided governmental macroeconomic policies. In both cases, employment and environmental pol-

---

[1] Much of the material in this chapter is taken from W. J. Baumol and W. E. Oates, "The Use of Standards and Prices for Protection of the Environment," which originally appeared in *Swedish Journal of Economics* LXXIII (March, 1971), 42–54 and was reprinted in P. Bohm and A. Kneese, Eds., *The Economics of the Environment: Papers from Four Nations*, London & Basingstoke: Macmillan, 1971.

icy, the approach is, in practice, basically of the "satisficing" variety, with acceptability standards based on individual judgments and, often, compromise. Yet, in both cases, the choice of effective *means* to achieve the established goals has been facilitated by a substantial body of economic theory. This theory suggests that fiscal measures can contribute to the efficiency of a program to control externalities. Moreover, the use of these fiscal measures in combination with standards for acceptable environmental quality, avoids, at least in part, the policy problems that have been raised in Chapters 7 and 8.

Although in this chapter we emphasize the efficiency properties of fiscal measures, we should not be taken to argue that these are always the best or the only ways to deal with externalities. In the following chapter, we adopt an analytic framework that permits the introduction of other policy tools and shows that, under certain circumstances, an optimal environmental policy requires the use of several such measures.

1. INFORMATION REQUIREMENTS FOR OPTIMIZATION POLICY

The use of predetermined standards as an instrument of environmental policy recommends itself primarily because of the vast information required by the alternative approaches. Economists have long been aware of the enormous amount of information necessary to achieve anything that can even pretend to approximate optimality by means of centralized calculation. This is a major component of the Mises-Hayek argument against the potential effectiveness of full-scale central planning and direction. For the case of externalities, the argument is, if anything, strengthened by the analysis of Chapters 7 and 8, which emphasizes that data relating only to the neighborhood of an economy's initial position are particularly likely, in the presence of externalities, to lead the planner in the wrong direction.

Prohibitive information requirements not only plague centrally directed environmental programs, they raise similar difficulties for the calculation of optimal Pigouvian taxes and subsidies. The proper level of the Pigouvian tax (subsidy) upon the activities of the generator of an externality is equal to the marginal net damage (benefit) produced by that activity, and it is usually not easy to obtain a reasonable estimate of the money value of this marginal damage. Kneese and Bower report some promising work constituting a first step toward the estimation of the damage caused by pollution of waterways, including some quantitative evaluation of the loss in recreational benefits.[2] However, it is hard to be sanguine about the availability, in the foreseeable future, of a comprehensive body of statistics reporting the marginal net

[2] Allen Kneese and Blair Bower, *Managing Water Quality: Economics, Technology, Institutions* (Baltimore: Johns Hopkins Press, 1968), Chapter 6.

damage of the various externality-generating activities in the economy. The number of activities involved and the number of persons affected by them are so great that, on this score alone, the task assumes Herculean proportions. Add to this the unquantifiable nature of many of the most important consequences—the damage to health, the aesthetic costs—and the difficulty of determining a money equivalent for marginal net damage becomes quite apparent.

This, however, is not the end of the story. The optimal tax level on an externality-generating activity is not equal to the marginal net damage it generates *initially*, but rather to the damage it would cause if the level of the activity had been adjusted to its *optimal* level. To make the point more specifically, suppose that each additional unit of output of a factory now causes fifty cents worth of damage, but that after the installation of the appropriate smoke-control devices and other optimal adjustments, the marginal social damage would be reduced to twenty cents. As our results in Part I indicate, the correct value of the Pigouvian tax is twenty cents per unit of output, that is, the marginal cost of the smoke damage *corresponding to an optimal situation*. A tax of fifty cents per unit of output corresponding to the current smoke damage would lead to an excessive reduction in the smoke-producing activity, a reduction beyond the range over which the marginal benefit of decreasing smoke emission exceeds its marginal cost.

The relevance of this point for our present discussion is that it compounds enormously the difficulty of determining the optimal tax and benefit levels. If there is little hope of estimating the damage that is currently generated, how much less likely it is that we can evaluate the damage that would occur in an optimal world that we have never experienced or even described in quantitative terms.

One alternative route toward optimality may seem to be more practical. Instead of trying to go directly to the optimal tax policy, as a first approximation, one could base a set of taxes and subsidies on the current net damage (benefit) levels. In turn, as outputs and damage levels were modified in response to the present level of taxes, the taxes themselves would be readjusted to correspond to the new damage levels. It might be hoped that this would constitute a convergent iterative process with tax levels affecting outputs and damages, these, in turn, leading to modifications in taxes, and so on.

Unfortunately, such an iterative process also requires information that is very difficult to acquire. At each point in the sequence of learning steps, one must be able to evaluate what the preceding step has achieved and to determine the directions to further improvement. But, knowing neither the relevant costs nor the incremental damages corresponding to each conceivable step, that is precisely what we cannot calculate. Because we are unable to measure social welfare, and because we do not know the vector of inputs and outputs that characterize "the optimum," we simply do not know whether a given change in the tax rate has moved us toward that optimum or has even been able to improve matters.[3] There seems to be no way in which we can get the information necessary to implement the Pigouvian tax-subsidy approach to the control of externalities.

2. THE ENVIRONMENTAL CHARGES AND STANDARDS APPROACH

The economist's predilection for the use of the price mechanism makes him reluctant to give up the Pigouvian solution without a struggle. There is a fairly obvious way to avoid recourse to direct controls and retain the use of the price system as a means to control externalities: it involves the selection of a set of standards for an acceptable environment.[4] On the basis of evidence concerning the effects of unclean air on health or of polluted water on fish life, one may, for example, decide that the sulfur-dioxide content of the atmosphere in the city should not exceed x percent, that the oxygen demand of the foreign matter contained in a waterway should not exceed y, or that the decibel (noise) level in residential neighborhoods should not exceed z, at least 99 percent of the time. These acceptability standards, x, y, and z, then amount to a set of constraints that society places on its activities. They represent the decision maker's subjective evaluation of the minimum standards that must be met in order to achieve what may be described as "a reasonable quality of life." The defects of this procedure are obvious, and, because we do not want to minimize them, we shall examine the problem of the choice of standards in a later section.

For the moment, however, we want to emphasize the role of the price system in the realization of these standards. The point here is simply that the public authority can levy a uniform set of charges that would, in effect, constitute a set of prices for the private use of social resources, such as air and water. The charges (or prices) would be selected so as to achieve specific acceptability standards rather than attempting to base them on the unknown value of marginal net damages. For example, one might tax all installations emitting wastes into a river at a rate $t(b)$ cents per gallon, where the tax rate,

[3] In practice, an iterative approach is, of course, likely to run into many other difficulties. The political process does not facilitate frequent and consistent changes in tax rates and the degree of fine tuning that may be required is not all that easy to achieve.

[4] This proposal is not new. Most attempts to write a system of effluent charges into law are based on a set of prescribed standards. For earlier variants of this proposal in the literature, see J. H. Dales, *Pollution, Property and Prices* (Toronto: University of Toronto Press, 1968). Dales stresses the auction of pollution "rights" as an alternative to taxes, an option we discuss only in our companion volume because we have nothing to add to the theoretical discussion of this device.

t, paid by a particular polluter, would, for example, depend on b, the BOD [5] value of the effluent, according to some fixed schedule. Each polluter would then be given a financial incentive to reduce the amount of effluent he discharges and to improve the quality of the discharge (that is, reduce its BOD value). By setting the tax rates sufficiently high, the community would presumably be able to achieve whatever level of purification of the river it desired. It might even be able to eliminate at least some types of industrial pollution altogether.[6]

In marked contrast to an attempt at optimization, should iterative adjustments in tax rates prove desirable in a charges and standards approach, the necessary information would be easy to obtain. They require no data on costs or damages—only figures on current pollution levels. If the initial taxes did not reduce the pollution of the river sufficiently to satisfy the preset acceptability standards, one would simply raise the tax rates. Experience might soon permit the authorities to estimate the tax levels appropriate for the achievement of a target reduction in pollution.[7]

One might even be able to extend such adjustments beyond the setting of the tax rates to the determination of the acceptability standards themselves. If, for example, attainment of the initial targets were to prove unexpectedly inexpensive, the community might well wish to consider making the standards stricter.[8] Of course, such an iterative process is not costless. It means that some of the polluting firms and municipalities will have to modify their operations as tax rates are readjusted. At the very least, they should be warned in advance of the likelihood of such changes so that they can build flexibility into their plant design, something that may itself not be cheap.[9] But at any rate it is clear that, through the adjustment of tax rates, the public authorities

[5] BOD, biochemical oxygen demand, is a measure of the organic waste load of an emission. It measures the amount of oxygen used during decomposition of the waste materials. BOD is used widely as an index of the quality of effluents, but it is only an approximation at best. Discharges whose BOD value is low may nevertheless be considered serious pollutants because they contain inorganic chemical poisons whose oxygen requirement is nil because the poisons do not decompose.

[6] Here it is appropriate to recall the words of Chief Justice Marshall when he wrote that "The power to tax involves the power to destroy." (*McCulloch* v. *Maryland*, 1819). In terms of reversing the process of environmental decay, the power to tax can be also the power to restore.

[7] Of course, the political problems likely to beset either iterative process must not be minimized.

[8] In this way, the charges and standards approach might be adapted to approximate the Pigouvian outcome. If the standards were revised upward whenever there was reason to believe that the marginal benefits exceeded the marginal costs, and if these judgments were reasonably accurate, the two might well arrive at the same end product, at least if the optimal solution were unique.

[9] See A. G. Hart, "Anticipation, Business Planning and the Cycle," *Quarterly Journal of Economics* LI (February, 1937), 273–97.

can usually realize whatever standards of environmental quality have been selected.

3. OPTIMALITY PROPERTIES OF THE PRICING AND STANDARDS TECHNIQUE

Although the pricing and standards procedure will not, in general, lead to Pareto-optimal levels of the relevant activities, it is nevertheless true that the use of unit taxes (or subsidies) to achieve specified quality standards does possess one important property: under appropriate conditions,[10] it is the least-cost method for the achievement of these targets.[11]

A simple example may serve to clarify this point. Suppose that it is decided in some metropolitan area that the sulfur-dioxide content of the atmosphere should be reduced by 50 percent. An obvious approach to this matter, and the one that often recommends itself to the regulator, is to require each smoke producer in the area to reduce his emissions of sulfur dioxide by the same 50 percent. However, a moment's thought suggests that this may constitute a very expensive way to achieve the desired result. If, at current levels of output, the marginal cost of reducing sulfur-dioxide emissions for Factory A is only one-tenth of the marginal cost for Factory B, we would expect that it would be much cheaper for the economy as a whole to assign A a much greater decrease in smoke emissions than B. Just how the least-cost set of relative quotas would be arrived at in practice by the regulator is not clear, because this obviously would require calculations involving simultaneous relationships and extensive information on each polluter's marginal-cost function.

It is easy to see, however, that the unit-tax approach can *automatically* produce the least-cost assignment of smoke-reduction quotas without the need for any complicated calculations by the enforcement authority. In terms of our preceding example, suppose that the public authority placed a unit tax

[10] These conditions are spelled out later in this and the next chapters. Specifically, we will see in the next chapter that the presence of stochastic influences can sometimes make other instruments of control more efficient than taxes.

[11] This proposition is not new. Although we have been unable to find an explicit statement of this result anywhere in the literature, it, or a very similar proposition, has been suggested in a number of places. See, for example, Kneese and Bower, *Managing Water Quality*, Chapter 6; and L. Ruff, "The Economic Common Sense of Pollution," *The Public Interest* XIX (Spring, 1970), 69–85. Since the publication of an earlier version of our discussion, our attention was called to a similar proof by Charles Upton in "Optimal Taxing of Water Pollution," *Water Resources Research* IV (October, 1968), 865–75. The theorem takes no explicit account of metering costs which can, of course, be substantial. However, there seems to be little reason to expect these to be out of line with the enforcement costs associated with other environmental protection methods.

on smoke emissions and raised the level of the tax until sulfur dioxide emissions were in fact reduced by 50 percent. In response to a tax on its smoke emissions, a cost-minimizing firm will cut back on such emissions until the marginal cost of further reductions in smoke output is equal to the tax. But, because all economic units in the area are subject to the same tax, it follows that the marginal cost of reducing smoke output will be equalized across all activities. This implies that it is impossible to reduce the aggregate cost of the specified decrease in smoke emissions by rearranging smoke-reduction quotas: any alteration in this pattern of smoke emissions would involve an increase in smoke output by one firm the value of which to the firm would be less than the cost of the corresponding reduction in smoke emissions by some other firm. A formal proof of this least-cost property of unit taxes for the realization of a specified target level of environmental quality is provided in the next section.

It is significant that the validity of this least-cost theorem does not require the assumption that the firms generating the externalities are profit maximizers or perfect competitors. All that is necessary is that they minimize costs for whatever output levels they select, as would be done, for example, by an oligopolistic firm that seeks to maximize its growth or its sales, and that the market prices of the inputs reflect reasonably well the opportunity costs of their utilization.[12]

The cost saving that can be achieved through the use of taxes and subsidies in the attainment of acceptability standards may by no means be negligible. In one case for which comparable cost figures have been calculated, Kneese and Bower report (p. 162) that, with a system of uniform unit taxes, the cost of achieving a specified level of water quality would have been only about half as high as that resulting from a system of direct controls. If these figures are at all representative, then the potential waste of resources in the choice between tax measures and direct controls may obviously be of a large order. Unit taxes appear to represent a very attractive method for the realization of specified standards of environmental quality. Not only do they require relatively little in the way of detailed information on the cost structures of different industries, but they lead automatically to the least-cost pattern of modification of externality-generating activities.

4. DERIVATION OF THE COST-MINIMIZATION THEOREM

Let us turn now to a formal derivation of the optimality property of the charges approach that was described in the preceding section. We will

---

[12] A similar argument suggests that the rationing of pollution by the sale of pollution licenses (rights) at a market-clearing price offers the same advantages in cost minimization.

show that, to achieve *any* given vector of final outputs along with the attainment of the specified quality of the environment, the use of unit taxes (or, where appropriate, subsidies) to induce the necessary modification in the market-determined pattern of output will permit the realization of the specified output vector at minimum cost to society.

Although this theorem may seem rather obvious (as the intuitive discussion in the last section suggests), its proof does point up several interesting properties. As already emphasized, unlike many of the propositions about prices in welfare analysis, the theorem does not require a world of perfect competition. It applies alike to generators of externalities who are pure competitors, monopolists, or oligopolists, so long as each of the firms involved seeks to minimize the private cost of producing whatever vector of outputs it selects and has no monopsony power (that is, no influence on the prices of inputs) and so long as input prices approximate their opportunity costs. The firms need not be simple profit-maximizers; they may choose to maximize growth, sales (total revenues), their share of the market, or any combination of these goals (or a variety of other objectives). Because the effective pursuit of these goals typically entails minimization of the cost of whatever outputs are produced, the theorem applies to whatever set of final outputs society should select (either by central direction or through the operation of the market). It does not judge the desirability of that particular vector of outputs; it only tells us how to make the necessary adjustments at minimum cost.

We shall proceed initially to derive the first-order conditions for the minimization of the cost of a specified overall reduction in the emission of wastes. We will then show that the independent decisions of cost-minimizing firms subject to the appropriate unit tax on waste emissions will, in fact, satisfy the first-order conditions for overall cost minimization.

Let

r_{ik} represent the quantity of input i used by plant k ($i = 1, \ldots, n$), ($k = 1, \ldots, m$);

s_k be the quantities of waste it discharges;

y_k be its output level;

$y_k = f^k(r_{1k}, \ldots, r_{nk}, s_k)$ be its production function;

p_i be the price of input i; and

s^* the desired level of $\sum s_k$, the maximum permitted discharge of waste per unit of time.

In this formulation, the value of s^* is determined by the administrative authority in a manner designed to hold waste emissions in the aggregate to a level consistent with the specified environmental standard (for example, the sulphuric content of the atmosphere). Note that the level of the firm's waste emissions is treated here as an argument in its production function; to reduce waste discharges while maintaining its level of output, the firm will presumably require the use of additional units of some other inputs (for example, more labor or capital to recycle the wastes or to dispose of them in an alternative manner).

The problem now becomes that of determining the value of the r_{ik} and s_k that minimize input cost for all firms together:

$$\min c = \sum_i \sum_k p_i r_{ik} \qquad\qquad (1)$$

subject to the output constraints

$$f^k(r_{1k}, \ldots, r_{nk}, s_k) = y_k \geq y_k^* = \text{constant} \qquad (k = 1, \ldots, m)$$

and the constraint on the total output of pollutants

$$\sum_k s_k \leq s^*.$$

It may appear odd to include, as a constraint, a vector of given outputs for the firms, because the firms will presumably adjust output levels as well as the pattern of inputs in response to taxes or other restrictions on waste discharges. This vector, however, can be *any* vector of outputs (including that which emerges as a result of independent decisions by the firms). What we determine are first-order conditions for cost-minimization that apply to *any* given vector of outputs no matter how it is reached.[13]

Using $\lambda_1, \ldots, \lambda_m$ and λ as our $m + 1$ Lagrange multipliers, we obtain as Kuhn-Tucker conditions

$$\begin{array}{ll}
\lambda - \lambda_k f_s^k \geq 0 & s_k(\lambda - \lambda_k f_s^k) = 0 \\
p_i - \lambda_k f_i^k \geq 0 & r_{ik}(p_i - \lambda_k f_i^k) = 0 \\
y_k^* - f^k(r_{1k}, \ldots, r_{nk}, s_k) \leq 0 & \lambda_k[y_k^* - f^k(r_{1k}, \ldots, r_{nk}, s_k)] = 0 \qquad (2) \\
\sum s_k - s^* \leq 0 & \lambda(\sum s_k - s^*) = 0
\end{array}$$

for all i, k, where we have written f_s^k for $\partial f^k/\partial s_k$ and f_i^k for $\partial f^k/\partial r_{ik}$.

---

[13] The reason for prespecification of the vector of output has its analogue in the elementary theory of the firm. Where we use a cost-minimization premise in the analysis of the firm's input choices, it is obviously not correct to assume that it seeks to operate at as low a cost per unit as possible, without specifying its output level. For the firm's output level is determined by demand relationships as well as costs, and the output it decides to produce may be far from that which minimizes average costs. It is, however, reasonable to posit that whatever the output level it selects for itself, the firm will seek to produce it at as low a cost as possible. Our premise here is the analogue of this last assumption.

Now let us see what will happen if the m plants are run by independent managements whose objective is to minimize the cost of whatever outputs their firm produces, and if, instead of the imposition of a fixed ceiling on the emission of pollutants, this emission is taxed at a fixed rate per unit, t_s. So long as its input prices are fixed, firm k will wish to minimize the cost of whatever output level it produces; that is, it will minimize[14]

$$c = t_s s_k + \sum_i p_i r_{ik} \tag{3}$$

subject to

$$f^k(r_{1k}, \ldots, r_{nk}, s_k) \geq y_k^*.$$

Direct differentiation of the m Lagrangian functions for our m firms immediately yields the first-order conditions (2); these are the same conditions as before,[15] provided t_s is set equal to λ where λ (and hence t_s) is the shadow price of the pollution constraint—the marginal social cost of an increase in the stringency of the pollution standard.[16]

We have thus proved

Proposition One. A tax rate set at a level that achieves the desired reduction in the total emission of pollutants will satisfy the necessary conditions for the minimization of the program's cost to society.[17]

The preceding discussion indicates, incidentally, that pricing can play an effective role as a substitute for part of the information that is pertinent in the presence of externalities. In an illuminating remark, S. C. Kolm reminds us that the choice of efficient measures for the control of externalities

---

[14] Note again that this assumes identity between the prices in (1) and (3), that is, that input prices to the private firm correspond to the cost of their use to society. Thus, although our result does not require pure competition in the regulated firm, it does call for input prices that are not too far from their competitive values.

[15] The last of the Kuhn-Tucker conditions, $\sum s_k \leq s^*$, obviously has no counterpart in the calculation of the individual firm. However, it will clearly be satisfied if the s_k corresponding to a given set of prices is unique.

[16] Clearly, the value of λ is an important datum and would be helpful in selecting a standard if that figure were available. Unfortunately, this information is lost in the standards and charges approach because no optimality calculation is carried out in the process. There are, indeed, no free lunches.

[17] In addition to satisfying these necessary first-order conditions, cost minimization requires that the production functions possess the usual second-order properties. An interesting treatment of this issue is available in Portes, "The Search for Efficiency in the Presence of Externalities," in *Unfashionable Economics*. We should point out also that our proof assumes that the firm takes t_s as given and beyond its control. Peter Bohm in "Pollution, Purification, and the Theory of External Effects," *Swedish Journal of Economics* LXXII, No. 2 (1970), 153–66, discusses some of the problems that can arise where the firm takes into account the effects of its behavior on the value of t_s. See also our discussion in Chapter 6.

requires, in principle, detailed information both about the benefits these measures offer the various members of the economy and the costs they impose on each of them.[18] The pricing mechanism offers no help with respect to the first of these because the very presence of externalities means that an individual decision maker's behavior does not reflect all of the relevant social benefits.

However, pricing does serve to eliminate the need for detailed cost information.[19] Under a system of central direction, a planner who wants to calculate the least-cost allocation of pollution quotas among the firms under his control must, as is shown in (2), have at his disposal data giving all of the f_s^k and f_i^k (that is, the marginal product figure for every input, i, and for every polluting plant, k). The Herculean proportions of the task of collecting this mass of information and then carrying out the requisite calculations is clear.[20] A pricing approach dispenses with the need for all these data and computations because it gives that portion of the optimization calculation over to an automatic process. This suggests that the charges and standards approach may be looked upon as a procedure that frankly abandons any attempt to obtain extensive information on benefits but which uses the pricing system where it is at its best, in the allocation of damage-reducing tasks in a manner that approximates minimization of costs, even though detailed data on the costs of these tasks are unavailable.

5. GEOGRAPHICAL AND OTHER APPROPRIATE VARIATIONS IN TAX RATE [21]

Even the cost-minimization claims for the standards and pricing approach must be qualified carefully. The theorem as stated runs into several problems in practice that may complicate its applicability.

---

[18] S. C. Kolm, "Économie de l'Environment" (unpublished manuscript), Chapter 2.

[19] "This advantage, not needing to know the value of the right to pollute, is one of the great points of interest of the method of regulation by taxation (or subsidy). It is a property of *decentralization* of decisions: by requiring everyone to pay a financial charge equal to the damage he causes, one leaves the necessity of knowing the value of the right to pollute entirely in the hands of the person who knows it best—the polluter himself." Kolm, *ibid.*, Chapter 2, p. 4.

[20] Although the calculation has ignored the costs of surveillance, obviously such outlays would be required under any system of environmental regulation. There seems to be reason to believe that, in many applications, the routine metering costs that would be needed will be considerably smaller than the costs of surveillance *and* judicial enforcement that are the instruments of direct controls.

[21] This section is based on comments by Elizabeth Bailey and on two illuminating papers: Thomas H. Teitenberg, "Taxation and the Control of Externalities: Comment," *American Economic Review* LXIV (June, 1974); and Susan Rose Ackerman, "Effluent Charges: A Critique," *Canadian Journal of Economics* VI (November, 1973), 512–28.

One relevant assumption implicit in the preceding analysis asserts that there is a direct and additive relationship between the emission of pollutants and the degree of welfare loss suffered by the community. However, that is not always the case. A firm that emits waste into the upper parts of a river may do more or less damage to the community than one that discharges the same amount of effluent downstream. The upstream emissions may be less damaging than those downstream if the upper part of the river is sufficiently unpolluted to permit natural processes to disperse or degrade a considerable portion of the wastes before anyone is affected by them. On the other hand, if there is little natural cleansing of the upstream discharges, they may well be more costly to society than discharges into the lower parts of the river because people and activities along the entire length of the river may be affected primarily by upstream emissions.

Because the social damage caused by upstream and downstream discharges obviously differs, it is not appropriate to tax them at the same rate. In such circumstances, an equal tax per unit of effluent in the two regions will generally *not* minimize the cost of a specified reduction in pollution as a simple counterexample demonstrates. Suppose that only the area near the mouth of the river is polluted so that the objective of the program is to reduce the level of pollution in that portion of the waterway. Suppose, moreover, that treatment of emissions will cost fifteen cents per gallon in a typical downstream plant but only ten cents per gallon upstream. Finally, assume that although all of the downstream firms' discharges add directly to the filth in the polluted part of the river, half of the upriver plants' discharges are eliminated automatically by natural processes. In that case, a tax of twelve cents per gallon of effluent will induce only the upstream plants to cleanse or reduce their emissions, because only their private costs of treatment per gallon are smaller than the tax rate. But to society this is an inefficient outcome, for ten cents nets it only a *half* gallon reduction in filth downstream, whereas treatment by a downstream plant would reduce pollutant discharge by a full gallon for only fifteen cents.[22]

Not only geographic accidents of location can lead to this problem. It may arise out of the range of decisions available to the firm itself, with the result that a uniform tax on discharges can induce management to make the wrong decisions. Turvey cites the case of a firm that has the option of building a high or a low chimney for its smoke.[23] If the high chimney can disperse pollutants sufficiently to render them harmless, it may yield the same contri-

[22] This is obviously a highly simplified illustration. Engineering models of waterways describing the differential impact on water quality of emissions at different locations use relationships that are much more complex. See Rose Ackerman's discussion of the Delaware Estuary Model, "Efficient Charges: A Critique."

[23] Ralph Turvey, "On Divergences Between Social Cost and Private Cost," *Economica* New Series XXX (August, 1963), 309–13.

bution to human welfare as the suppression of smoke emissions and do so at a lower cost in resources. However, a tax based on emissions will clearly always favor smoke suppression rather than dispersion via higher chimneys, whatever their relative social costs.

The upshot of all this is that, for the minimum-cost theorem to hold, it is necessary for the tax to be based on the *effect* of an emission on the community, and not necessarily on the amount generated. In practice this can sometimes be done in a rough and ready way (for example, by basing effluent charges on, say, two parameters—the quantity emitted and the quality of the receiving waters, or the amount of smoke emitted and on chimney height). Another device that may sometimes work reasonably well involves the establishment of different zones, based on concentration of population and current pollution levels, with different tax rates imposed in different zones.[24] Where some such simple provision will do the trick, the issues raised in this section create no insuperable difficulties for the charges and standards procedure. However, where delicate differentiations are essential, the attractive simplicity of the proposal can dwindle rapidly.[25]

One instructive way of looking at the matter is that differences in the effects of equal quantities of emission upon the effective level of pollution require the policy maker to retreat part way toward explicit evaluation of the social damage resulting from an emission. He must determine the extent to which various emissions influence the level of pollution. Note, however, that the charges and standards procedure still does not require the calculation of the effects of pollution on health, recreation, and psychic pleasure, and the translation of each of these into common (money) units.

What all this suggests is that, although the charges and standards procedure should never be as difficult to implement as the ideal Pigouvian tax,[26] it may still be quite complicated to take advantage of the cost savings it offers in theory, in applications where the level of pollution damage responds differently to emissions from alternative sources or locations. The importance of this qualification obviously depends upon the circumstances at hand. As was just noted, where such differential effects of emissions are unimportant or where some simple device, such as variations in the charge by zone can

---

[24] See Teitenberg, "A Note on Taxation and the Control of Externalities," *American Economic Review*, for further discussion of this proposal. Deliberate differences in tax rates of the sort discussed here are of course not to be confused with the fortuitous differences arising from variations in local policies that are rightly deplored by J. L. Stein, "The 1971 Report of the President's Council of Economic Advisors: Micro-Economic Aspects of Public Policy," *American Economic Review* LXI (September, 1971), 531–37.

[25] Rose Ackerman, "Effluent Charges: A Critique," describes a condition under which a uniform tax on emissions can conceivably be even more costly as a means to reduce pollution than a system involving an equal percentage reduction of emissions by all polluters.

[26] Obviously the ideal Pigouvian tax would also have to be adjusted for the differential effects of emissions that we have discussed in this section.

deal with them (at least roughly), the appeal of the charges and standards procedure seems to us to remain very compelling.

6. THE STANDARDS-CHARGES APPROACH AND MULTIPLE LOCAL OPTIMA

In one important respect, the charges and standards approach avoids completely the problem posed for the Pigouvian solution and for central planning by nonconvexities and the resulting presence of a multiplicity of local optima. Because it is a satisficing procedure, it makes no attempt to search for an optimum, and so there is no occasion for the decision maker to aim mistakenly for what is in fact a local optimum instead of the global one.

So long as the emission of a pollutant is a monotonically decreasing function of the magnitude of the charge imposed on it, a function that is not bounded away from zero, one can choose a set of tax levels sufficient to guarantee attainment of whatever standards happen to have been selected. If the quantity of pollutant S still exceeds the level called for by the adopted standards, one need merely increase the charge upon the emission of S until its quantity has been reduced to the "acceptable" level, and that is all there is to the matter.

The presence of a multiplicity of maxima does, however, require one significant qualification of the cost-minimization theorem. For although, at least in principle, the use of charges guarantees that a given set of standards will be achieved at some sort of minimum cost, this may, in fact, be a local rather than a global minimum. Suppose, for example, that there are two ways of avoiding the pollution produced by some commodity X, an increase in the output of smoke suppressors, or the substitution of another commodity, Y, which emits little pollution. Assume, moreover, that there are decreasing average costs both in the production of smoke suppressors and in the manufacture of Y. In that case, there will be two cost-minimizing ways of getting the pollution down to the desired level, the elimination of a sufficient amount of X and its replacement by a suitable amount of Y, or through the production of a sufficient quantity of pollution-suppression equipment. Toward which of these minima the market process will converge depends on the initial position, for that will determine the relative initial costs of Y and suppressors. There certainly is no guarantee that the process will converge toward the less costly of the two minima.

However, the likelihood that this problem will be encountered is apparently unrelated to the presence or absence of externalities. Unlike the issues discussed in Chapter 8, the multiplicity of equilibria that is relevant for the cost calculation does not seem to be made more likely by the presence of externalities. For the nonconvexities induced by externalities stemming from *X* arise both in the social production possibility set for *X* and the activity *Z*, that is damaged by it. But the externality caused by *X* need not affect activities *W* and *V* whose purpose is to offset the pollution produced by *X*. Thus, it need not introduce nonconvexities into the *XW* or the *WV* production sets, which are the production sets pertinent for the determination of the cost-minimizing program of pollution control corresponding to a given output vector. Consequently, although it is true that the cost-minimization property of the charges and standards approach can run into multiple maximum problems, it seems no more likely to encounter these difficulties than a decision process in some other economic area. There seems to be no special reason to expect it to run afoul of the nonconvexities that are built into the economy by the presence of externalities and which serve as booby traps that threaten the effectiveness of any attempt to design an *optimal* externalities policy.

7. WHERE THE CHARGES AND STANDARDS APPROACH IS APPROPRIATE

As we have emphasized, the most disturbing aspect of the charges and standards procedure is the somewhat arbitrary character of the criteria selected. There does presumably exist some optimal level of pollution (that is, quality of the air or a waterway), but in the absence of a pricing mechanism to indicate the value of the damages generated by polluting activities, one knows no way to determine accurately the set of taxes necessary to induce the optimal activity levels.

Although this difficulty should not be minimized, it is important to recognize that the problem is not unique to the selection of acceptability standards. In fact, as is well known, it is a difficulty common to the provision of nearly all public goods. In general, the market will not generate appropriate levels of outputs where market prices fail to reflect the social damages (benefits) associated with particular activities. As a result, in the absence of the proper set of signals from the market, it is typically necessary to utilize a political process (that is, a method of collective choice) to determine the level of the activity. From this perspective, the selection of environmental standards can be viewed as a particular device utilized in a process of collective decision making to determine the appropriate level of an activity involving external effects.

Because methods of collective choice, such as simple majority rule or decisions by an elected representative, can, at best, be expected to provide only rough approximations to optimal results, the general problem becomes one of deciding whether the malfunction of the market in a certain case is sufficiently serious to warrant public intervention. In particular, it would seem to us that such a blunt instrument as acceptability standards should be used only sparingly, because the very ignorance that serves as the rationale for the adoption of such standards implies that we can hardly be sure of their consequences.

In general, intervention in the form of acceptability standards can be utilized with a degree of confidence only where there is reason to believe that the existing situation imposes a high level of social costs *and* that these costs can be significantly reduced by feasible decreases in the levels of certain externality-generating activities. If, for example, we were to examine the functional relationship between the level of social welfare and the levels of particular activities that impose marginal net damages, the argument would be that the use of acceptability standards is justified only in those cases where the curve, over the bulk of the relevant range, is both decreasing and steep. Such a case is illustrated in Figure 10–1 by the curve *PQR*. In a case of this kind,

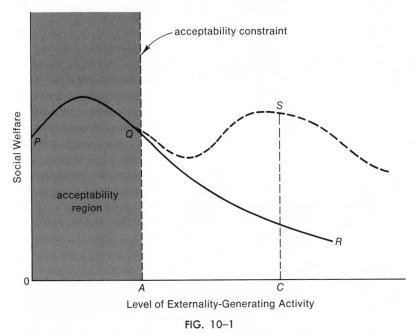

FIG. 10–1

although we obviously will not have an accurate knowledge of the relevant position of the curve, we can at least have some assurance that the selection of an acceptability standard and the imposition of a unit tax sufficient to achieve that standard will lead to an increase in social welfare. For example, in terms of the curve *PQR* in Figure 10–1, the levying of a tax sufficient to reduce smoke outputs from level *OC* to *OA* to insure that the quality of the air meets the specified environmental standards would obviously increase social welfare.[27]

On the other hand, if the relationship between social welfare and the level of the externality-generating activity is not monotonically decreasing, the changes resulting from the imposition of an acceptability standard (for example, a move from S to Q in Figure 10–1) clearly may lead to a reduction in welfare. Moreover, even if the function were monotonic but fairly flat, the benefits achieved might not be worth the cost of additional intervention machinery that new legislation requires, and it would almost certainly not be worth the risk of acting with highly imperfect, inconclusive information.

In some cases, notably in the field of public utility regulation, some economists have criticized the employment of acceptability standards on both these grounds; they have asserted that the social costs of monopolistic mis-allocation of resources are probably not very high (that is, the relevant portion of the social welfare curve in Figure 10–1 is not steep), and that the regulation can itself introduce inefficiencies into the operations of the regulated industries.

Advocacy of environmental pricing and standards procedures for the control of externalities must therefore rest on the belief that, in this area, we do have a clear notion of the general shape of the social welfare curve. This will presumably hold true where the evidence indicates, first, that a particular externality really does have a substantial and unambiguous effect on the quality of life (if, for example, it makes existence very unpleasant for every-one or constitutes a serious hazard to health); and, second, that reductions in the levels of these activities do not themselves entail huge resource costs. On the first point, there is growing evidence that various types of pollutants do in fact have such unfortunate consequences, particularly in areas where

----

[27] The relationship depicted in Figure 10–1 is to be regarded as an intuitive device employed for pedagogical purposes, not in any sense as a rigorous analysis. However, some further explanation may be helpful. The curve itself is not a social welfare function in the usual sense; rather it measures, in terms of a numeraire (for example, dollars), the value, summed over all individuals, of the benefits from the output of the activity minus the private *and* net social costs. Thus, for each level of the activity, the height of the curve indicates the *net* benefits (possibly negative) that the activity confers on society. The ac-ceptability constraint indicates that level of the activity that is consistent with the specified minimum standard of environmental quality (for example, that level of smoke emissions from factories that is sufficiently low to maintain the quality of the air in a particular metropolitan area). There is an ambiguity here in that the levels of several different activities may jointly determine a particular dimension of environmental quality (for example, the smoke emissions of a number of different industries will determine the quality of the air). In this case, the acceptable level of polluting emissions for the firm or industry will clearly depend on the levels of emissions of others. If, as we discussed earlier, unit taxes are used to implement the acceptability standards, there will result a least-cost pattern of levels of the relevant externality-generating activities. If we understand the constraint in Figure 10–1 to refer to the activity level indicated by this particular solution, then this ambiguity disappears.

they are highly concentrated.[28] Second, what experience we have had with, for example, the reduction of waste discharges into waterways suggests that processes involving the recycling and reuse of waste materials can frequently be achieved at surprisingly modest cost.[29] In such cases, the rationale for the imposition of environmental standards is clear, and it seems to us that the rejection of such crude measures on the grounds that they will probably violate the requirements of optimality may well be considered a kind of perverse perfectionism.

[28] See on this, L. Lave and E. Seskin, "Air Pollution and Human Health," *Science* CLXIX (August 21, 1970), 723–33.

[29] Some interesting discussions of the feasibility of the control of waste emissions into waterways, often at low cost, are contained in Kneese and Bower, *Managing Water Quality*. In particular, see their description of the control of water quality in the Ruhr Valley in Germany.

chapter 11

Stochastic Influences, Direct Controls, and Taxes

This chapter seeks to show that, in addition to the tax measures advocated in the preceding chapter, there is room in a well-designed environmental policy for at least one instrument that has attracted virtually no defenders among economists—the direct controls, so popular outside the profession.

After the demonstration in the preceding chapter that tax methods have important efficiency advantages over direct controls, our advocacy of the use of the latter may appear somewhat inconsistent. However, we are not suggesting that the preceding discussion is basically incorrect, but rather that it omits an important consideration. Environmental problems do not always develop smoothly and gradually. Instead, they are often characterized by infrequent but more or less serious crises whose timing is unpredictable. Such emergencies may require rapid temporary changes in the rules of the control mechanism, and it is here that tax policy appears subject to some severe practical limitations.[1] In this chapter, we will show how the uncertainty associated with environmental conditions greatly complicates the implementation of a program of fees or subsidies.

We will not conclude from this that taxes are useless. We still believe that they have an important role to play and that economists have been right in trying to convince policy makers of their advantages. Rather, we suggest that the ideal policy package contains a mixture of instruments, with taxes,

---

[1] As was already noted, another recent work has questioned, on theoretical grounds, the universal superiority of tax methods to control externalities. See S. Rose Ackerman, "Effluent Charges: A Critique."

direct controls, and even moral suasion each used in certain circumstances to regulate the sources of environmental damage.

Before proceeding further, it is desirable to indicate more formally how we distinguish between direct controls and taxes or fees. This is not as obvious a difference as one might think at first blush, for direct controls are presumably enforced through fines or other penalties and the difference between a fine and a tax requires some elucidation. To us, a direct control must involve a directive to *individual* decision makers requiring them to set one or more output or input quantities at some specified levels or prohibiting them from exceeding (or falling short of) some specified levels. If the activity levels satisfy these requirements, they are considered legal and no penalty is imposed. However, if they are violated, whether by small or large amounts, the individual is considered to be a lawbreaker who is subject to punishment. With taxes or fees on the other hand, even if they are based on standards *for the community as a whole,* no individual is told what input or output levels to select. Moreover, taxes and fees utilize no knife's-edge criterion. The amount of the decision maker's payment will vary with his pertinent activity levels, with no imputation of illegality to the activity levels he chooses.

1. EXOGENOUS INFLUENCES AND THE SOCIAL COST OF EMISSIONS

In some cases, the damage done by an emission depends almost exclusively upon its magnitude and on the number of persons whose location makes them vulnerable to its effects. The annoyance generated by a loud noise may plausibly be taken to depend largely on its decibel level and on the number of persons within earshot.

However, under many other circumstances, the social costs of a particular activity depend on variables beyond the control of those directly involved. For example, the polluting effects of a given discharge of effluent into a river will depend upon the condition of the waterway at that time— whether it has just been replenished by rainfall or depleted by a drought. The amount of water and the speed of its flow are critical determinants of the river's assimilative capacity. Similarly, stagnant air can trap atmospheric pollutants, perhaps even collecting them until they become a danger to health and life.[2]

The point of all this is that emission levels that are acceptable and

---

[2] Note, however, that the latest of the very careful studies by Lave and Seskin of the evidence on the mortality effects of air pollution suggests that fears about the consequences of air pollution *crises* may be exaggerated considerably. See Lester Lave and Eugene Seskin, "Acute Relationships Among Daily Mortality, Air Pollution and Climate," to appear in Edwin Mills, ed., *Economic Analysis of Environmental Problems* (New York: Columbia University Press).

rather harmless under usual conditions can, under other circumstances, become intolerable. Moreover, these conditions depend on the values of variables that are largely outside the control of the policy maker and often are not predictable much in advance. Meteorological conditions, for example, must, for most purposes, be considered largely exogenous and only imperfectly foreseeable.[3]

Such exogenous influences contribute to an important class of serious environmental problems: the occasional crises that call for the imposition of emergency measures and that, in some instances, have grown into widely publicized disasters. Typically, we cannot predict these crises much in advance or with any degree of certainty; we can, however, be certain that at some unforeseen time they will recur. An environmental program incapable of dealing with such emergencies is hardly likely to be greeted with overwhelming enthusiasm.

2. ADMINISTRATIVE OBSTACLES TO THE EFFECTIVE USE OF TAXES

Whatever their other virtues, taxes and subsidies suffer from at least one serious practical liability as a means for the regulation of externalities: they are very difficult to change on short notice. Anyone who has followed the history of recent attempts at tax reform knows how slow and painful a process it is. Even during periods when unemployment and disappointing growth rates called for rapid tax reductions, there have been delays running into months and, in some cases, years. Certainly, the few days that are as much advance notice as one can reasonably expect for an environmental emergency are hardly enough to effect a change in the tax regulations.

Moreover, even if an environmental administrator possessed a substantial degree of flexibility in the setting of tax rates so that he could adjust them rapidly, he would still find the instrument ill-suited to short-term crises. For the sort of response one hopes to elicit from the imposition of Pigouvian taxes characteristically is not achieved overnight. One expects them to lead to the use of cleaner fuels, of production processes that emit smaller quantities of pollutants, to the adoption of equipment for the cleansing of emissions, and so on. These are measures that normally are effective only in the long run,

---

[3] Similar arguments apply to the state of the quality of life more broadly interpreted. The effects of deterioration of a neighborhood upon crime rates clearly depend on a number of noneconomic and largely exogenous influences: the level of drug addiction, whether the country is currently engaged in military combat, on the current rainfall and temperature (recall the "hot summers" of the 1960s with their frequent outbreaks of urban violence and looting). Forecasts of the timing of the resulting disturbances are consequently highly uncertain.

and that it is neither reasonable, nor often possible, to press into service in a brief emergency period.

This second point really involves two sorts of problems in the implementation of a system of fees to cope with occasional periods of severe environmental deterioration. First, the response to a given level of fees is difficult to predict accurately. And, second, the period of adjustment to new levels of activities is typically uncertain. These problems may not be very serious for a long-run policy designed to achieve desired standards of environmental quality. As we discussed in the preceding chapter, the environmental authority can set tax rates, observe the response in levels of polluting activities over time, and, where necessary, seek further adjustments in the level of the fee. Our point is that, *given sufficient time for the adjustment of fees to achieve the desired response*, the case for effluent fees (or taxes) is a very compelling one.

However, environmental conditions may, under certain situations, alter so swiftly that fees simply may not be able to produce the necessary changes in behavior quickly (or predictably) enough to avoid a real catastrophe. This suggests one major attraction of direct controls: *if enforcement is effective*, controls can induce, with little uncertainty, the prescribed alterations in polluting activities.[4]

Direct controls may offer another source of flexibility that is difficult to achieve with taxes. It is certainly true, as many economists have pointed out, that programs of direct controls frequently require essentially the same monitoring system (and costs of enforcement) as a program of fees. A plant that is prohibited from discharging more than x units of sulphur from its smoke stacks should have its emissions recorded just as it would if it were to be taxed t dollars per unit of sulphur emitted.

But during periods of severe environmental distress, it may be necessary to regulate activities that in normal times are left to pursue their own course. Bans or limitations on motor vehicle travel, the cessation of certain types of waste disposal, all of which are not normally of sufficient concern to require regulation, may be convenient temporary expedients. Because of the infrequency of these controls and, perhaps, the suddenness of their need, comprehensive monitoring and metering systems may not be sensible, economically. Instead, the authorities may have to be content to catch only some of the violators, imposing penalties sufficiently severe to make them an

---

[4] This, incidentally, suggests another reason for the popularity of direct controls among regulators. Having had little experience in the use of effluent taxes, they seem to fear that a program introducing a fee for the first time will fall far short of its intended goal and that a subsequent increase in tax rates sufficiently high for the purpose will prove unacceptable politically. A set of quotas, they argue, does not proceed so indirectly; it can give the community far greater assurance of achieving its objectives than can an untried program of taxes.

effective deterrent to others. Then punishment itself becomes a stochastic process, with penalties higher than those that would be appropriate if their imposition were certain and universal.[5] The landlord whose incinerator continues to run despite an emergency prohibition on trash burning may be jailed for sixty days rather than being fined the relatively small fee that would otherwise be called for. This seems not to be too bad a description of the way in which direct controls actually work in emergency situations.

Just because they do not require metering, direct controls of this sort can be imposed cheaply and quickly, avoiding the fixed costs that supplementary taxes may require.[6]

3. TAX RATES AND EXOGENOUS DETERMINANTS OF DAMAGE: AN ILLUSTRATIVE MODEL

Using an elementary model, we can illustrate an environmental process and see why fiscal controls by themselves can sometimes be an excessively costly instrument for environmental protection.

The basic relationship is built about a random variable, k_t, where $0 \leq k_t \leq 1$. We take k_t to depend on exogenous forces (which, for convenience, we call *wind velocity*); in particular, k_t represents the proportion of the previous period's pollution that is not dispersed by the time the current period begins. The current pollution level, P_t, equals this residue from the previous quantity of pollution, $k_t P_{t-1}$, plus current emissions:[7]

[5] Presumably, in a stochastic punishment process, the expected value of the penalty to a violator who has (as yet) not been caught should bear some direct relation to the fee rates appropriate where a charge is certain and universal.

[6] One might argue that any degree of reduction in polluting activities can be achieved by a tax that is sufficiently high. A tax of $100,000 per motor vehicle on the streets of a city should effectively curtail all motor traffic. Moreover, such a tax can also be imposed haphazardly, falling only on those who happen to be caught violating the pertinent rules or standards. Aside from the purely semantic problem of distinguishing between such randomly collected taxes and the fines used to enforce direct controls, the preceding example also suggests that in practice an environmental protection agency is unlikely to have the authority to levy taxes of such magnitudes, although it is likely to be able to enlist the support of the police and the courts in imposing emergency controls.

[7] We believe that this is not a bad representation of the facts of the matter. Rather similar relationships have long been used in the engineering literature in the field of water quality analysis. See, for example, H. W. Streeter and Earle B. Phelps, *A Study of the Pollution and Natural Purification of the Ohio River*, U.S. Public Health Bulletin, #146 (Washington, D.C.: Government Printing Office, February, 1925); J. Donald O'Connor, "The Temporal and Spacial Distribution of Dissolved Oxygen in Streams," *Water Resources Research* III, No. 1, (1967) pp. 65–79; W. E. Dobbins, "BOD and Oxygen Relationships in Streams," *Journal of Sanitary Engineers Division*, American Society of Civil Engineering, XC, No. SA3, (June, 1964) pp. 53–78. We note also that the logic of our analysis holds for a much broader range of functional forms, say $P_t = \phi(P_{t-1}, k_{1t}, \ldots, k_{qt}) + nf(r)$, where the k_{jt} are random variables. All is well so long as we can, from the probability distribution for the k_{jt}, calculate G, the distribution for P_t.

$$P_t = k_t P_{t-1} + nf(r) \tag{1}$$

where

  n is the number of polluters in the commuhity
  r is the tax rate on emissions[8] and
  $f(r)$ is the level of emission of a representative polluter.

Equation (1) is, of course, a linear, first-order difference equation with a stochastic coefficient, and it is nonhomogeneous.

  Let us illustrate the workings of the model by starting off with the case where wind velocity is not subject to stochastic influences. Then the equilibrium solution of (1) for $k_t = k$ (nonrandom) is

$$P_e = nf(r)/(1 - k). \tag{2}$$

  If, in addition, we assume that the waste emissions by a representative firm are a linear function of the tax rate (they can be expressed as $f(r) = a - br$ where r is the tax rate),[9] then the equilibrium level, P_e, is given as

$$P_e = n(a - br)/(1 - k). \tag{3}$$

Let D be the maximum level of accumulated pollutants consistent with a given set of standards; then the tax rate, r, necessary to maintain the equilibrium level of P_e at the critical level is obtained as a solution to

$$P_e = \frac{n(a - br)}{1 - k} = D.$$

Or, solving for the tax rate, r,

$$r = \frac{a}{b} - \frac{D(1 - k)}{nb}. \tag{4}$$

  This gives us a non-increasing linear relation between r and the pollution dispersion rate, $(1 - k)$. In Figure 11–1, we depict this relationship for various values of D. For example, in the case $D = 0$, the second term in the RHS of (4) drops out so that r takes the constant value a/b as indicated by horizontal locus QR in the figure. This, of course, is the case of zero waste emissions. As D rises, indicating a higher permissible level of discharges, the

  [8] In this chapter we depart from our notation elsewhere, using r rather than t to represent the tax rate to avoid confusion with the conventional time subscript, t.

  [9] $f(r)$ depends in part on how the polluter's costs are affected by the quantity of his emissions. This relationship will enter the discussion explicitly later in the chapter when we construct a model for an optimal mixed policy, that is, a policy using both taxes and direct controls.

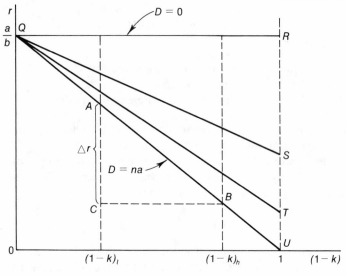

FIG. 11-1

curve pivots down about the fixed vertical intercept, a/b. All the loci have this same vertical intercept because, for $(1 - k) = 0$, we have $r = a/b$ for all values of D.

The linear case we have just discussed assumes implicitly that the marginal cost of pollution control is constant. In fact, the cost of eliminating pollution normally rises sharply as its level approaches zero. To illustrate this possibility, we can utilize the emissions function $f(r) = ce^{-vr}$, which implies that the reduction in emissions resulting from a given rise in the tax rate will level off asymptotically. Arguing as before, we now obtain

$$D = P_e = \frac{nf(r)}{1 - k} = \frac{nce^{-vr}}{1 - k}$$

$$\frac{D(1 - k)}{nc} = e^{-vr}$$

$$-vr = \ell n\, D + \ell n\, (1 - k) - \ell n\, (nc)$$

$$r = \frac{\ell n\, (nc)}{v} - \frac{\ell n\, D}{v} - \frac{\ell n\, (1 - k)}{v}. \tag{5}$$

The relationship[10] between r and $(1 - k)$ is illustrated by curve $R'R$ in Figure 11–2.

[10] Note that because $0 \le (1 - k) \le 1$, then $\ln (1 - k) \le 0$, and approaches zero as $1 - k$ approaches unity.

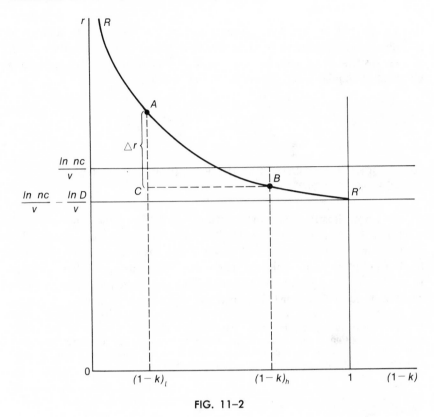

FIG. 11-2

4. SOME QUALITATIVE OBSERVATIONS

Several broad conclusions are suggested by these simple deterministic models: i) Increasing D (a lowering of standards) permits a reduction in r but does so at a declining rate (because it restores pollution whose elimination is decreasingly expensive). This result follows directly from (5). It obviously depends on the assumption that the marginal cost of reducing waste emissions rises as the level of emissions falls. For example, as (4) indicates, this result does not hold in the linear model. ii) An increase in n, the number of polluters, increases r, but at a decreasing rate. With more sources of emission there will be more pollution, but each increase in r also elicits the associated decrease in emissions from a correspondingly larger number of polluters. In both (4) and (5), it is easy to show $\partial^2 r / \partial n^2 < 0$. This suggests that, to maintain a given level of waste discharges, a pollution tax rate in more densely populated cities should be higher than that in smaller communities, but the increase should be less than proportional to the rise in the number of polluters.[11] iii) Finally, as is to be expected, a rise in $(1 - k)$, the rate of natural dispersion of pollutants, reduces the tax rate necessary to meet a given set of standards, for from (2), setting $D = P_e$,

$$f'(r)\frac{\partial r}{\partial(1 - k)} = \frac{D}{n} \quad \text{so} \quad \frac{\partial r}{\partial(1 - k)} < 0.$$

5. STOCHASTIC MODELS AND THE POTENTIAL SUPERIORITY OF DIRECT CONTROLS

We now illustrate the workings of the model when the wind velocity is subject to stochastic influences. Unlike the deterministic case, the level of pollution in each period is a random variable; consequently, the equilibrium level of pollution is not uniquely determined but is also a random variable. It has been proved by V. S. Bawa that, for our stochastic relationship (1), the limiting or equilibrium distribution of the pollution level always exists and

[11] The declining rate of increase in r with rising n is *not* dependent on our exponential response assumption. On the contrary, the increasing cost of pollution control (that is, the $f''(r) > 0$) works *against* that relationship. Indeed, it is only guaranteed to hold if $f''(r) \leq 0$. To show this we return to our basic general relationship,

$$f(r) = \frac{D(1 - k)}{n}$$

(which includes both the linear and exponential models as special cases). Consequently,

$$f'(r)\frac{\partial r}{\partial n} = -\frac{D(1 - k)}{n^2}, \quad \text{or} \quad \frac{\partial r}{\partial n} = -D(1 - k)n^{-2}f'(r)^{-1}.$$

Because $f'(r) < 0$, it follows that $\dfrac{\partial r}{\partial n} > 0$.

Differentiating again, we have

$$\frac{\partial^2 r}{\partial n^2} = D(1 - k)\left[f'(r)^{-1}2n^{-3} + n^{-2}f'(r)^{-2}f''(r)\frac{\partial r}{\partial n}\right].$$

Here $D(1 - k)$, $2n^{-3}$, $f'(r)^{-2}$ and $\partial r/\partial n$ are all positive and $f'(r)^{-1}$ is negative, and so, if $f''(r) \leq 0$, the entire expression will be negative (that is, then r does increase at a decreasing rate with n). However, if $f''(r) > 0$, the first term in the brackets will still be negative but the second will be positive so that the net result will depend on their relative magnitudes as it does in our exponential model. In economic terms, the reason for the ambiguity introduced by the last term is that, with $f''(r) > 0$, the higher value of r required by a larger n runs into diminishing returns and this offsets the scale advantages of having more persons reduce their emissions in response to a given rise in r.

is given uniquely as a function of the distribution of the random variable,[12] k_t.

First, for illustrative purposes assume that the dispersion rate, $(1 - k)$, of Equation (2) can take two values: the high usual value $(1 - k)_h$ that occurs on most days, and the low emergency-dispersion rate $(1 - k)_l$ that occurs only infrequently. Then the maximum level of emissions during emergency periods is (approximately) [13] $nf(r)/(1 - k)_l$, but the normal emission level is (approximately) $nf(r)/(1 - k)_h$. The tax rate necessary to keep pollution levels acceptable under ordinary wind conditions is illustrated by B in Figures 11–1 and 11–2, and the higher tax rate A is required to be certain of coping with emergencies.[14] Note that, if the tax were set high enough to deal with crises and were not reduced at other times, it would require the community to pay an "excess" tax rate, $\Delta r = CA$, during most of the year when $(1 - k)$ is at its normal level. The expected excess cost to society per period is the resulting outlay on the reduction of emissions below normal levels, multiplied by the probability that the tax rate is excessive.

The concept of the excess tax is, of course, not dependent on our use of the probability distribution encompassing only two possible states, which we have introduced purely for expository simplicity. Using Bawa's results described in the Appendix to this chapter, one can, in an analogous manner, calculate the expected excess cost for any given distribution of k_t.

This result is important because it follows that

Proposition One. In the presence of stochastic influences, taxes may sometimes be more costly to society than direct controls as a means to limit environmental damage.[15]

If the cost induced by the excess tax is sufficiently high, it can always offset the static allocative efficiency offered by the tax program that we discussed in the preceding chapter. That is, even if taxes incur only a fraction of the social costs imposed by direct controls in stationary conditions, with unforeseeable variability in those conditions, safety may require the maintenance of an extremely high tax rate that generates heavy, unnecessary costs in nonemergency periods. We cannot simply assume that taxes will always be the more efficient of the two regulatory instruments.

---

[12] Bawa derives these results formally in the Appendix to this chapter. If $G(P_t)$ is the distribution of P_t, we define the equilibrium or limiting distribution as the limit of G as P_t approaches P_e.

[13] We must say "approximately" because we have not accounted for the level of pollution not yet dispersed from earlier periods. The actual pollution level will always be lower than this if the value $(1 - k)_l$ does not hold indefinitely, because pollution can then be expected to approach the "equilibrium level," $nf(r)/(1 - k)_l$, asymptotically from below, and hence will never actually reach that level.

[14] In Figure 11–1, this assumes $D = na$ so that the relevant locus of r and $(1 - k)$ values is QU.

[15] Of course, this result depends on our earlier argument that taxes are subject to short-run rigidities and uncertainty that can be circumvented by direct controls.

6. MIXED SYSTEMS OF REGULATION

Indeed, the analysis suggests that neither reliance solely on fiscal methods nor on direct controls will constitute an optimal regulatory strategy. Rather, it may be less costly to society to employ a mixed system that makes use both of taxes and direct controls. The environmental authority would set effluent charges and other pollution tax rates so as to meet prescribed environmental standards during normal periods. Flexible direct controls might then be adopted on a standby basis, to be put into effect when (unforeseeable) circumstances call for them. The environmental authority, for example, might have available a series of regulations of increasing severity, with the choice among them depending on the magnitude of the threatened danger at the time the decision is made. During a mild intensification of air pollution, apartment house incinerators may, for example, be shut down. If atmospheric conditions continue to deteriorate, the environmental agency could ban private passenger cars from the streets, and so on. In fact, several cities have already defined and formulated corresponding policy measures for sequences of increasingly serious "air pollution alerts."

In this way, we may be able to realize the best of both worlds by taking advantage of the efficiency properties of tax measures in normal circumstances and invoking direct controls to cope with temporary periods of accentuated environmental deterioration.

7. AN OPTIMAL MIXED PROGRAM: GRAPHIC DISCUSSION [16]

We can use our model to show, at least formally, how to determine an optimal mixed policy to achieve a prescribed environmental standard. Assuming for illustrative purposes that we have only one type of direct control, there is only one degree of freedom in the selection of the mixed policy. Specifically, once the effluent tax rate is determined, the remainder of the policy follows directly.

This is illustrated in Figure 11–3, which shows schematically how the level of pollution in some particular area might vary over time with the tax rate set for the entire period at some specific level, $r = r_0$ (the upper curve). If the inviolable pollution standards call for pollution levels that never exceed danger level, D, it is clear that there are four periods of time, t_a, t_b, t_c, and t_d, when the environmental authority will have to invoke direct controls. The extent of the controls will vary with the amount of excess pollution that might otherwise be expected, as indicated by the shaded areas above line DD'. Now suppose that the tax rate had instead been set for the entire period at some

---

[16] Formal proofs of the results used in this section are given in the Appendix.

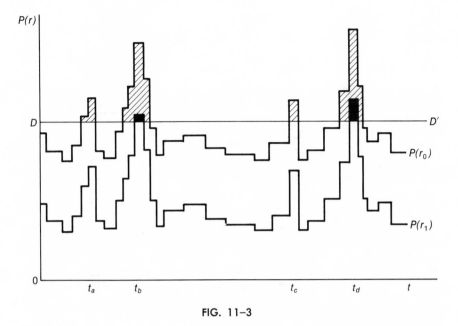

FIG. 11–3

higher level, $r = r_1 > r_0$. Emissions will now be lower than they would have been otherwise, and the pollution curve must shift downward corresponding-ly, say, to the lower curve in the figure. Now, two of the periods that formerly required direct controls, t_a and t_c, will no longer need them. More-over, the two remaining periods of high potential pollution, t_b and t_d, will now require much milder doses of controls, as indicated by the black areas remaining above DD'.

We see that the choice of the value of r determines unambiguously, in retrospect, both the periods when direct controls are invoked and the strength of these measures. But an optimality calculation must, of course, be prospec-tive rather than retrospective. We must therefore deal with the *probability* distribution of $P_t(r)$ and with the corresponding expected values of the pollution-control costs.

V. S. Bawa has proved that for our stochastic relationship,

$$P_t = k_t P_{t-1} + nf(r),$$

given the probability distribution of our random variable, k_t, the equilibrium or limiting distribution of P_t exists and can in principle be determined (though its precise calculation can be very difficult). Let us then take $G[P(r)]$ to repre-sent that distribution.

We will now describe our optimality calculation graphically and then express it more explicitly with the aid of algebraic notation. Figure 11–4

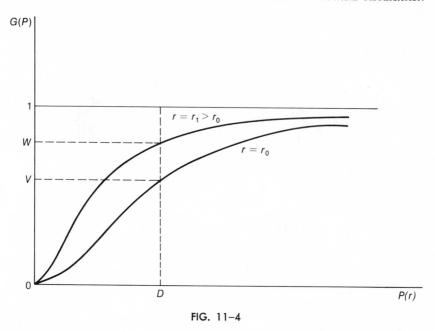

FIG. 11–4

shows two probability distributions of $P(r)$ corresponding to $r = r_0$ and $r = r_1 > r_0$. The curve corresponding to r_0 lies below that for r_1 because the former involves larger frequencies of higher pollution levels. Once again, we see that as r is reduced, the expected use of direct controls will automatically increase. That is, there will be a greater expected frequency of $P(r) > D$, represented by VW in Figure 11–4, as r decreases from r_1 to r_0.

Figure 11–5 now translates this observation into cost terms. The curve TT' shows the total social cost of the reductions in emissions induced by the taxes. This will obviously be a monotonically increasing function, because a rise in the tax rate will normally induce less (and certainly no more) waste emissions. The curve CC' is the same relationship for the program of direct controls. The slope of this curve will, of course, be negative, because with an increased tax rate, r, the use of direct controls will fall and so will the total cost they impose on polluters. Adding these two costs vertically, we obtain curve SS' giving the total cost of the mixed program.[17] The minimum point

---

[17] We should note that SS' measures the cost to polluters of various combinations of tax rates and controls that will maintain the level of environmental quality at *or above* the prescribed standard *at all times*. This calculation does not allow for the added social benefits that a higher tax rate generates by providing environmental quality in excess of the standard during normal times. The analysis is still framed in terms of the objective adopted in Chapter 10: the attainment of *prescribed* standards at minimum cost.

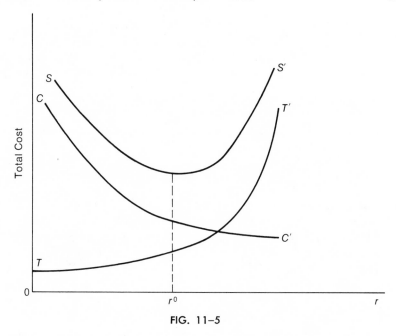

FIG. 11–5

on SS', at which the marginal cost of the two component programs are equal, yields the optimal tax rate r^o.[18]

8. A MODEL FOR DETERMINATION OF THE OPTIMAL MIXED POLICY

To formalize this process, we will formulate an expected social cost function that is to be minimized by a suitable choice of tax rate, r. This minimization process is, of course, constrained by a set of relationships restricting pollution to a level no higher than D and invoking direct controls whenever the tax rate does not suffice to do the job. We will first describe the constraints, leaving specification of the objective function until later.

Assume that for each polluter, i, there is a cost function

$$c_i(s_i, \ldots)$$

[18] The curve SS' can have a number of local minima. Monotonicity of CC' and TT' is not enough to prevent this possibility. We can be confident that SS' will have at least one minimum in any closed interval because CC' and TT' cannot take negative values. CC and TT can be expected to take *very* high values toward the left and rightward ends of the diagram, respectively, so that we may expect SS' to be roughly U-shaped. However, that is not necessary for the curve to have at least one minimum.

representing total cost as a function of his emission level, s_i, among other variables that, for our current purposes, we need not specify.

Then, with tax rate r and no direct controls, we will presumably have

$$c_{is} = \frac{\partial c_i}{\partial s_i} = r \tag{6}$$

or, assuming we can solve for the inverse, $c_{is}^{-1}(r)$, of this derivative we have in the absence of direct controls[19]

$$s_i = c_{is}^{-1}(r). \tag{7}$$

That is, the emission level of firm i will be adjusted to the level at which the cost of reducing emissions by one additional unit equals the unit tax.

However, in times of crisis in the absence of further restraints for all firms together, this level of emissions will be unacceptably high. For these circumstances we may define[20]

$$\text{Excess emissions} = \Delta = \sum_i c_{is}^{-1}(r) + k_t P_{t-1}(r) - D. \tag{8}$$

Excess emissions are the excess of accumulated pollutants over the maximum acceptable level, D. Note that this includes new emissions of all firms plus pollutants undispersed from the previous period. To meet the prescribed standard corresponding to D, we require direct controls to reduce total emissions by the amount Δ *if* $\Delta > 0$, (if there really are excess emissions); but we require no direct controls if $\Delta \leq 0$, so that there is no threat of emergency. More formally, we require direct controls to reduce emissions by the amount δ, where

$$\delta = \Delta \text{ if } \Delta > 0$$
$$\delta = 0 \text{ if } \Delta \leq 0.$$

This is equivalent to requiring[21]

---

[19] Note that $\sum_i c_{is}^{-1}(r)$ equals $nf(r)$ of Equation (1).

[20] Note again that, although for concreteness of illustration we continue to use $k_t P_{t-1}$ to represent the pollutants left over from the previous period, obviously such a multiplicative relationship need not always hold. But nothing is changed by substituting into (8) the more general relationship $f(P_{t-1}, k_{1t}, \ldots, k_{qt})$ for $k_t P_{t-1}$, where the k_{it} are all random variables, provided we can determine probability distributions for the k_{it}, and from them can calculate a probability distribution for $P_t(r)$, in accord with Bawa's results.

[21] The purpose of relationships (9), (10), and (11) is to express the two regimes, the situation requiring the imposition of direct controls and the one that does not, in a single set of constraints. Equation (10) assures us that either $\delta = \Delta$ or $\delta = 0$. The other two conditions then guarantee the use of direct controls ($\delta \neq 0$) if, and only if, there are excess emissions ($\Delta > 0$).

$$\delta \geq \Delta, \tag{9}$$

$$\delta(\delta - \Delta) = 0 \tag{10}$$

and

$$\delta \geq 0. \tag{11}$$

The direct controls on emissions must in some way assign to each polluter, i, an emission quota

$$s_i = c_{is}^{-1}(r) - w_i\delta \tag{12}$$

where

$$\sum w_i = 1 \tag{13}$$

so that total emissions will be reduced by the required amount $\sum w_i\delta = \delta$. Note that relationship (12) holds at all times whether it is a "normal" or a "crisis" period, because during the latter, we will have $\delta > 0$, but during the former, (9), (10), and (11) guarantee that we will automatically have $\delta = 0$.

Relationship (12) is a rough, but not necessarily a bad, representation of emergency direct controls. For example, a directive simply to "shut down incinerators" amounts to an assigned quota for reduction of emissions independent of what other emissions the polluter finds it convenient and profitable to continue. Relation (12) distinguishes between the effect of the tax on waste emissions and that of the controls. The first term on the *RHS* represents the former and obviously corresponds to the necessary condition (6) for private cost minimization in the presence of emissions taxes. On the other hand, the second term is the direct controls component whose value is determined by the assignment of the weights w_i.

We turn finally to our objective function, which requires us to minimize the *expected* costs of emissions control

$$C = \int_0^\infty \sum_i c_i(s_i)dG[P(r)]. \tag{14}$$

That is, we minimize the sum over all firms, i, of the costs, c_i, of their emission levels, s_i, where the emission levels are in turn determined by the current pollution level, $P(r)$, all this multiplied by $dG(P)$, representing the probability of occurrence of that pollution level. Thus (14) is to be minimized subject to the constraints (8)–(13) and the additional nonnegativity conditions

$$r \geq 0, \qquad s_i \geq 0.$$

The solution to this nonlinear programming problem will yield the specifications of our optimal mixed policy by determining the optimal tax rate, r, and residually [by (9)–(11)] the amount, δ, the expected excess emissions to be eliminated by direct controls. It will represent the tax rate that incurs the lowest possible social cost of the overall program of pollution controls when direct controls are assigned the task of removing any unacceptable emissions that escape the influence of the fiscal incentives.

9. CONCLUDING COMMENT

The models of this chapter clearly have not encompassed all there is to be said for the usefulness of direct controls in environmental policy. Much of their appropriate function, arising out of issues such as relative monitoring costs, can be discussed effectively only on a more pragmatic level, as is done in the companion volume. We have intended to show here that, even considered in their own arena, that is, cost minimization, tax-subsidy measures do not have the field entirely to themselves. In many important cases, there is a significant role to be played by direct controls and other types of nonfiscal measures. We are convinced that economists are justified in continuing to emphasize the advantages of fiscal methods; their relative neglect by policy makers has very likely incurred heavy costs. But we economists should also broaden the scope of the methods we are willing to espouse and should attempt to determine the appropriate functions and use of the several policy instruments that are available.

APPENDIX TO CHAPTER 11
BY V. S. BAWA

As in Section 3 of this chapter, the pollution level P_t in period t, $t = 1, 2, \ldots$ is taken to be given by the following recursive relation:

$$P_t = k_t P_{t-1} + nf(r), \tag{A1}$$

where k_t, $0 \le k_t \le 1$, a random variable, represents that proportion of the previous period's pollution not dispersed by the current period. We assume that $k_1, k_2, \ldots$ are a sequence of independent and identically distributed random variables with common probability distribution $F(\cdot)$.

Using (A1), we note that P_1, the pollution level in period 1, is given as

$$P_1 = k_1 P_0 + a, \tag{A2}$$

where we denote $nf(r)$ by a for typographical simplicity. P_1 is a random variable because k_1 is a random variable. Thus, if we let $G_1(\cdot)$ denote the probability distribution of P_1, then

$$
\begin{aligned}
G_1(y) &= Pr\{P_1 \leq y\} \\
&= Pr\{k_1 P_0 + a \leq y\} \\
&= Pr\{k_1 \leq (y - a)/P_0\}
\end{aligned}
$$

or

$$G_1(y) = F[(y - a)/P_0]. \tag{A3}$$

Thus, knowing $F(\cdot)$, the distribution of the basic random variable k, the distribution, $G_1(\cdot)$, of P_1, the random level of pollution in period 1, is given by (A3). Similarly, using (A1), the level of pollution in period 2, P_2, is also random and given as

$$P_2 = k_2 P_1 + a, \tag{A4}$$

and if $G_2(\cdot)$ denotes the probability distribution of P_2, then

$$
\begin{aligned}
G_2(y) &= Pr\{P_2 \leq y\} \\
&= Pr\{k_2 P_1 + a \leq y\} \\
&= \int_0^1 Pr\{P_1 \leq (y - a)/x \,|\, k_2 = x\} \, dF(x)
\end{aligned}
$$

or

$$G_2(y) = \int_0^1 G_1[(y - a)/x] \, dF(x). \tag{A5}$$

Thus, knowing $F(\cdot)$, $G_2(y)$ can be calculated recursively using (A3) and (A5). In general, it follows from this reasoning that for $t \geq 1$, P_t given by (A1) is a random variable with probability distribution function $G_t(y)$ given as

$$G_t(y) = \int_0^1 G_{t-1}[(y - a)/x] \, dF(x), \tag{A6}$$

and hence for any value of $t \geq 2$, $G_t(y)$ can be calculated by using (A3), (A5), and (A6) recursively. Although for a general distribution function $F(\cdot)$, $G_t(y)$ cannot be expressed as an explicit function, $G_t(y)$ can be evaluated numerically quite efficiently using the recursive relation (A6).

We are interested in the equilibrium, steady state, or limiting value of the pollution level. If $k_t = 1$ with probability one (that is, zero pollution is carried away each period), then it follows from (A1) that $P_t = P_0 + ta$ where $a > 0$. Hence, as would be expected intuitively, as $t \to \infty$, $P_t \to \infty$ and thus there is no way to control the pollution level. We are interested in the other, more realistic, case when $E(k_t) < 1$ (that is, at least some pollution is carried away each period). In this case, it can be shown, using standard asymptotics, that the equilibrium or steady state pollution level, denoted P, is a proper random variable, and, as would be expected intuitively from (A6), its probability distribution, $G(\cdot)$, is given uniquely as a solution to:

$$G(y) = \int_0^1 G[(y - a)/x] \, dF(x). \tag{A7}$$

If we let $G_r(y)$ denote the distribution of P when r is the tax rate, then the effect of the tax rate r on the equilibrium pollution level P is summarized by the following:

Lemma: If $r_1 > r_0$, then for all y

$$1 - G_{r_1}(y) \leq 1 - G_{r_0}(y).$$

Proof: Using (A1), we see that P_t is a stochastically increasing function of a; thus, it follows that P, the equilibrium pollution level, is a stochastically increasing function of a. Because $a = nf(r)$ is a decreasing function of the tax rate r, it follows that P is a stochastically decreasing function of r. This completes the proof of the Lemma.

This result has the intuitive interpretation that as the tax rate r decreases, the probability of a higher equilibrium pollution level increases. This is illustrated in Figure 11–4 of this chapter. The result is also useful in proving the existence of an optimal tax rate r^o. To do that, we note that the steady state total expected social costs $TSC(r)$ for a pollution control policy with tax rate r is given as

$$TSC(r) = T(r) + \int_D^\infty c(x - D) \, dG_r(x), \tag{A8}$$

where $T(r)$ represents the total social costs of emission reductions induced by tax rate r and $c(x - D)$ represents total direct control costs necessary to reduce the pollution level from x to critical level D [where $c(x - D) = 0$ for $x \leq D$]. $T(r)$ is assumed to be a monotonically increasing function of r. (This is illustrated by TT' in Figure 11–5.) It is also plausible that $c(x - D)$ is an increasing function of $(x - D)$; as the level of excess pollution (that is, the amount over the critical level D) increases, the total costs of reducing the pollution level to acceptable level D increases.

Integrating by parts, (A8) can be rewritten as

$$TSC(r) = T(r) + \int_D^\infty [1 - G_r(x)]c'(x - D) \, dx. \tag{A9}$$

Thus, using the Lemma, it follows that the second term in (A9), represented by CC' in Figure 11–5, is a decreasing function of the tax rate r. In other words, as tax rate r is increased, there is a decrease in the frequency with which direct controls are used in short term crises or emergencies to keep pollution levels acceptable and, hence, the expected direct control cost decreases. Moreover, both terms in (A9) are certainly nonnegative. Hence, their sum, $TSC(r)$ (represented by SS' in Figure 11–5), that is, the sum of the tax costs and expected direct control costs, must have at least one minimum in any closed interval $0 \leq r \leq r^*$, where we take the constant, r^*, to represent a tax rate so high that the probability of $P(r^*) > D$ is less than some arbitrarily small G. Thus, there exists a tax rate, r^o, that minimizes $TSC(r)$. We have proved the following:

Proposition Two. Given some maximal level of pollution, D, that is not to be exceeded, the optimal pollution control policy is a mixed policy completely specified by an optimal tax rate, r^o.

We note that, from the monotonicity of $T(r)$, it follows that r^0 is finite. However, depending on the rate of change of $T(r)$ relative to direct control costs, it may happen that $r^o = 0$. In such a case, the optimal policy for pollution control is to impose no taxes and use only direct controls. (This may be viewed as a special case of a mixed policy with $r^o = 0$.) We also note that to guarantee the uniqueness of the optimal tax rate r^o and to obtain practical methods for the calculation of r^o, we need some more assumptions about the cost functions (for example, $T(r)$ is a convex function). Such issues are considered in detail in Bawa [1].

The multiplicative model (A1) considered in this chapter is an appropriate choice for problems of air pollution where there is no constraint on the level of pollution that can be carried away in each period. In some other cases (for example, water pollution problems), there may be a constraint on the level of pollution that can be carried away in a period by the natural sources and the following model may be more appropriate:

$$P_t = \max(0, P_{t-1} + a - k_t). \tag{A10}$$

For this and some other general stochastic models, it can be shown that the preceding results still hold. These general models are considered in detail in [1] and some additional results on optimal pollution control policies are obtained.

REFERENCE

[1] Bawa, V. S., "On Optimal Pollution Control Policies," (forthcoming).

Taxes vs. Subsidies:
A Partial Analysis

We can rest assured that firms and municipalities that are asked to reduce their damage to the environment will look to state and federal agencies for financial assistance. Such a request may seem uncomfortably analogous to the case of a holdup man who appeals to his victims to finance the costs of his going straight. Sometimes, however, a persuasive case *can* be made in terms of equity. What of the firm that built its smoking factories well away from the centers of population only to find itself surrounded by inhabitants a few decades later? Is it really the company that is responsible for the damage generated by its emissions of smoke?

We must admit to feeling that too much has probably been made of such cases in the literature, and that there usually is some presumption against rewarding government agencies and private enterprises for the damage they have done to the environment in the past. But whatever the virtues of the matter, the issue is a real one. There will continue to be calls for subvention of industrial activities that may otherwise find themselves at a competitive disadvantage and of local agencies whose budgets are already under heavy strain.

The central question here is whether or not it is possible to attain an optimal pattern of resource use through a program of subsidies rather than fees. In Chapter 4, we showed that there is a set of Pigouvian taxes that will sustain optimal levels of externality-generating activities in a competitive system. Can this also be achieved by some specified set of payments?

The literature has occasionally suggested an affirmative answer to this question. Some writers (including one of the present authors[1]) have argued that the public authority can use either the stick or the carrot to induce socially desirable patterns of behavior. In recent years, however, a short series of articles has shown that, on any reasonable interpretation, this is simply untrue. Kamien, Schwartz, and Dolbear[2] have demonstrated that where the polluter recognizes the effects of his actions on the regulatory authority, a subsidy scheme may make it profitable for the firm to start off by polluting more than it would have otherwise in order to qualify for larger subsidy payments.[3] Wenders, moreover, has suggested that, where there is this sort of interaction between the polluter's behavior and regulatory standards, there is less of an inducement for new pollution-abatement technology from a system of subsidies than a program of taxes.[4] Consider a firm that is evaluating a pollution-reducing innovation. If the introduction of the new technique (and the resulting lower level of waste emissions) is likely at some future time to induce the public authority to reduce fiscal incentives, then the decision of the firm may well depend upon whether the agency is employing taxes or subsidies. In the former case, the prospective tax reduction would promise increased profits to the firm and thus encourage the introduction of the new technology, but under a system of subsidies, the change in fiscal incentives would take the form of a reduction in the future rate of *payments* from the agency and hence reduce the profitability of the innovation.

Bramhall and Mills[5] have pointed out what to us seems to be the most important distinction between the two types of stimuli: the fact that an enterprise that would be unprofitable under a tax may be made profitable by a subsidy.

[1] See W. J. Baumol, *Welfare Economics and the Theory of the State*, 2nd ed. (Cambridge, Mass.: Harvard University Press, 1965), p. 104.

[2] M. I. Kamien, N. L. Schwartz, and F. T. Dolbear, "Asymmetry between Bribes and Charges," *Water Resources Research* II, No. 1 (1966), 147–157.

[3] In this case, the firm need not be very large for this sort of interdependence to arise. The pollution benchmark will presumably have to be set for each firm in light of its product line, its output level, and its inherited plant and equipment. As with price-control mechanisms, it would not be surprising to see the firm's benchmark pollution level, s^*, against which improvement is to be measured, set on the basis of its emissions during some arbitrarily chosen period. The firm might then have much to gain by emitting a great deal of pollution during that period to increase the value of the base level of its subsidies.

[4] J. T. Wenders, "Asymmetry between Fees and Payments and the Rate of Change in Pollution Abatement Technology," (unpublished).

[5] D. E. Bramhall and E. S. Mills, "A Note on the Asymmetry between Fees and Payments," *Water Resources Research* II, No. 3 (1966), 615–16. On this see also the papers by A. M. Freeman, "Bribes and Charges: Some Comments," *Water Resources Research* III, No. 1 (1967), 287–88; and T. D. Tregarthen, "Collective Supply Problems in the Allocation of an Air Basin," paper delivered to the Economics of Pollution Section of the 1971 Annual Meetings of the Western Economic Association, Simon Fraser University, August, 1971.

However, the literature seems not to have noted that, as a result, whereas a tax will typically drive firms out of a competitive industry and so generally lead to a decrease in its output, a subsidy may increase entry and induce an expansion in competitive outputs. We shall explore this issue in some depth in this chapter and will contend that it is far more significant than a casual reading of the literature would suggest. We will show, for example, that, under pure competition, although a subsidy will tend to reduce the emissions of the *firm*, it is apt to *increase* the emissions of the industry beyond what they would be in the absence of fiscal incentives! Moreover, paradoxically, the more the subsidy succeeds in limiting the emissions of the firm, the more it may stimulate those of the industry. Similar problems may well arise under oligopoly where the relevant exit and entry may, preponderantly, take the form of the opening and closing of *plants* rather than firms.

Before turning to these propositions, however, it is important to note the element of truth in the contention that there can be equivalence between the carrot and the stick. We will show formally that, *in principle*, there does exist a program(s) of subsidies that can sustain optimal levels of polluting activities. But the very character of this program suggests immediately that, although it may be an interesting theoretical construct, it is virtually inconceivable that any such program would ever be adopted in practice. We will see that any plausible systems involve fundamental asymmetries between fees and subsidies.

For expository convenience, we will for the most part deal only with detrimental externalities so that, according to the analysis of Chapter 4, the appropriate instrument for the achievement of Pareto optimality is always a set of taxes. We will find it convenient in this discussion to deal with just one polluting industry and with the firms that compose it. Thus, for most of this chapter, we leave our general-equilibrium framework and turn temporarily to a partial analysis.

One more matter remains to be settled before getting to the substance of our discussion: the nature of the subsidy program we will consider. This is not as obvious as it may seem on first thought. Several different types of subsidy programs have in fact been proposed and their effects may well differ considerably. For example, some proposals have called for a tax credit for investment in pollution-control equipment or for some other device to help cover some proportion of the cost. However, as Kneese and Bower point out, such a subsidy is, at least in principle, likely to prove quite ineffective in stimulating pollution abatement.[6] For, if the equipment adds to a firm's costs

---

[6] See A. V. Kneese and B. T. Bower, *Managing Water Quality: Economics, Technology, Institutions* (Baltimore: Johns Hopkins Press, 1968), pp. 175–78. They point out that various bills have recently been introduced in Congress offering this type of subsidy in a variety of forms including rapid tax write-offs and tax credits. They argue that aside from the fact that such subsidies can never by themselves make abatement investments

and contributes nothing to its revenues, the absorption of k percent of the cost by a government agency cannot turn its acquisition into a profitable proposition. So long as k is less than 100 percent, the installation of the equipment will lose money for the firm, and its attractiveness to management will remain doubtful, except perhaps as a public-relations gesture or as a pure act of conscience by the businessman.

The type of subsidy with which we will be concerned in most of this chapter is of quite another sort. It involves a payment to the firm based on the *reductions* in its output of a pollutant or in some other sort of damage to the environment. That is, taking s to be the firm's output of the pollutant, and s^* to be the base (benchmark) against which improvement is to be measured,[7] the subsidy payment can be described by the relationship $g(s^* - s)$, where $dg/d(s^* - s) > 0$ (that is, the payments to the firm increase with the amount by which it decreases its emissions). In the bulk of our discussion we will assume that the subsidy payment per unit reduction in emissions is constant, so that the payment becomes

$$v(s^* - s), \tag{1}$$

where v and s^* are constants. Expression (1) immediately indicates one fundamental difference between programs of taxes and subsidies. With taxes, we need concern ourselves with only one parameter, the tax rate, but a system of subsidies requires that we specify values for two parameters: the unit subsidy (v) and the benchmark level of emissions (s^*).

In the subsidy programs with which we will concern ourselves, payments are made only to firms that are actually engaged in an activity that is (potentially) polluting. The firm that closes its doors ceases to receive any such payments, and no subvention is given to a firm that is considering entry into the area but has not actually done so. These are features we would expect to characterize any real subsidy program. Their critical significance for the analysis will become clear presently.

---

profitable, they suffer from at least three other defects: first, they increase the "excess burdens" imposed by the tax system; second, this sort of arrangement rewards only the installation of particular types of equipment (for example, treatment equipment), and, hence, may not induce the adoption of the most efficient pollution-control methods; and, third, this type of subsidy aids only firms that are profitable enough to invest and may not be very helpful to marginal concerns. We may note, however, that, from the point of view of efficiency, failure to rescue marginal firms may well be desirable socially.

[7] Note that s^* may, but need not be, based on observation of the firm's past behavior (for example, its previous levels of smoke emission).

1. THE FORMAL SUBSIDY RELATIONSHIP AND THE GENERAL CASE

Assume that firm k is subject to a fixed Pigouvian tax per unit of emission. Its profit function is

$$\pi_k^t = y_k p^k(y_k) - c^k(y_k, a_k) - ts^k(y_k, a_k) \tag{2}$$

where
$$y_k = \text{the output produced by firm } k$$
$$a_k = \text{its abatement outlay}$$
$$p^k(y_k) = \text{the price of its product}$$
$$c^k(y_k, a_k) = \text{total production cost}$$
$$t = \text{the tax rate per unit of emission}$$
$$s^k(y_k, a_k) = \text{the total emission of pollutant}$$

and where we assume

$$s_y^k = \frac{\partial s^k}{\partial y_k} > 0, \qquad s_a^k = \frac{\partial s^k}{\partial a_k} < 0. \tag{3}$$

Similarly, it is clear that if the firm is instead offered the subsidy (1), its profit function becomes[8]

$$\pi_k^v = y_k p^k(y_k) - c^k(y_k, a_k) + v[s_k^* - s^k(y_k, a_k)]. \tag{4}$$

2. THE EQUILIBRIUM OF THE INDIVIDUAL FIRM [9]

It is convenient to begin by comparing directly the subsidy profit function (4) with the tax-profit function (2); this comparison immediately yields a significant result about the relative effects of the two types of fiscal incentive on the equilibrium of the individual firm. We see at once that if $v = t$, the two profit functions differ only by the constant quantity vs^*. If the company is a profit maximizer and *continues to engage in the same types of activity*

---

[8] We should note that the profit function (4) for the firm receiving a subsidy for the reduction of emissions can be taken to represent the profit function in the general case encompassing all three of the relevant possibilities: a subsidy program, a tax program, or the absence of either. The function, as it stands, is the subsidy relationship. By setting $v = 0$, we at once obtain the case with neither taxes nor subsidies. Finally, setting $s^* = 0$, we are left with the pure tax case, with the firm having vs deducted from its profits and thus paying the tax rate v per unit of emission. This observation about the generality of (4) will prove useful to us in Section 4 of this chapter.

[9] For an illuminating discussion of the subject of this section, see Kneese and Bower, *Managing Water Quality*, pp. 98–109. See also A. P. Lerner, "Pollution Abatement Subsidies," *American Economic Review* LXII (December, 1972), 1009–10.

under either fiscal program, we see that the choice between a tax and subsidy system will not affect *any* of its decisions one iota. Whatever values of its decision variables it will find most profitable in the one case will also maximize profits in the other.[10]

There is another way that this conclusion has been described in the literature. The subsidy program (1) has been interpreted as equivalent to a tax on pollution, vs (with v being the per-unit tax rate), plus a lump-sum subsidy given by the constant vs^*. Because, by definition, a lump-sum subsidy does not affect behavior, it should hardly come as a surprise that the choice between a tax and a subsidy policy does not influence any of the firm's decisions. This, then, is the basic argument rationalizing the intuitive notion suggested at the beginning of this chapter that a tax and a subsidy, like the carrot and the stick, should be able to achieve the same result.[11]

Strictly speaking, this conclusion is, however, incorrect. For suppose that, in the absence of taxes and subsidies, our firm's maximum profits are zero. Then the imposition of a tax would ultimately force it to close its doors, but the subsidy program could end the precariousness of its existence. Put another way, it is not quite legitimate to describe the component vs^* in the subsidy (1) as a lump-sum payment, for it may influence the firm's decision between continuation and cessation of operations.

This suggests immediately the provision that is required for the subsidy program to establish a set of incentives identical to those of the tax: the lump-sum payment (vs^*) must not be contingent upon the firm's decision to stay in business.[12] In principle, this payment must be made to the polluter, whether potential or actual, so that it has no direct influence on any choice that confronts him.[13] Note that once this stipulation is introduced, the choice of the benchmark level of emissions becomes wholly arbitrary in terms of

[10] In an unpublished note, Yakov Amihud has argued that in the presence of risk the lump-sum payment, vs^*, may reduce the marginal risk of the subsidized firm and may therefore induce it to maintain an output level larger than that of the taxed firm. On this see, for example, E. Sandmo, "On the Theory of the Competitive Firm Under Price Uncertainty," *American Economic Review* LXI (March, 1971), pp. 65–73.

[11] There is a different argument whose invalidity is shown in Section 5. Suppose there are two industries, *A* and *B*, and that a tax rate of *t* on *A*'s output will achieve the desired reallocation of resources from *A* to *B*. Then surely the same thing can be accomplished by an *r* dollar subsidy to *A* if a sufficiently greater subsidy is provided to *B* and (fiscal and monetary) policy keeps the levels of employment of resources from changing. As will be shown later, this argument is, in fact, incorrect so long as the relative prices corresponding to a given optimum for the economy are unique, *and* the absolute prices are fixed by some normalization rule or otherwise.

[12] Kneese and Bower note this condition (*Managing Water Quality*, p. 104).

[13] We must say no "direct" influence here, because a set of lump-sum taxes or subsidies will have income effects leading, in general, to a new general equilibrium set of relative prices. The point is that such a program has no direct price effects in the sense of altering the terms of choice in the initial equilibrium situation.

any implications for optimal resource use; the selection of a value for s^* affects only the magnitude of the subsidy payment.

The administrative infeasibility of such a system of payments is evident. The lump-sum subsidy must be paid not only to those who continue polluting activities, but also to any *potential* polluters. For example, a firm that chooses to cease its operations altogether must continue to receive the subsidy payment *indefinitely* (otherwise the subsidy program might have induced the firm to remain in business). Similarly, potential entrants into the polluting activity must be eligible for the subsidy to prevent them from initiating waste generation simply to qualify for the lump-sum payment. The difficulty of identifying these economic units (along with the obvious political obstacles to such a system of payments) imply that we must restrict our consideration of this form of subsidy program to the conceptual realm, as it does not represent a real policy alternative.

Throughout this chapter, it is therefore assumed that subsidy payments in any period t are limited to firms that are actively in business during this period. The equivalence of the incentives under the tax and subsidy programs then vanishes, and we conclude

Proposition One.   For the individual firm, the choice between a tax and a subsidy program to induce a decrease in pollution emissions may determine whether or not the firm continues its operations. However, other things being equal, no other decision of the profit-maximizing firm will be influenced by the choice between the two fiscal measures provided the marginal tax and subsidy rates are equal.

Note that Proposition One does not enable us to reach any unambiguous conclusions about the relative desirability of taxes and subsidies in practice. *If* the firm stays in business, its level of output will be identical under the two fiscal programs. However, we know (ignoring any external effects) that monopoly outputs are normally less than optimal.[14] It is thus conceivable that a subsidy, if it permits a monopoly to continue its operations, may be a second-best solution superior to a tax that leads to the cessation of production. However, when we turn next to the case of pure competition, the conclusions are unambiguous. As we have already shown in Chapter 4, the appropriate taxes imposed on detrimental externalities are indeed capable of yielding a Pareto optimum. In the next section, we will see, however, that, for the competitive *industry*, subsidies may be expected to produce

---

[14] As we noted in Section 1 of Chapter 6, Buchanan has pointed out recently that the imposition of effluent charges on monopoly firms may actually reduce welfare, because they will induce a fall in the level of an output that is, perhaps, already less than optimal. See his "External Diseconomies, Corrective Taxes, and Market Structure," *American Economic Review* LIX (March, 1969), 174–77.

pollution levels very different from those corresponding to a Pigouvian tax program. We find that subsidies must unavoidably violate the necessary conditions for Pareto optimality (Table 1 of Chapter 4).[15,16]

Before turning to the behavior of the industry in the next section, the reader should note that Proposition One refers explicitly to the *individual firm* and applies only with "other things being equal." This means that, *if* the tax or subsidy has no effect on the price of the firm's output, then the firm (if it stays in business) will operate at the same level of output with the same level of waste emissions under both fiscal programs. However, as we shall see in the next section, a system of taxes in a competitive industry will generate a different industry supply curve (and hence a different price) than a subsidy program. As a result, the new equilibrium output and emissions level for the competitive firm will differ under the two sets of fiscal incentives.

[15] In most of this chapter, we will take the utilization of resources achieved by the Pigouvian tax as the standard of optimality against which to measure the subsidy program. It is easy to argue the propriety of this procedure intuitively. After all, the tax merely makes the individual pay *all* of the social costs of his activity. The optimality of a system of pure competition in the absence of externalities follows in part from this characteristic of its operation. The tax program, in effect, internalizes all externalities and makes a competitive system operate as if no externalities were present. That is why the tax system always yields optimal results and why, if a subsidy program leads to a different pattern of resources utilization, it is likely not to be optimal.

However, we must be careful in using this argument. Because a Pareto optimum is normally not unique, one cannot be certain from the observation that the allocation of resources under the subsidy program differs from that under taxes that the former is not itself Pareto optimal. This point will be examined further in Section 5.

[16] Note that Table 1 of Chapter 4 shows that Pigouvian taxes will sustain Pareto optimal exit and entry decisions by all the firms in a competitive economy and not just optimal decisions on nonzero activity levels. The exit-entry decisions relating to emissions of pollution are represented by conditions 5° and 5° in Chapter 4, which show that the equilibrium emissions of the firm will be zero under a Pigouvian tax regime if, and only if, that is true in the corresponding Pareto optimum. On the other hand, it is important to recognize that Pigouvian taxes can introduce a systematic bias into the exit-entrance decision in a world of second-best in which the polluting firm is not a perfect competitor or if the industry is not in long-run equilibrium. This has been shown by Susan Rose-Ackerman using the following argument: Let *msc* represent the marginal social cost of the firm's emissions, and msc^o be its value with an optimal level of emissions, s^o. Then, if it decides to operate and to do so at an optimal level, the firm's total Pigouvian tax payment will be

$$\text{(a) } s^o msc^o,$$

whereas its total social damage will be

$$\text{(b) } \int_0^{s^o} msc \ ds.$$

If *msc* rises with the emission level, as seems often to be true, (a) will be larger than (b). Hence the tax savings the firm obtains by ceasing the emission of *s*, as given by (a), will exceed the corresponding social gains, (b), and so Pigouvian taxes may tend to induce the exit of more firms than is desirable. See S. Rose Ackerman, "Effluent Charges: A Critique."

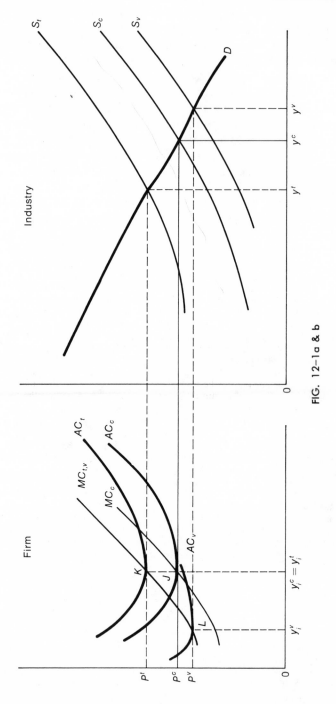

FIG. 12–1a & b

3. THE CASE OF THE COMPETITIVE INDUSTRY

Matters turn out quite differently in the competitive industry, because exit and entry are an integral element in the determination of total output. Here we can expect the choice between a tax and a subsidy to have a significant effect on total output. In fact, the results of a subsidy may well prove surprisingly unsatisfactory, as we will now show. In this section the argument will proceed on the simplifying premise that emissions are a single-valved function of industry output, and in the next section it will be generalized to take account of the possibility of changing emissions independently of output (abatement).

It may be helpful to consider the argument first in diagrammatic terms. In Figures 12–1a and 12–1b, we depict the equilibrium positions of a representative competitive firm (firm i) and the corresponding competitive industry under three different sets of circumstances: the equilibrium point, (y^c, p^c), when there is no public environmental program; point (y^t, p^t) with a unit tax on pollution emissions; and point (y^v, p^v) when there is a unit subsidy, v (equal to t), for reductions of emissions below some benchmark level. Starting from the no-program solution, we note that the unit pollution tax produces an upward shift in the firm's marginal and average cost curves (to $MC_{t,v}$ and AC_t).

If, instead of having no environmental program, a system of subsidies is instituted (under which we assume there are no negative subsidy payments), the firm's marginal cost shifts up to $MC_{t,v}$, but its average cost is now reduced (to AC_v). From our earlier results, we know that the tax and subsidy programs have identical effects on the firm's marginal costs. Consequently, in Figure 12–1a, the sole difference in the firm's cost relationships under the two programs is that its average cost under the system of subsidies (AC_v) will be less than its average costs (AC_t) under the pollution tax or in its absence (AC_c). However, entry and exit can be depended upon to drive price down to the firm's minimum level of average cost.

The result may actually be no change or even an increase in the equilibrium emissions of the individual firm under an emissions tax. For example, if emissions are strictly proportionate to output, the equilibrium output of the representative competitive firm must be exactly the same with and without the tax, for a fixed tax per unit will then shift its average cost curve directly upward by a uniform vertical distance (it will not be increased by full amount of the unit tax because rent will also be affected by the accompanying change in industry output) and so the firm's cost minimizing output and emissions levels will remain completely unaffected by the tax.

However, a subsidy program will generally decrease the equilibrium emissions of the competitive firm. Geometrically, we see this by noting that the new marginal cost curve $MC_{t,v}$, must now cut the original (no-program) cost curve, AC_c, at a point that lies to the left of the old equilibrium point, J. But, AC_v, the average cost curve with subsidy, must lie below AC_c, and so, given a positive slope of the marginal cost curve, the new equilibrium point, L, must lie still further to the left[17] of J.

Turning now to the emissions of the industry, which are, of course, the primary concern of policy, we note that the tax program, because it raises every firm's average and marginal costs, must result in a leftward shift of the industry supply curve, from S_c to S_t; price rises from p^c to p^t and *industry output falls* from y^c to y^t with a consequent decline in the *industry's* emission of pollutants. This happens though each firm that continues to operate produces the same output in both cases, because the tax will drive some firms from the industry. Similarly, the subsidy will induce the entry of firms (producing the rightward shift of the industry supply curve from S_c to S_v); the result is a fall in price (to p^v) and an increase in industry output (to y^v) and in industry emissions. Note that, although the individual firm produces less under the subsidy than it would under *either* the tax or in the absence of any program, the industry output under the subsidy (y^v) exceeds both y^t and y^c; thus, the entry of new firms more than offsets the reduction in emissions by the individual firm.

More specifically, if waste emissions are a fixed and rising function of the volume of industry output (no abatement technology available), Figures 12–1a and 12–1b suggest the disturbing conclusion that, although a subsidy program may reduce the emissions of each firm by itself, the subsidies, far from yielding a reduction in total industry emissions like a pollution tax, may, in fact, increase emissions from their unregulated level! It is easy to show that this paradox *must* result if emissions increase with output, and if the slopes of the industry supply and demand curves are respectively positive and negative, as we normally assume. For, on the premise that the subsidy program as described by (1) never involves a negative subsidy payment (that is, a payment by the firm to the government), some reduction in average cost to the industry must result. Hence, with a subsidy, the long-run competitive supply curve must shift downward and so, with a negatively sloping demand curve, equilibrium output *and pollution* must be increased above the levels they would have reached in the absence of government intervention. In sum:

[17] If emissions are strictly proportionate to output, so that we may write $s = by$, this result is trivial if the average curve has a single minimum and a continuous first derivative. For if $g(y)$ represents the firm's average cost in the absence of a tax or subsidy, with minimum point given by $dg(y)/dy = 0$, at that point the slope of the average cost curve with subsidy is

$$d[g(y) - vb(y^* - y)/y]\, dy = dg(y)/dy - d[vby^*/y]\, dy = vby^*/y^2 > 0,$$

so that the average cost minimizing output in the absence of subsidy must be greater than that under subsidy.

Proposition Two. In a competitive industry, where polluting emissions are a fixed and rising function of the level of industry output, equal tax and subsidy rates will normally *not* lead to the same output levels or to the same reductions in total industry emissions. Other things being equal, the subsidy will yield an output and emission level not only greater than those that would occur under the tax, but greater even than they would be in the absence of either tax or subsidy.

As already noted, the explanation of our paradox is straightforward. The subsidy does indeed reduce the level of emissions per firm. But it necessarily attracts into the industry enough additional firms to offset this reduction and more. Thus, we can hardly expect the effect of the subsidy on the decision of the firm to continue or discontinue operations to be an insignificant matter.

A further examination of the case in which emissions depend exclusively on output can sharpen these results and offer some additional insights. Let us simplify still further by assuming emissions to be strictly proportionate to output. Then we may write $s = by$ (b some constant) as the emissions-output relation and let

$s^* = $ the base pollution level for calculation of the subsidy,

$y^* = $ the corresponding output level where $s^* = by^*$,

$s^v = $ the emissions of the representative firm after imposition of subsidy rate, v, per unit of emissions, and

$y^v = $ the output of the representative firm under a subsidy program with a pollution benchmark, s^*, and a subsidy rate $v = t$ per unit of reductions in emissions, $s^v = by^v$.

With subsidy rate v, the total subsidy payment to the representative firm must be

$$v(by^* - by^v)$$

so that the subsidy per unit of output will be

$$vb(y^* - y^v)/y^v = vb[(y^*/y^v) - 1]. \qquad (5)$$

This will be positive if, and only if, $y^* > y^v$ (that is, so long as the benchmark emission level at which zero subsidy is paid is set higher than the firm's level of emissions under the subsidy program). Thus, so long as $y^* > y^v$, the subsidy program must produce a uniform downward shift in the industry supply curve by the amount indicated by (5), though one that is not generally equal to the upward shift that results from a tax program. This, incidentally, points up the importance of the value of the second parameter in a subsidy program: the benchmark pollution level (s^*). The larger s^*, the more the industry supply curve shifts down and the larger will be the industry's output (and emissions). This is in contrast to our earlier conceptual subsidy that was made equivalent to a tax by paying the subsidy to all "potential" polluters; there, the benchmark pollution level had no direct effect on the industry supply curve.

Now from (5), we can immediately derive a second paradoxical conclusion:

Proposition Three. If emissions rise monotonically with industry output, the more effective the subsidy program is in inducing the individual firm to reduce its emissions, the larger is the *increase* in total industry emissions that can be expected to result from the subsidy.

This follows at once, for the smaller the value of y^v relative to y^*, the larger will be the unit subsidy payment (5) and so the larger will be the resulting downward shift in the industry supply curve. In other words, the more effective the subsidy program is in inducing the desired behavior on the part of the individual firm, the worse for society the corresponding subsidy program will be! [18]

To summarize, we see that in a competitive industry the consequences of a given tax and subsidy rate are far from similar; a subsidy intended to curb pollution may produce exactly the opposite outcome by inducing increases in total emissions. Note also that the problem need not be limited to competitive industries. Under oligopoly, for example, a subsidy program may induce the entry of new firms or the opening of additional plants that can produce precisely the same sort of result.[19]

4. INDUSTRY EQUILIBRIUM WITH ABATEMENT TECHNOLOGY

As was shown in Chapter 4, appropriate taxes will always lead to optimal industry outputs even when the emissions of the firm depend not only

[18] A moment's thought shows that this proposition must hold where the output-emissions function for the industry takes the more general form $g = G(y)$ where $G' > 0$. The result is in no way dependent on our simplifying proportionality premise $s = by$. It does, however, depend upon our assumption that there is no pollution-abatement technology so that the firm is unable to reduce emissions per unit of output. We will relax this condition in the next section.

One way to get around the difficulty of Proposition Three is to reduce the unit subsidy with the number of firms so that, with n firms in operation, the individual firm will receive $(v^*/n)(s^* - s^v)$ instead of $v(s^* - s^v)$ where v^* is a constant. There would appear to be serious practical difficulties to such a variable-subsidy arrangement. In any event, it does not help in the more fundamental difficulty described in Proposition Two, for any positive subsidy payment must, in the conditions we are discussing, increase rather than decrease the pollution emissions of a competitive industry.

[19] We are grateful to Lionel Robbins for this observation.

on its outputs but also on the resources it devotes to their abatement. However, we have seen in Section 6 of Chapter 7 that, where emissions depend
on the levels of both of these types of activities by the firm, the level of the
polluting output may very well be *increased* by the imposition of a tax simply
because the corresponding Pareto optimal level of that output is greater than
it would be in a competitive market equilibrium. Indeed, if several industries
produce the pollutant or if the community has several different pollutants to
contend with, the optimal tax may conceivably result in an increase in the
industry's emissions of the pollutant.

The more pertinent issue for us, however, is the consequence of a set
of subsidies. To examine their consequences we construct a formal model
of industry when abatement is possible. Using the same notation as before in
our subsidy-profit relation (4), we have the equilibrium condition that the
industry earns zero profit after taxes and subsidies

$$yp(y) - c(y, a) + v[s^* - s(y, a)] = 0. \tag{6}$$

Moreover, because a competitive industry's expansion path involves an input use that minimizes its total *private* cost for whatever level of output is
chosen, it will select a value of a that minimizes $c(y, a) - v[s^* - s(y, a)]$,
so that

$$c_a + vs_a = 0, \qquad c_{ca} + vs_{aa} > 0. \tag{7}$$

To determine how a change in the marginal subsidy (tax) rate, v, and the
benchmark subsidy payment, s^*, affect total payments, we utilize a comparative statics approach, differentiating the equilibrium conditions (6) and (7)
totally, and setting the results equal to zero. We obtain, writing mr for
$dyp(y)/dy$ and mc for $d[c - v(s^* - s)]/dy$,

$$(mr - mc)\, dy - (c_a + vs_a)\, da = (s - s^*)\, dv - v\, ds^*$$
$$(c_{ay} + vs_{ay})\, dy + (c_{aa} + vs_{aa})\, da = -s_a\, dv. \tag{8}$$

We note first that if $da = 0$ (no change in abatement level possible),
we must have

$$\frac{\partial y}{\partial s^*} = \frac{-v}{mr - mc}. \tag{9}$$

But because the competitive output level is presumably larger than that of a
monopoly, if the profit-maximizing output for the industry is unique, we may
take $mr - mc < 0$ for the competitive output level so that (9) must be positive. Hence, in this case, output must be increased by the introduction of a
subsidy (that is, the increase of s^* from zero to ds^*); this confirms our earlier
result.

However, we are now interested in the case in which we do not neces-sarily have $da = 0$. To simplify the expressions for $\partial y/\partial s^*$ and $\partial a/\partial s^*$ that indicate the effects of an increase in subsidy payments on output and abate-ment outlays, we write D for the determinant of the system. Because $c_a + vs_a = 0$ by (7), we have

$$D = (mr - mc)(c_{aa} + vs_{aa}) < 0. \tag{10}$$

We then obtain directly from (8),

$$\frac{\partial y}{\partial s^*} = -v(c_{aa} + vs_{aa})/D = -v/(mr - mc) > 0 \tag{11}$$

$$\frac{\partial a}{\partial s^*} = v(c_{ay} + vs_{ay})/D. \tag{12}$$

The expression for $\partial y/\partial s^*$ then reduces back to (9) and so must still be positive. In other words, industry output will still increase unambiguously in response to an increase in subsidy payments. In particular, the mere insti-tution of a subsidy, by increasing the lump-sum payment from zero to $v \, ds^* > 0$, must have this effect. Moreover, though this is not certain, abate-ment outlays may be decreased by a rise in subsidy payments. For if a rise in output increases marginal private abatement costs so that

$$c_{ay} + vs_{ay} > 0, \tag{13}$$

then it follows directly, from (12) and (10), that $\partial a/\partial s^* < 0$.

Thus, with s^* increasing y and perhaps decreasing a, the subsidy can once again increase emissions. This possibility can be brought out more directly by rewriting our model, using y and s rather than y and a as the industry's decision variables. Now the conditions requiring zero profits and minimization of costs for any given level of output are, respectively,

$$yp(y) - c(y, s) + v(s^* - s) = 0 \tag{14}$$

$$c_s + v = 0, \qquad c_{ss} > 0, \tag{15}$$

which, when differentiated totally, yield

$$(mr - mc) \, dy - (c_s + v) \, ds = -vds^* + (s - s^*) \, dv$$

$$c_{sy} \, dy + c_{ss} \, ds = -dv.$$

We obtain directly

$$D = (mr - mc)c_{ss} < 0$$

$$\frac{\partial y}{\partial s^*} = \frac{-vc_{ss}}{D} = \frac{-v}{mr - mc} > 0$$

$$\frac{\partial s}{\partial s^*} = \frac{vc_{sy}}{D} > 0 \text{ if } c_{sy} < 0.$$

That is, a smoke abatement subsidy will actually increase smoke emissions if c_{sy} is negative! But $c_{sy} < 0$ is tantamount to the very plausible premise that the industry will find it profitable to increase its emissions when its output rises (at least in the absence of environmental policy measures). For let s_1 be an initial emissions level at which $c_s = 0$ (the marginal private benefit of emissions must be zero for equilibrium). If greater emissions are to become profitable when industry output increases, at s_1, the old emissions level, c_s must become negative, bringing the[20] point of minimum total costs to the right of s_1. Hence the rise in output, y, reduces c_s from zero to a negative value; we must have $c_{sy} < 0$ as asserted.

It is easy to proceed next from equilibrium conditions (6), (7), (14), and (15) to evaluate the effects of an increase in the tax rate, t, on our variables, y, a, and s. It follows by the same arguments as before, substituting t for v and setting $s^* = 0$ to transform our subsidy model into a tax model, that we will have $\partial y/\partial t < 0$. That is, the tax, unlike the subsidy, will reduce the polluting output, just as where abatement is impossible. Similarly, where (13) holds, so that $\partial a/\partial s^* < 0$, then $\partial a/\partial t > 0$, so that, in this case, the effects of the tax and subsidy are again opposite to one another. Finally, if $c_{sy} < 0$ then $\partial s/\partial s^* > 0$ but $\partial s/\partial t < 0$; that is, an increased tax rate will help to suppress the industry's emissions, but an increased subsidy payment will increase them.

We can, then, sum up the results of this section in

Proposition Four. Where the competitive industry adjusts both output and abatement outlays, the comparative static effect of an increase in subsidy payments will be an increase in the polluting output and possibly a decrease in abatement expenditures and a rise in total emissions. On the other hand, a rise in the emissions tax rate will reduce the polluting output and, probably, total emissions.

5. UNIQUENESS OF THE TAX SOLUTION FOR PARETO OPTIMALITY

The argument that a subsidy is not usually an adequate substitute for a tax, because the former will generally not satisfy the conditions for a Pareto

[20] Note that the argument assumes the minimum to be unique.

optimum, may at first leave the reader uncomfortable because of the non-uniqueness of the Paretian solution that is inherent in the concept. We know that there will usually be a substantial set of Pareto optima with each optimum corresponding to a different distribution of benefits among the affected parties. Must it not be true then that one can get from one such solution to another with a suitable redistribution (that is, with different combinations of unit taxes and subsidies of the activities of the affected parties)? Will not all such tax and subsidy programs be Pareto optimal?

There is an element of validity to this argument. Either by changes in the initial income distribution or through *lump-sum* taxes or subsidies, one can get from one of the optimal solutions to any other. But *any* Pareto optimum achieved in this manner must always end up satisfying the necessary optimality conditions derived in Chapter 4. If those necessary conditions call for a tax per unit of output, then a per-unit subsidy on just that item simply will not do; it will generally prevent the attainment of optimality. That is, of course, the nature of a necessary condition.

That the move from one Pareto optimum to another will not change the Pigouvian taxes into subsidies follows immediately from one highly plausible assumption: that the change from one optimum to another does not transform any activity from a generator of external benefits into one that yields detrimental externalities, or *vice versa*. The product whose manufacture yields noxious fumes does not begin to emit Arpege. Our result follows at once, for we have demonstrated in Chapter 4 that optimality always requires taxation of activities that produce detrimental externalities and subsidization of those that yield external benefits in accord with the standard Pigouvian formula.

Similarly, if the victims of an undepletable (public) externality continue to suffer from it when one shifts from one optimum to another, but in both cases generate no externalities themselves, they will be required in both cases to receive zero compensation for the damage they suffer (neglecting lump-sum payments). Thus, a shift between Pareto optima can *not* introduce compensation of the victims of externalities.

In sum, we have

Proposition Five. If every activity that yields detrimental externalities in one Pareto optimal solution also does so in some other solution, both solutions will call for Pigouvian taxation of these activities. Moreover, there will always be zero compensation and zero taxation of the victims if the externality is undepletable. The analogous proposition (with unit subsidies instead of taxes) applies to external benefits.

However, as we will see now, for any particular Pareto optimum, there is a formal sense in which a complex system of subsidies can generally be substituted for a simple Pigouvian tax. For the choice of unit of account does offer a degree of freedom in the selection of the price, tax, and subsidy values called for by the solution in Chapter 4. It is easy to show that the solution summarized in Table 1 of Chapter 4 is unique except for the factor of proportionality permitted by our price normalization convention.[21]

This is, of course, what we would expect: for a particular competitive equilibrium, *relative* prices will be determined uniquely, with taxes serving as prices for the generation of externalities. Thus, we can multiply all prices, taxes, and subsidies by the same constant, call it $(1 - k)$, without violating the optimality requirements. Now it is true that in a formal sense, by using some appropriate value of k, we do get a system in which taxes and subsidies replace one another.

As an illustration, assume for simplicity that any increase in taxes produces an equal increase in price and that, as in Chapter 4, only commodity 1 produces externalities, requiring the imposition on that good alone of a tax at rate t. Then the price of that item is changed from p_1 to $(p_1 + t_1)$.

Now, if all prices and taxes are reduced by the factor $(1 - k)$ this becomes

$$(1 - k)(p_1 + t_1) = p_1 + [t_1 - k(p_1 + t_1)] = p_1 + t_1^* \qquad (16)$$

which is tantamount to the original price plus a subsidy t_1^*, if $t_1^* < 0$, that is, if

$$t_1^* = t_1 - k(p_1 + t_1) < 0 \quad \text{or} \quad 1 > k > t_1/(p_1 + t_1) > 0. \qquad (17)$$

However, any other good, $i \neq 1$, that was previously untaxed will now have its price changed from p_i to

$$p_i(1 - k) = p_i - kp_i = p_i + t_i^*, \qquad t_i^* = -kp_i < 0. \qquad (18)$$

Thus, for k sufficiently large to satisfy (17) (that is, to permit a subsidy to the production of commodity 1), (18) must represent a set of universal subsidies that together with (16) will yield exactly the same Pareto optimum as the simple Pigouvian tax, t_1, on commodity 1 alone. Of course, the subsidy option is extremely cumbersome because it requires one subsidy value to be determined for each activity in the economy in place of the one tax on the externality-generating output. Nevertheless, it is true that

Proposition Six.   If the necessary conditions for any specific Pareto

[21] Recall the condition $p_i* = \omega_i*$ (9) of Chapter 4, where ω_i* is the Lagrange multiplier corresponding to the labor constraint. This condition may be interpreted as setting the price of labor (leisure) equal to the marginal utility derivable by consumers from a unit addition to society's labor supply. Comparison of optimality relationships (3°)–(5°) of Chapter 4 with market equilibrium conditions (3°)–(5°) indicates immediately that all optimal prices and taxes can simply be multiplied by the same factor, q.

optimum can be satisfied by a set of Pigouvian taxes, it is generally possible to satisfy those conditions also with a subsidy to the externality-generating activity, counterbalanced by subsidies to other activities. However, this substitution, in effect, amounts only to a variation in the unit of account that leaves all relative prices and taxes unchanged.[22]

Of course, this sort of substitution can hardly be considered a practical proposal, and it certainly is not what the advocates of subsidy proposals have in mind. Yet it is perhaps useful to recognize to what (very limited) extent there is, theoretically, a choice in the matter.

6. CONCLUDING COMMENT

This chapter has shown that, although there is some degree of symmetry in the effects of taxes and subsidies designed to regulate externalities, the two are far from perfect substitutes. Although it is possible to conceive of a system of subsidy payments that would establish the same set of incentives as a unit tax on pollution (by making lump-sum payments to all potential polluters), the obstacles to the implementation of such a subsidy program are so formidable as to render it a theoretical curiosity. For any plausible version of a subsidy policy, where a Pigouvian tax is appropriate, a subsidy will generally lead to an inefficient use of resources. By inducing the entry of more polluting firms, a simple subsidy may well even increase the emissions of an industry, though the reverse is desired and intended. In terms of efficient resource allocation, the theory offers little support for the use of subsidies as a substitute for taxes in the regulation of externalities.

[22] In reality, this is complicated by cash balance effects, fixed contractual relations, and so on, which makes it extremely difficult to institute a pure change in the unit of account, particularly through a clumsy system of universal subsidies that must vary from commodity to commodity by just the right amount after allowance for differences in shifting.

chapter 13

Environmental Protection
and the Distribution
of Income

At least from a reading of the newspapers, one gets the impression that environmental policies are an issue in which income class plays a significant role. The poor and the wealthy seem to assign different degrees of priority to environmental protection: the proposed construction of an oil refinery is likely to produce anguished cries from middle- and upper-income inhabitants of a potential site and yet be welcomed as a source of more remunerative jobs by residents whose earnings are low. Similarly, proposals to ban DDT have been received with somewhat less enthusiasm in underdeveloped countries than they have encountered in the wealthier nations. This should, of course, come as little surprise to an economist. Assuming environmental quality to be a normal good, we would expect that wealthier individuals would want to "buy" more of it.

In addition to these differences in the demand for environmental quality, distributive elements also enter when we consider how the costs of a policy of environmental protection are likely to be distributed among individuals with differing incomes. To offer a prediction on so broad a subject is hazardous, because the methods that will be used to finance such policies are unsettled. Nevertheless, by making some reasonable assumptions and exploring the available evidence, we can reach some inferences concerning the likely pattern of incidence of these costs.

Obviously, the distributive side of externalities policy is of interest in and of itself in a world in which inequality and poverty have assumed high priority among social issues. In addition, without adequate consideration of this aspect of the matter, we may not be able to design policies that can obtain the support they require for adoption. Thus, by ignoring the redistributive effects of an environmental policy, we may either unintentionally harm certain groups in society or, alternatively, undermine the program politically.

In the first section of this chapter, we consider the relation between Pareto optimality and equity in environmental programs. In particular, we will present a theorem that shows that, under certain conditions, *all* users of common-property resources who impose external costs upon one another may actually be made worse off by the introduction of the Pareto-optimal tax! This suggests a possible source of conflict between objectives in the design of environmental measures.

In the next two sections, we construct two polar models describing the consumption of environmental quality; with these, we explore the extent to which individuals with differing incomes will succeed in obtaining their desired level of consumption of environmental services. From this background, we then use these models along with some admittedly fragmentary evidence to examine the incidence, first, of the benefits of environmental programs, and, second, of their costs.

The results suggest that strong measures to improve environmental quality may indeed have a very uneven pattern of incidence, particularly during the period of adjustment to a new composition of output and employment. Moreover, the evidence suggests that we can typically expect a somewhat regressive pattern of distribution of the benefits and costs from environmental programs; we find some basis for the contention that environmental concern "is not the poor man's game."

Yet, because there is strong evidence that health and longevity are affected substantially by pollution and by other types of environmental damage, we continue to believe that the interests of society, including those of its less-affluent members, require a relatively efficient environmental program even taking account of its distributive consequences. But the pious hope that the "distributive branch" of the fiscal authority can be trusted to compensate for the regressive effects of a new set of taxes carries little conviction. This suggests that programs to improve the quality of the environment should incorporate provisions specifically designed to help offset any distributive consequences; we discuss two such provisions in the concluding section.

1. EFFICIENCY AND EQUITY IN THE PROVISION OF ENVIRONMENTAL QUALITY

The efficiency conditions we have derived in earlier chapters of this book are all founded on the criterion of Pareto optimality. That is, in each case, we determined a state, or set of conditions, necessary for maximization of the welfare of any one individual, selected arbitrarily, without reducing the level of welfare (also selected arbitrarily) of any other member of the community. This may appear to avoid entirely the issue of income distribution, for if the proposal harms no one, it would seem, almost by definition, to be unobjectionable to everyone.

The matter can be put another way. It is tempting to argue that, whatever the distribution of income that is desired or with which one starts, an allocation of resources that is not Pareto optimal must be unsatisfactory. For, given any such allocation, there must exist some reshuffling of resources that benefits some individuals and harms no one. This *is* true by definition, for if no such alternative were available, the initial allocation would have satisfied the conditions of Pareto optimality. It is all too easy to conclude from this that it is irrational to oppose a policy measure necessary or, perhaps, sufficient for the achievement of Pareto optimality, for with a supplementary program capable of achieving whatever distribution is desired, the policy maker can always increase social welfare by combining the socially desired distributive measure with one that achieves a Pareto-optimal allocation of resources.

Although all this is unimpeachable at a formal level, the difficulty of implementing such policy packages in practice is well known. Nevertheless, it is often ignored by economists who advocate concrete policies derived directly from welfare theory. This section offers a specific example that illustrates dramatically how dangerous it can be to disregard the redistributive consequences of environmental policies.

In general terms, the issue is a simple one. Given any initial resource allocation, A, that is not Pareto optimal, it is of course true that there must exist at least one other allocation, say B, that leaves everyone unharmed in comparison with A and makes some individuals better off. But now select randomly some other Pareto optimal allocation, C. There is no way of knowing from this whether or not some persons will be harmed by the move from the nonoptimal point, A, to the optimal point, C. The distinction here is between a *state* of Pareto optimality and a *move* that can be described as a *Paretian improvement*. Any point on the utility-possibilities frontier obviously represents a Pareto-optimal state; no one can increase his level of welfare without reducing that of someone else. However, a *move* from some position in the interior of utility-possibilities space to a point on the frontier may not itself be Pareto optimal, for it can make someone worse off. Thus, somewhat paradoxically, a *move* to a *state* of Pareto optimality may not itself be a Paretian improvement.

Recently, Martin Weitzman and Uwe Reinhardt independently constructed striking examples of this point with direct implications for environmental policies.[1] We describe Reinhardt's simpler, but less formal, analysis because it is easier to follow and its rigor is sufficient for our purposes.

A standard illustration of the effects of externalities is road crowding. An additional car that enters an overcrowded highway adds to the congestion and imposes a time loss on everyone else. The driver's entry thus generates a marginal social cost that exceeds the marginal private costs. In this case, every driver is both a generator of these externalities and a victim of the same externalities produced by other drivers. The drivers constitute a self-contained group engaged in inefficient levels of driving activity. In accord with the conclusions of Chapter 4, optimality requires the imposition upon each driver of a toll equal to the marginal social damage resulting from his presence, *with no compensation to him for the damage he suffers from the presence of others.*

So far there is nothing new in our discussion. But the novel and rather startling observation offered by Weitzman and Reinhardt is that this optimal Pigouvian tax, far from benefiting some drivers without harming anyone, may, on the contrary, result in a loss in welfare to each and every one of the road users.

The proof is easily provided with the aid of a supply-demand diagram, Figure 13–1. For simplicity, we assume that there is a fixed rate of exchange between time spent on the journey and money. That is, we take one hour to be worth some specified number of dollars to all individuals.[2] We deal with the demand for and cost of travel along some specified stretch of road. DD' is the analogue of the ordinary market demand curve that we interpret, subject to the usual qualifications, as an approximation to a curve of marginal social benefits.

Curve CA indicates the money value of the amount of time spent per vehicle on the journey (that is, it is a curve of average social time cost per vehicle trip).[3] We assume that CA is increasing over some range, which simply implies that the presence of additional vehicles can slow traffic.

[1] M. Weitzman, "Free Access vs. Private Ownership as Alternative Systems for Managing Common Property," (Working Draft, April 12, 1972); U. Reinhardt, "Efficiency Tolls and the Problem of Equity," (Working Draft, 1973).

[2] For a notion of time-price that is justified more rigorously, see Gary Becker, "A Theory of the Allocation of Time," *Economic Journal* LXXV (September, 1965), 493–517. Becker's treatment is much more complex than ours: time-price varies from individual to individual according to each person's opportunity cost. We assume here that the cost of time is the same for everyone. Weitzman's approach, incidentally, does not require this simplification.

[3] The shape of CA may require a bit of comment. It is horizontal over the stretch CH, which indicates that up to some level of utilization, the road is completely uncongested so that additional vehicles do not slow anyone down. The later backward bend in the curve represents a phenomenon that has been substantiated empirically: after some point, a further increase in the number of vehicles attempting to enter the road increases the time-costs so severely that the number of vehicles able to traverse it in a given period of time is

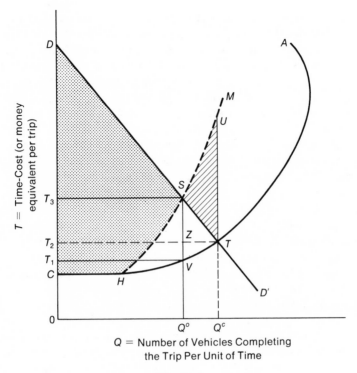

Q = Number of Vehicles Completing
the Trip Per Unit of Time

FIG. 13–1

The curve labelled CM is the marginal social cost of an additional vehicle.[4] The net benefit to this group of drivers is given by the area between the marginal social cost curve, CM, and the marginal benefit (demand) curve, DD'. This is at a maximum (dotted area) at traffic volume $0Q^o$. However, left to itself, traffic will settle at the "competitive" level, $0Q^c$, at which the demand curve crosses the average cost curve. This must be so because, at any smaller volume of traffic, marginal private benefit exceeds marginal private cost so that traffic will expand (and conversely). Relative to the optimal level of usage, $0Q^o$, the competitive level, $0Q^c$, involves a net loss to the drivers equal to the cross-hatched area, STU.

---

actually reduced. The analysis, however, does not depend in any way on the two properties of the average cost curve discussed in this note; it requires only that the marginal costs of congestion be increasing at least over some range.

[4] Note that CA, not CM, is the curve of marginal *private* costs. Consider an individual traversing the stretch of road we are examining. If traffic is at level $0Q^o$, the individual who embarks on the road can anticipate a time-cost for his journey of Q^oV. That is, if the total time-cost of his day's activities would otherwise be (x), the decision to add this trip to his other activities will increase his total time-cost to $(x + Q^oV)$.

Our theory tells us that society can eliminate this loss by imposing a road tax, T_1T_3 equal to VS, the marginal social damage at the optimal level of usage, $0Q^o$. However, it is easy to see that this must leave every driver worse off. For as compared with the unregulated usage, the individual saves T_1T_2 in time-cost per trip, but for this saving he pays the additional amount T_1T_3 per trip. Because with a negatively sloping demand curve, the latter *must* be greater than the former by the amount $ZS = T_2T_3$, he will inevitably suffer a net loss in welfare.

The result seems paradoxical, for here we have a move to a Pareto optimum that appears to be detrimental to *everyone* involved. But this is, of course, not so. Assuming that the level of employment remains the same, *some* members of the economy must gain in the process. The taxes must either finance the supply of additional public goods or, by decreasing prices or taxes paid by others, it must add to the private-goods consumption of other persons. The point is that, so long as the users of the road do not share in the proceeds made possible by the additional public revenues,[5] they will actually suffer a loss in welfare from the imposition of the "optimal" tax.[6] There is thus a net gain to the community, but it is associated with a loss to drivers on the taxed road.

Although we have used the case of highway congestion to illustrate the theorem, it should be clear that this proposition also applies to at least some other sorts of environmental usage. More specifically, the argument shows that, wherever a common-property resource is subject to rising costs of congestion, the imposition of the optimal Pigouvian tax will reduce the welfare of the users of that resource so long as they are excluded from the benefits accruing from the tax revenues. We may see here why opposition to "optimal" taxes is to be expected, unless special provisions are made to assist the losers.

2. THE DEMAND FOR ENVIRONMENTAL QUALITY BY INCOME CLASS

In later sections of this chapter, we will offer some empirical evidence and tentative conclusions on the probable pattern of incidence of the benefits

---

[5] Because compensation of the victims was shown, in Chapter 4, to be incompatible with Pareto optimality, the road users *cannot* share in the proceeds of an optimal tax program if that share depends to any extent on their own use of the road.

[6] This suggests, incidentally, that the argument will not hold if every member of the community uses the road. In this case, the welfare gain arising from the move to a Pareto-optimal pattern of resource use must get back to (at least some of) the road users. Indeed, as the preceding footnote argues, in this case, no tax program may even be able to achieve Pareto optimality. However, if the real tax proceeds are channeled back in a manner that is sufficiently indirect, they may not cause significant deviations from Pareto optimality.

and costs of programs to enhance the quality of the environment. However, to examine the issue theoretically, it is necessary first to consider in this and the next two sections how the demand for environmental quality is likely to vary with income and how these variations in demand can, to some extent, be accommodated through the individual's choice of location.

As suggested earlier, there is good reason to believe that the demand for environmental quality will rise with income. Such a case is illustrated in Figure 13–2, where we see that a rise in the individual's budget constraint from AA' to BB' leads to an increase in his desired level of environmental quality from q_p to q_r. We might therefore expect higher-income groups to have a greater demand than poorer individuals for such things as clean air and water.

This conclusion depends upon three assumptions implicit in Figure 13–2. The first is that, for a typical individual, environmental quality is a

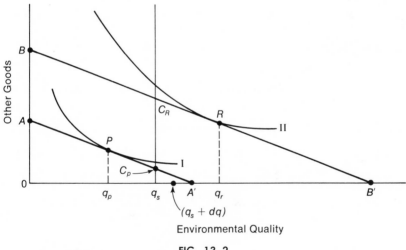

FIG. 13–2

normal good, so that his desired degree of, say, air cleanliness rises with income, an assumption that seems quite reasonable. Second, this proposition assumes at least roughly similar preference *functions* for rich and poor; or, more accurately, it presumes that lower-income groups do not possess systematically stronger preferences for environmental quality than the more wealthy. Otherwise, the poor, because of their more intense preferences for clean air, might, in spite of their lower incomes, still be willing to pay more than the rich for a given level of environmental quality. This second assumption also seems to us a valid one. In fact, if preferences themselves diverge significantly among income groups, it would be our guess that the stronger predilection for environmental protection is to be found among those with higher incomes. The dangers, both in health and aesthetic terms, of environmental deterioration are frequently complex and sometimes apparently remote and so are more likely to be recognized by those reached regularly by the media that offer extensive discussions of the issues. Some have actually characterized the growing concern with environmental protection as an "upper-class" movement.[7]

The third, and most problematic, of the conditions implicit in Figure 13–2 is that there is a fixed price for environmental quality, a price that is invariant with respect to income. It is certainly conceivable that, with a progressive tax system, the price of environmental programs will be higher for the rich than for the poor. In fact, we can even have a situation like that illustrated in Figure 13–3, where the effect of the price differential outweighs

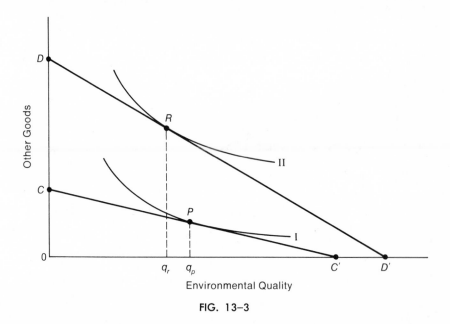

FIG. 13–3

that of income, so that the poorer individual actually demands a higher level of environmental quality (q_p) than that (q_r) desired by the wealthier person.

---

[7] See, for example, J. Harry, R. Gale, and J. Hendee, "Conservation: An Upper Class Social Movement," *Journal of Leisure Research* I (Summer, 1969), 246. This, of course, does not prove that there exist systematic disparities in the preference maps of rich and poor for environmental quality; the apparently greater concern of the wealthy for environmental protection may result simply from a positive income effect like that illustrated in Figure 13–2. Our point here is simply that there seems to be no persuasive evidence that the poor exhibit stronger preferences for environmental quality than do the rich.

We will have more to say about this later, when we examine the various ways in which individuals can "buy" varying degrees of environmental quality. Let us say here that we frankly doubt that the situation depicted in Figure 13–3 is plausible as a typical case. For one thing, what is relevant here is not the progressivity of the initial tax structure, but rather that of the *incremental* taxes needed to finance increased outlays on environmental protection. Progressivity of current taxes by no means implies that the tax-price of a given *increase* in environmental protection need be greater to the rich than to the poor. In fact, if the current tax system is already highly progressive, it may be quite difficult politically to make *increases* in taxes progressive. However, there are even more compelling reasons for believing that situations like that represented in Figure 13–3 are atypical; we shall explore these in subsequent sections of this chapter.

3. A PUBLIC-GOOD MODEL OF THE PROVISION OF ENVIRONMENTAL QUALITY

In this section and the next, we want to consider two polar cases of the consumption of environmental quality. In the first model, we take environmental quality to be a pure, Samuelsonian public good; this is a world in which all individuals in society consume exactly the same quality of air, water, and other environmental goods. Returning to Figure 13–2, let indifference curve *I* and budget constraint *AA'* represent the situation of our typical poor individual, while curve *II* and budget constraint *BB'* are associated with a rich person. As noted earlier, the wealthier individual will, in this case, demand a level of environmental quality, q_r, higher than q_p, the amount desired by his poorer counterpart. If, however, environmental quality is a pure public good, all persons must, by definition, consume the same set of environmental services. This means that a single level of environmental quality (or vector of environmental characteristics) must be settled upon by society. If this decision is made through democratic processes, let us say by simple majority rule, we might expect to obtain (roughly) the level of environmental quality most preferred by Duncan Black's median voter.[8] The point here is that a likely outcome is a compromise in which the quality of the environment will be less than that desired by the wealthy and more than that preferred by the poor, say q_s in Figure 13–2. To the extent, therefore, that environmental quality is a relatively pure public good, we should find upper-income groups pushing for greater outlays on environmental programs in opposition to the

[8] D. Black, "On the Rationale of Group Decision Making," *Journal of Political Economy* LVI (February, 1948), 23–34.

wishes of the poor, who want more income to devote to the consumption of other goods. We will return to this point later.

4. THE MODEL OF PERFECT ADAPTATION BY CHOICE OF LOCATION

As many writers have pointed out, environmental quality is, at least under most circumstances, far from a pure public good. The quality of air, for example, varies substantially even within the confines of a single metropolitan area. This means that an individual does have some choice as to his environment: he can determine to some extent his environmental surroundings by his selection of location.[9] We can envision, at the opposite pole from our pure public-good case, a Tiebout type of world in which a continuum of environmental quality is available at differing points in space.[10] Individuals choose, in accordance with their demands, a location that provides the most desired quality of the environment. Locations offering superior environmental quality obviously rent for a higher price and thus command an economic rent. Moreover, in line with our earlier discussion, we can expect higher-income groups to satisfy their relatively high demands for environmental quality by selecting sites with comparatively little air pollution, noise, and so on. In contrast, the poor can be expected to occupy the less-attractive parts of the metropolitan area in exchange for lower rents. In fact, if differentials in environmental quality are perfectly capitalized into differentials in property values and rents, we can visualize a locational pattern that is economically efficient in that the marginal rate of substitution (MRS) between environmental quality and other goods of each individual would, in equilibrium, equal the opportunity cost of a "unit" of environmental quality; equality of MRSs among individuals would then hold. Although poorer individuals would consume an inferior quality of environment (as depicted in Figure 13–2), their marginal valuation, as measured by their willingness to sacrifice other goods for another unit of environmental quality, would be identical with that of wealthier persons if the (marginal) costs of environmental improvement were the same for everyone.

Although the Tiebout polar case, like that of pure public good, is surely an oversimplification, it contains more than a little truth. Empirical studies have verified that, within metropolitan areas, property values do indeed

---

[9] Even in the same locality within a particular city, environmental quality may vary. The rich, for instance, can insulate themselves from such annoyances as noise and the discomforts of hot and dirty air through the purchase of appropriately constructed apartments, air conditioners, and so on.

[10] See the classic article by Charles Tiebout, "A Pure Theory of Local Expenditures," *Journal of Political Economy* LXIV (October, 1956), 416–24.

reflect differences in environmental quality. In one such study (and there are others with similar results), Ridker and Henning found, in the St. Louis metropolitan area, that property values displayed a significant inverse relationship with a measure of the extent of air pollution (specifically, a measure of atmospheric sulfation levels).[11] Moreover, Freeman, in a study of three metropolitan areas, determined that exposure to air pollution varies inversely with income; he concludes that, "Air quality is distributed in a pro-rich manner." [12] It is thus clear that geographical location has, to some degree, permitted individuals to purchase different environmental qualities in accord with the differences in their effective demands and, as is to be expected, this bears a strong relationship to income. The poor live in the most heavily polluted sections of metropolitan areas, while the wealthier seek out the more attractive sites.

Reality, of course, lies somewhere between the two worlds that we have dealt with: the community in which public goods are supplied to everyone in equal quality and the range of geographic areas offering a wide variety of levels of public outputs. The rich and the poor cannot afford to live too far apart; the latter offer jobs to the poor, and the former offer services to the rich. Geographic separation imposes heavy time and money costs of commuting on one or both parties. For this and other reasons, one often finds slum neighborhoods cheek by jowl with the homes of the wealthy. If the air is foul, neither of them escapes it completely, and purification of the atmosphere affects both neighborhoods directly. Most environmental programs thus have strong elements of "publicness."

5. THE DISTRIBUTION OF BENEFITS OF ENVIRONMENTAL PROGRAMS

We turn now to the issue of central concern: the incidence by income class of the costs and benefits of environmental programs. We will consider, first, the distribution of the benefits from these programs, and, second, the pattern of incidence of their costs. At the outset, we stress that it is difficult to reach firm conclusions on these matters; in some cases, a single program has both propoor and prorich elements. Nevertheless, the bits of evidence that are available, along with some reasonable conjectures, suggest to us (as it has

[11] Ronald Ridker and John Henning, "The Determinants of Residential Property Values with Special Reference to Air Pollution," *Review of Economics and Statistics* XLIX (May, 1967), 246–57. This is a multiple-regression study that attempts to hold constant the other determinants of property values.

[12] A. Myrick Freeman, "The Distribution of Environmental Quality," in A. Kneese and B. Bower, eds., *Environmental Quality Analysis: Theory and Method in the Social Sciences* (Baltimore: The Johns Hopkins Press, 1972), p. 264.

to others) that, without specific redistributive measures as part of an environmental policy, we can expect programs of environmental improvement to be typically prorich in their redistributive effects.

Let us first consider the distribution of benefits of a program of environmental improvement in the pure public-goods case; we will then reexamine the issue in the model of geographic specialization. Suppose, for example, that the public authority undertakes to reduce the level of air pollution in a metropolitan area. Where the improvement is a pure public good, it must, by definition, be available to everyone on equal terms. Thus, it will not be provided preponderantly either to the rich or to the poor. Nevertheless, the public-goods model suggests that the dollar value placed on these *benefits* will be greater among higher-income recipients. We recall that our public-goods solution (q_s in Figure 13–2) was one in which the marginal valuation of a unit of environmental quality is higher for a rich man than for a poor man. This implies that an incremental increase in the quality of the environment will be worth more (as measured by willingness to pay) to those with higher incomes than to the poorer members of the community. In this model, therefore, an environmental program must be more favorable to the rich than to the poor providing there is no offsetting differential in the apportionment of the cost burden.[13]

However, in a Tiebout world we can reach no such simple and categorical conclusion. Because there the poor and the rich inhabit separate areas, it is possible to devise (a) programs whose benefits flow to both parties, (b) programs that exclusively, or at least primarily, affect the poor alone or (c) programs directed mainly to localities inhabited by the wealthy.

In fact, one encounters each of these three types of measures in practice. A general tax on emissions, for example, is likely to improve air and water quality everywhere to some extent and thus is a measure of type (a). A set of minimum standards for air and water quality (for example, a regulation limiting emissions in different communities sufficiently to achieve an acceptable level of sulphur dioxide in the atmosphere in all localities) may have its primary impact on poorer neighborhoods, because the wealthy may inhabit areas in which the standards were already met prior to the adoption of the regulation. Finally, a program designed to protect the more unspoiled areas, and so to preserve "sanctuaries of cleanliness," is likely to focus on the areas inhabited by the wealthy rather than the localities in which the poor live and in which deterioration may be well under way. We want to consider next somewhat more systematically the effects of each of these three types of policies. Because in our Tiebout world pollution is likely to be most serious

---

[13] Note that we cannot say that the program is strictly regressive. Although the marginal benefits to the rich are greater than those to the poor, it still remains possible that the incremental benefits would be larger *as a proportion of income* for the poor than for the rich.

in poorer neighborhoods, we might suppose that a program of type (a) that improves environmental quality (for example, reduces levels of air pollution) in all localities generates benefits of more critical importance to the poor than to the rich.

However, this conclusion requires several important qualifications. First, although such programs may bring greater improvement *measured in physical terms* to areas of poorer residents, it cannot be stated unequivocally that the *value* of these increases in environmental quality will be greater to the poor than to the rich. Depending on the geographical pattern of the improvements, the income elasticity of demand for environmental quality, and current income differentials, the value *in money terms* of a lesser increase in, say, air quality may still be greater in rich, than in poor, areas. Our formal analysis is consistent with this conclusion.

As Figure 13–2 suggests, in a Tiebout equilibrium there *need not* be a significant difference in the rich and poor individual's MRS between environmental quality and private goods, even though this quality is far more abundantly supplied to the former. True, the equal MRSs displayed in the figure depend on the highly questionable premise that the marginal cost of environmental improvements are the same in the two types of area. However, there seems to be no clear presumption that the relative costs will differ systematically in such a way that the relative marginal value of a given improvement will tend to be higher for the poor than it is for the rich.

Second, suppose that our cleansing of the atmosphere effected a dramatic improvement in, say, the air quality in what has been a low-income area. In our Tiebout world, this should make these sites more attractive, and thereby lead to a bidding up of rents in the area. To the extent that they are renters, the poor may well find that much of the benefit of living in a cleaner environment is largely offset by the higher rents they must pay. The force of this argument at a practical level is difficult to evaluate. As Freeman points out, the sunk investment in housing and other neighborhood configurations generally make changes in local land-use patterns a relatively slow process.[14] It *may* thus be a long period before the improvements in environmental quality become capitalized into higher rents. However, over the longer run, alterations in locational patterns and levels of rents may reduce significantly the net benefits realized by the poor.

Programs of type (b), requiring, for example, the attainment of certain minimum environmental standards in all localities, obviously have the greatest potential for a propoor incidence of benefits. Even here, however, the extent of this propoor pattern of benefits may be eroded by one response noted above: the bidding up of rents, in areas inhabited by the poor, as a result of the improvement in environmental quality in these neighborhoods.

[14] "Distribution of Environmental Quality," pp. 268–69.

We turn finally to the apparently prorich [type (c)] environmental programs. Because of the heavy costs of maintaining high levels of environmental quality in all areas, the environmental authority may decide to confine polluting activities to specific locations so as to preserve other localities from environmental degradation.[15] Such a result can be obtained in a rather inefficient manner by zoning devices, or more efficiently by some variety of tax measure (for example, one in which taxes on emissions of fumes vary *directly* with the initial purity of the atmosphere in the area).

There is, clearly, a strong presumption that such an environmental policy will work counter to the interests of the poor in a Tiebout economy.[16] Because they may be assumed to inhabit the dirty areas to begin with, the imposition of these policies is likely to make their communities dirtier still, as polluting activities are driven there from the protected areas. Moreover, rents in the unprotected regions may be expected to increase as well, as more polluters are induced to locate there! [17] Thus the poor will find themselves

[15] As we saw in Chapter 8, this may be an optimal strategy in the presence of non-convexities caused by the presence of externalities. For then there may be virtue in a corner solution in which polluting activities are segregated.

[16] The Samuelson model is not relevant to this case, which requires, as one of its premises, differentiation in the environmental quality of different communities.

[17] Actually, this is not inevitable. For example, a tax that varies directly with initial air cleanliness will to some extent discourage pollution in *both* areas. If the tax on the *relatively* unprotected area is still not too far below that in the other, it may offset the resulting migration of polluting activities from the more protected areas.

To show this, assume that a firm produces in two areas: A, which is unprotected, and B, which is protected, and let x_a and x_b be its outputs in the two locations, which are produced at respective costs $c_a(x_a)$ and $c_b(x_b)$; its total revenue is $r(x_a + x_b)$; and assume that the tax rates on polluting production in the two locations are, respectively, kt and t where $0 \leq k < 1$. Then if the firm's objective is to maximize profits, its problem is to

$$\text{Max } \pi = r(x_a + x_b) - c_a(x_a) - c_b(x_b) - ktx_a - tx_b,$$

yielding the first-order conditions

$$r' - c_a' - kt = 0$$
$$r' - c_b' - t = 0.$$

Differentiating totally with respect to t, x_a, and x_b, we obtain

$$(r'' - c_a'') \, dx_a + r'' dx_b = kdt$$
$$r'' \, dx_a + (r'' - c_b'') \, dx_b = dt.$$

Solving and letting D represent the determinant of the system (where $D > 0$ by the second-order conditions), we have

$$\frac{dx_a}{dt} = [k(r'' - c_b'') - r'']/D.$$

Thus, if as we might expect, $r'' < 0$ and $c'' > 0$, then dx_a/dt will be negative if k is sufficiently close to unity (that is, if the tax differential is not great enough, x_a, the firm's living in less-attractive areas and receiving less of a rent advantage relative to the cleaner areas than they would in the absence of the program.

So far, we have largely followed our intention of dealing exclusively with the distribution of the benefits of an environmental program. But in the Tiebout model, this procedure forces us to ignore a particularly critical issue. Suppose that the programs we have been considering require the individual communities to pay the bulk of the costs of their environmental improvements. Then, from the point of view of the members of each individual locality, its own environmental program is, *on net*, detrimental to their interests. For in the pure Tiebout case, everyone will have achieved precisely the level of environmental quality that he desires, given the cost of improvement. Consequently, any measure that forces further improvement on a community must impose on its inhabitants something they do not want. In terms of our figures, it forces them to the right of their preferred positions.

Thus in this case, programs of type (b) (the setting of uniform standards), rather than benefiting the poor, will be disadvantageous to them and to them alone, and programs of type (a) that affect the environment in every type of community will be somewhat less antipoor because they will be disadvantageous to rich and poor alike! [18]

When we bring the analysis to a lower level of abstraction, the prorich orientation of the benefits from environmental programs seems even more likely. For example, substantial funds have been directed into the provision of outdoor recreation facilities: national parks, the preservation of surface waters for recreational purposes, and so on. We might guess that the use of such facilities would be related directly to income, particularly in view of their significant distance from densely populated areas. Empirical studies confirm this. In the most comprehensive study of the economics of outdoor recreation, Cicchetti, Seneca, and Davidson have found (using multiple-regression analysis) that level of income was a significant determinant of the probability and frequency of usage by an individual of a wide variety of outdoor recreational activities.[19] Expenditures on such facilities thus appear to have a prorich orientation.

---

output in the unprotected area may actually be reduced by the tax), and so its demand for land there may fall, with rents following suit. A very similar argument holds for a competitive *industry*.

[18] To the extent that community environmental programs have beneficial external effects on environmental quality in other jurisdictions, they may of course benefit everyone if all communities undertake measures, say, to achieve certain standards of environmental quality. In a Tiebout world, the case for additional incentives to communities for environmental improvement appears to rest primarily on such external effects.

[19] C. J. Cicchetti, J. J. Seneca, and P. Davidson, *The Demand and Supply of Outdoor Recreation* (Washington, D.C.: U.S. Department of the Interior, 1969).

6. THE DISTRIBUTION OF TRANSITIONAL COSTS

In our public-goods model, we used the simplifying assumption that the cost per unit of environmental quality was the same for rich and poor. This is admittedly rather unlikely: the incidence of the costs of an environmental program will obviously depend on the means adopted to implement the program, be they effluent charges, government subsidies, or direct controls that, in turn, influence the structure of prices. In examining this issue, we will consider two kinds of costs: the *transitional* costs involved in a program of improving the environment and the *continuing* costs of maintaining a given state of environmental quality. By transitional costs, we mean the costs of the process of adjustment from one state of environmental quality to another; continuing costs then become the costs of maintaining, over time, the newly achieved quality of the environment.

The most striking feature of the transitional costs of environmental programs is the likelihood of a highly uneven pattern of incidence. Whether the improvement of the environment (involving, say, reduced emissions into the atmosphere and waterways) is achieved by effluent charges or by direct regulation, the effects will hit some industries much harder than others. Heavy polluters, such as those chemical and paper plants that are located in populous areas, may be forced to curtail their operations significantly and perhaps even to stop them completely. This suggests, as testified to by frequent opposition in industrial towns, that one of the most significant transitional costs of environmental programs will be a loss of jobs.

The employment-restricting effects of environmental measures may be increased by the fact that such policies are not instituted in all regions simultaneously. The area that imposes them unilaterally or in concert with only a few other jurisdictions will find itself at a competitive disadvantage in the production of the polluting items. Whether or not this will reduce the level of employment in the region as a whole, it will certainly make for a decrease in the demand for labor in the industries directly affected.

There are some obvious automatic offsets to these employment effects and some that are optional. Measures that penalize the emission of pollutants will stimulate the manufacture of recycling and purification equipment. Moreover, appropriate monetary and fiscal programs can be used to minimize any loss in employment entailed in an environmental protection policy. However, it is difficult, as we have learned, for conventional stabilization policy to cope effectively and promptly with highly localized unemployment resulting from cutbacks in particular lines of activity. The short-run costs for the newly unemployed are thus likely to be heavy.

In principle, this burden need not inevitably fall more heavily on the poor. A new refining plant, for example, may offer an unusually high proportion of jobs to executives and technicians. The pattern of transitional costs by income class will thus depend on the relative change in demand for high- and low-income employees. It is difficult to generalize on the matter; however, where environmental protection does restrict job opportunities, it is our conjecture that the costs are likely to fall most heavily on those in the lowest-income stratum. Professional personnel frequently have a greater occupational and geographical mobility than lower-wage employees; as a result, lower-income workers may well have more to lose than higher-salaried employees. This at least appears to be how workers themselves view the matter. When one reads newspaper accounts of local opposition to the curtailing of activities of some plant, the invariable rallying cry of its proponents (who are usually reported to be drawn largely from the community's lower-income groups) is that restriction of the enterprise will mean a loss of jobs that are "badly needed." [20]

This discussion has a direct bearing on the diagrammatic analysis of earlier sections. It suggests that, at least in the eyes of the poor themselves, and, very likely, in fact as well, the transitional costs of environmental measures may be much higher for the poor than they are for the wealthy. The slope of the price line in Figure 13-3, interpreted as a curve of total real cost per unit of environmental quality, rather than being less steep for the poor, may actually be steeper for those whose jobs are jeopardized by programs for environmental improvement. In such cases, income as well as transitional "price" effects will make environmental measures more attractive to higher- than to lower-income groups.

7. THE DISTRIBUTION OF CONTINUING COSTS

The continuing costs of programs to sustain a given level of environmental quality relate more to the change in the structure of prices of goods and services. If we assume that, following a transitional period of temporarily unemployed resources, full (or approximately full) employment is reestablished, the incidence of the steady-state environmental programs becomes a matter of the equilibrium set of prices (including levels of wages). Our expectation here is that there will be a rise in the relative price of those goods whose production involves substantial external costs (at least where techniques of production that reduce destructive emissions are significantly more costly than "free" dumping of wastes into the atmosphere or local waterways).

[20] Even if employment is not hurt by environmental protection measures, real output, conventionally measured, will tend to be reduced because a given set of inputs will yield a smaller bundle of outputs than before. In many cases, this cost, too, will probably fall most heavily on the poor. If a ban on DDT undermines the "green revolution" with its spectacular contribution to grain outputs in less-developed areas, can there be any serious doubt about the income group that will suffer the resulting malnutrition or starvation?

Suppose, for example, that we were to impose a set of effluent charges on emissions of the sort discussed in Chapter 10; the level of charges would be adjusted to achieve desired targets of environmental quality. What can we say about the pattern of incidence of such a set of charges? In principle, the approach to this problem is a straightforward one. Effluent fees simply amount to excise taxes on certain activities of the industry; the problem thus becomes one of determining, first, the effect of the tax on the cost and price of each commodity (including inputs) and, second, of establishing the incidence of the price changes by income class. Although this is simple enough at the general level, those who have worked with problems of fiscal incidence in a general-equilibrium framework are well acquainted with the complexities inherent in such analyses.[21]

It is not too difficult to enumerate those industries that would be prime candidates for environmental taxation. At least the superficial evidence suggests that the list would include petroleum and other fuels, electricity generation, pulp and paper production, chemicals, the use of automobiles and. perhaps, aircraft, and various mining and minerals-processing operations. This list is not intended to be exhaustive, but it does appear to provide a reasonable beginning.

The analysis becomes much more difficult from here on. One needs, for example, some information on the production functions for these various activities to determine how their response to effluent charges would affect their costs. In some industries, very modest alterations in production processes may permit large reductions in waste emissions at little additional cost; for others, the cost increases may be substantial. The extent to which the increases in costs then become transformed into higher prices depends to some extent upon the competitive character of the industry and on its elasticity of demand. This is further complicated by the fact that the outputs of many of the industries on our list are themselves inputs in the production of other commodities; it can become difficult to trace the path of cost and price increases from one product to another and possibly yet others. To reach definitive conclusions on the incidence of the burdens of a program of effluent fees (or any other control technique) is thus virtually impossible given our present state of knowledge.

Nevertheless, there is some evidence that provides a few clues as to the likely pattern of incidence of such programs. Studies by Freeman, Roberts, and Schaeffer all indicate that consumption expenditures for electricity and other forms of fuel for household use constitute a lower proportion of the

---

[21] The classic general-equilibrium study of incidence is Arnold Harberger, "The Incidence of the Corporation Income Tax," *Journal of Political Economy* LXX, (June, 1962), 215–40. Harberger's paper illustrates well the difficulties in incidence analysis.

incomes of higher-income families.[22] This suggests that increased prices for fuel for household purposes exhibit a regressive pattern of incidence. It must be noted, however, that only one-third of U.S. electricity output is consumed by households; the rest is used in the industrial sector. How the cost increases would be distributed among different commodities is, at this point, a matter of conjecture. If, however, we were to assume that it increased the price of all commodities in the same proportion, we may again get a regressive pattern of incidence, if consumption as a fraction of income falls with the level of income. We are, in effect, treating the increased cost of electricity for industrial use as a general sales tax, the pattern of which is likely to be somewhat regressive.[23] Roberts' tentative conclusion is that, ". . . the distribution of well-being in the society will probably become more unequal as a result of controlling the environmental side effects of electric power—the rich will gain more than they pay, the poor will either lose or not gain as much as the rich." [24]

Other bits of evidence point in the same direction. Freeman finds, for example, that household consumption of paper supplies as a fraction of income is higher for lower-income families;[25] Roberts suggests that higher prices for automobiles resulting from emission-control devices and design are likely to exhibit a regressive pattern, because the number of automobiles owned rises more slowly than income.[26] All this points in the direction of a somewhat regressive incidence of the costs of environmental programs.

8. DISTRIBUTIVE CONSIDERATIONS IN ENVIRONMENTAL POLICY

In sum, our models and the available evidence lend support to the view that, on balance, programs for environmental improvement promote the interests of higher-income groups more than those of the poor; they may well increase the degree of inequality in the distribution of real income. Low-income families are more likely to feel that basic needs, such as better food and housing, constitute more pressing concerns than cleaner air and water.

[22] Freeman, "Distribution of Environmental Quality," Table 7.1, p. 259; Marc Roberts, "Who Will Pay for Cleaner Power?", mimeo, Table 3; and Jeffrey Schaeffer, "Sales Tax Regressivity under Alternative Tax Bases and Income Concepts," *National Tax Journal* XXII (December, 1969), 516–27.

[23] See Joseph Pechman, *Federal Tax Policy*, rev. ed. (New York: W. W. Norton, 1971), pp. 156–58.

[24] Roberts, "Who Will Pay for Cleaner Power?" p. 32.

[25] Freeman, "Distribution of Environmental Quality," Table 7.1, p. 259.

[26] Roberts, *op. cit.*, p. 32.

Moreover, where new environmental programs threaten jobs, including higher-paying as well as lower-wage work, redistributive effects may weigh particularly heavily on certain individuals.

In fact, the rich and the poor seem often to have realized instinctively the difference in what they stand to gain from environmental programs. In a recent case study, Perry Shapiro examined voting patterns in a referendum in Santa Barbara County.[27]

> At issue was the development of a large ranch (El Capitan) fronting on the sea in the rural part of the county. The voters were to decide whether or not a private developer should be allowed a zoning variance to develop home-sites in an established agricultural open space area. The project promised to generate an increase in local economic activity at the expense of environmental quality. The issue, as related in pre-election press reports, was one of environmental quality versus income, and there is good reason to believe this was the alternative between which voters chose in the polling booth.[28]

Using probit analysis to study the election results by wealthier and poorer districts, Shapiro found a clear, direct relationship between mean income and the proportion of voters opposing the project; only in the lowest income class was there substantial support for the grant of a variance for increased housing density.

There are two obvious polar reactions to these observations. An over-simplification of the reaction of the pure economist might assert that resource allocation and income distribution are two separate issues and that one should not be permitted to interfere with a rational resolution of the other. No matter what their distributive implications, one should seek to institute policies that make for efficiency in resource utilization, leaving it to some other (unclearly identified) branch of government to take the steps required to achieve a more just distribution of income.

The other extreme view, again one that is probably rarely held in its strongest form, asserts that the elimination of poverty is a matter of much higher priority than the (primarily aesthetic) issue of environmental protection. If the latter interferes with the former, so much the worse for it; it is a luxury whose attainment must at the very least be postponed until the more pressing problem of inequality is reduced to reasonable proportions.

We find neither of these views acceptable. The past performance of redistributive policy does not make us confident that the undesired redistributive consequences of environmental programs will somehow be offset.

[27] Perry Shapiro, "Voting and the Incidence of Public Policy: An Operations Model and an Example of an Environment Referendum," Working Paper in Economics #8, University of California at Santa Barbara, (May, 1972). In several subsequent studies of voting patterns on other environmental issues, Professor Shapiro has obtained very similar results.

[28] *Ibid.*, pp. 1–2.

Moreover, at a more pragmatic level, the failure to redress at least the most glaring redistributive insults will generate strong opposition to the adoption of appropriate environmental programs.

On the other hand, postponement of environmental measures is not an appealing option. If these are vital matters of public health and perhaps ultimately of survival, even the poorest citizen may not have much reason to thank the legislator who resists effective action, even if it apparently is resisted for his sake. The issues of allocation raised by the literature on externalities cannot be brushed aside lightly on distributive grounds.

What this suggests to us is the need to incorporate sensible redistributive provisions into environmental programs, both as a matter of justice and as a means to enhance their political feasibility. We should not, however, lose sight of the fact *that the primary purpose of environmental programs is allocative:* their basic rationale is the direction of resource use to achieve desired levels of environmental quality.[29] We are inclined to agree with Freeman's contention that environmental programs are generally not very well suited to the achievement of distributional objectives.[30]

The goal should rather be to neutralize the more serious of the objectionable redistributive consequences of our environmental policies. Two promising lines of strategy have been suggested. First, as we noted earlier, the most drastic redistributive effects are likely to occur during periods of transition with individuals displaced from jobs in badly located, heavily polluting plants. Such transition problems can be met, at least in part, by the use of *adjustment assistance*, outlays common under legislation to reduce tariffs; such provisions typically offer unemployment compensation, retraining programs, and relocation assistance to minimize the costs to those displaced by the altered patterns of output and employment resulting from the legislation. Adjustment assistance can be an important component in an aggressive program of environmental protection, a component that would spread the transition costs of the program more evenly across society.

Second, we have suggested that the continuing costs of environmental measures are likely to have a somewhat regressive pattern of incidence. To offset this to some extent, Roberts has argued that, where public expenditures are necessary to finance certain parts of environmental programs (for example, the construction of dams, treatment facilities, and so on), they be funded largely by revenues collected by the federal government.[31] Roberts's point is that, because the federal tax system is more progressive than most state and

---

[29] This is admittedly a tricky issue. As Henry Aaron and Martin McGuire show at a formal level, the appropriate level of provision of a public good can, under certain circumstances, become, largely, an ethical decision. See their "Efficiency and Equity in the Optimal Supply of a Public Good," *Review of Economics and Statistics* LI (February, 1969), 31–39.

[30] Freeman, "Distribution of Environmental Quality," pp. 274–78.

[31] Roberts, "Who Will Pay for Cleaner Power?" p. 36.

local taxes, this serves to allocate at least some of the costs in a more propoor manner. This approach does have substantial appeal, although as we mentioned earlier, it is the progressiveness of incremental revenue collections that is important here; one might expect, however, that at the margin (as well as on the average), federal revenues are likely to be generated in a more progressive manner than state and local funds.

chapter 14

International
Environmental Issues[1]

Almost invariably, public discussion of programs for the protection of the environment has emphasized their international implications. Two central issues have emerged from the debates. First, questions have been raised about the effects upon the competitive position in international trade of the country undertaking the program. It has been suggested, particularly by representatives of industries likely to bear the costs, that the proposed measures would impose on exporters a severe handicap in world markets that is certain to have an adverse effect on the nation's balance of payments, its employment levels, and its GNP. This problem has proved particularly frightening to the less-affluent nations, but even in wealthy countries it has been a persistent concern.

The second issue in this area is quite a different matter; it involves the transportation across national boundaries, not of commodities desired by the recipient nation, but of pollutants whose influx it seems powerless to prevent. Although there is a good deal of talk of international cooperation in the control of transnational pollution, joint programs like those we have already discussed will undoubtedly prove difficult to institute. Therefore, it is important to consider whether the victim nation can do anything to protect itself in the absence of something better in the form of effective collective measures. Obviously, where international cooperation *can* be achieved, the

[1] Much of this chapter is taken from the 1971 Wicksell Lectures, W. Baumol, "Environmental Protection, Spillovers and International Trade" (Stockholm: Almqvist and Wiksell, 1971).

213

theoretical analysis that has been described in earlier chapters applies equally to international and domestic policy. It is only in the absence of joint action that an analysis of special measures for an effective international policy is required.

International trade theory offers some illumination on both these issues. Accordingly, this chapter is divided into two largely unrelated parts. The first examines the effects of a domestic pollution control program on the initiating country's balance of payments and on international patterns of specialization; the second part concerns itself with transnational pollution issues. To avoid unnecessary complications, we will assume away each problem in turn when discussing the other. That is, when examining the balance of payments and related issues, we will assume that the pollution in question remains within the borders of the country that generates it, and in discussing transnational pollution problems, we will ignore the issues relating to specialization and trade considered in the first part of the chapter.

1.   DOMESTIC EXTERNALITIES AND TRADE OBJECTIVES

Just as the management of an individual firm may feel that it cannot undertake unilateral measures to reduce its emission of pollutants for fear of being priced out of the market by its competitors, as a matter of national policy, a government may be reluctant to institute significant pollution control measures for fear of the effects on its production costs and hence on its balance of trade.[2] Our objective in this section is to examine what theoretical analysis can tell us about the validity of such fears.

Let us then consider a world composed of two countries, i and w, which it may be suggestive to think of as a more impecunious and a wealthier country, respectively, though that interpretation plays no role in our formal analysis. In our model each country produces, among other goods, a commodity, D, whose production can, *but need not*, be dirty. Suppose for example that, unless preventive measures are taken, D generates smoke, all of which

---

[2] Some very preliminary calculations by Ralph C. d'Arge and Allen V. Kneese suggest that the trade and income consequences of the imposition of strong environmental controls would, in some cases, be very substantial though they would differ from country to country. On the basis of data consisting partly of available statistics and partly of very rough guesses, they estimate that each of the countries examined would experience about the same relative increase in export prices, something on the order of a 3.5 to a 9 percent rise. However, assuming that a country were to impose environmental protection measures unilaterally, the effect on gross national income varied considerably from country to country. In several cases, the effects were negligible, but in others, the loss in income exceeded 25 percent. See Allen V. Kneese, "The Economics of Environmental Management in the United States," in *Managing the Environment: International Economic Cooperation for Pollution Control*, Allen V. Kneese, Sidney E. Rolfe, and Joseph W. Harned, eds., (New York: Praeger Publishers, 1971), pp. 3–52.

falls in the vicinity of the factory. We assume that there exists a method of producing D that is smokeless but more expensive than the alternative production method. Assume that country w has already chosen its environmental policy, say it prohibits the production of D by the smoky method. Our central concern is the effect of the decision of the other country, i, between a policy of controls and no controls. In the next two sections we examine the (short-run) consequences of this unilateral choice for the balance of payments in i and for the demand for employment of its labor. Then, a later section considers the more permanent effects on international patterns of specialization (that is, on the types of industry located in the two countries).

We are concerned, then, with a comparative-statics question: the difference in its foreign exchange earnings and employment levels that will result if i decides to continue its cheap but smoky production methods as against the smokeless alternative. The shorter-run effects on balance of payments and employment have attracted the bulk of public attention, and they also happen to lend themselves to formal analysis. Consequently, they will occupy most of our discussion. However, it is the longer-run consequences for specialization patterns that, we believe, will have the more profound consequences for the welfare of the nations concerned, and they deserve more attention than they seem to have received.

2. SHORTER-RUN EFFECTS

Figures 14–1a and 14–1b are the standard supply-demand diagrams used to examine such issues in a partial analysis. In the case of country i, two alternative supply curves are considered: the lower curve, S_{ic}, corre-

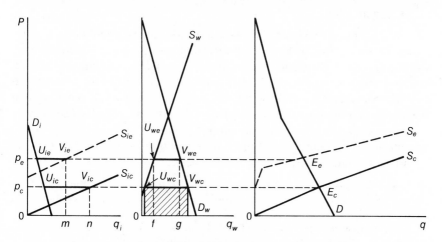

FIG. 14–1a, b, & c

sponds to the cheap, dirty method of production, and S_{ie}, the higher broken curve, corresponds to the choice of the expensive production process in which pollution is eliminated.

Ignoring differences introduced by transportation costs, tariffs, and the like, we shall assume in our discussion that p, the price of D, is the same in both countries. This premise simplifies the analysis but does not really alter its substance. Figure 14–1c then represents total supply and demand in the two countries together, corresponding to each alternative price. There are two total supply curves, one corresponding to each of the alternatives available to i. The solid combined supply curve, S_c, corresponds to the case where i decides to keep its costs low by not prohibiting pollution. The corresponding international equilibrium point is E_c, and it yields equilibrium price p_c. In the diagrams as drawn, at this price, i is a net exporter of D, shipping out quantity $U_{ic}V_{ic}$ (with w, clearly, importing the same amount). Similar magnitudes correspond to the expensive production case. We obtain the following conclusions whose derivation will be examined in the following section:

1. In general, we may expect that a decision by i to use the less expensive (dirty) production process will keep down the world price of the commodity (p_c lower than p_e). This will be true so long as the supply curves have positive slopes or, if those slopes are negative, so long as they are less steep than the demand curves.[3]

2. World demand for the commodity, and the demand for it in each country, will be higher as a result of the lower price. The higher world demand when the cheaper production method is employed is indicated in Figure 14–1c by the position of E_c, which lies to the right of E_e. Similarly, the rise in quantity demanded in country w is indicated by the comparative position of V_{wc} and V_{we}, and so on.

3. Country i will certainly produce more of the commodity if it refrains from adoption of the more expensive process, because the lower price will increase both domestic demand (from U_{ie} to U_{ic} in Figure 14–1a) and foreign import demand (from $U_{we}V_{we}$ to $U_{wc}V_{wc}$ in Figure 14–1b). As a corollary of items 2 and 3, we have the not very surprising result that the total world emission of pollutants is likely to be increased as a result of country i's failure to undertake the pollution control program, for with greater world demand for commodity D and more of it produced by the dirty process in country i, the output of pollutant can be expected to be increased.

4. However, employment in industry D of country i may fall as a result. Although more of the commodity will be produced, less labor (and

---

[3] To be a bit more precise, we will show in the next section that this result requires the sum of the slopes of the supply curves to exceed the sum of the slopes of the two demand curves.

other inputs) will very likely be required per unit of output and so it is conceivable, at least in principle, that the net consequence will be a decline in employment.[4] In Figure 14–1a, the total cost of i's production of D with the cheaper polluting process is represented by the rectangle $OnV_{ic}p_c$. Similarly, with the more expensive process, the corresponding rectangle is $OmV_{ie}p_e$. The relative magnitude of the rectangles depends on the slopes of the alternative supply curves for country i and the distance between them, and one cannot generalize about their relative sizes. The effects on country i's wage bill will therefore also be indeterminate. Specifically, we know that total expenditures on output in i will fall when its price is lowered if domestic demand for D and foreign import demand for D are both price inelastic, so we may expect that, in the absence of other measures to keep up the level of employment, in these circumstances, demand for labor will also fall.[5]

5.   Whether i's foreign currency earnings are increased by failure to introduce pollution control must be considered separately for the case where it is a net importer and that where it is a net exporter of the item.

a)   If i is a net importer of D, the fact that its domestic cost of production has been kept down means that the cost of its imports must have been held down as well. This reduced cost results in the production of more D in i and less in w. Note that the marginal costs of producing D in the two countries will (neglecting transport costs) remain equal despite the more costly production process used by w. By keeping down both the amount of its imports and the price of what it does continue to import, it follows that i will gain in terms of its foreign exchange position.[6]

b)   If i is a net exporter of D, it is no longer clear that the adoption of the dirty method of production will increase its net foreign exchange earnings.[7] True, it will now export more than if it had banned smoky production processes within its borders. But it also receives a lower price for its product. Hence, its exchange position will have improved only if w's price elasticity of demand for imports of D is greater than unity. Otherwise, i may actually

---

[4] This is not meant to suggest that environmental policy is the appropriate means to deal with employment issues. But complete disregard of its employment consequences is equally inappropriate.

[5] Of course, this need not be the case if the clean method of production is less labor-intensive than the dirty technique.

[6] This abstracts from side effects on exports and imports of the other good, C. If, for example, pollution control raises the world price of D, demand may shift to C. If i is the exporter of C, then this could conceivably swamp the worsening of its import position described in the text.

[7] It is noteworthy that the d'Arge-Kneese estimates of the trade effects of environmental protection measures, which were mentioned earlier, suggest that for virtually all of the countries studied, the result of their unilateral adoption would be an *improvement* in the trade balance! That is, the country that refused to institute such measures would very likely *lose* in terms of its exchange position. Of course, the calculations were very rough, as the authors are careful to stress.

earn a smaller quantity of foreign exchange for its exports.[8] We see, in Figure 14–1b, that receipts of foreign exchange will be less under the smoky production technique if the shaded area, representing the total import expenditure on D by w at the lower price, is smaller than the area of the corresponding rectangle at the higher price, the rectangle $U_{we}V_{we}gf$.

In sum, what appear to be obvious consequences of pollution controls by our poorer country are by no means as certain as widely supposed. A decision by its government that leads to elimination of the polluting production process *may* produce a deterioration in its balance of payments and an increase in domestic unemployment, but neither of these is a foregone conclusion. Without examining the relevant elasticities, it is never safe to argue that a rise in production cost and price will lead to a reduction in revenues and input demand.[9]

3.   FORMALIZATION OF THE SHORTER-RUN ANALYSIS

We will now generalize somewhat the arguments of the preceding section, though we continue to utilize a partial analysis in the sense that we will ignore the effects of changes in the price of the polluting commodity on the exports, imports, and price of the other commodity. We use the following notation:

$$p = \text{price}$$
$$D^i(p), D^w(p) = \text{demand for the commodity in } i \text{ and } w, \text{ respectively}$$
$$S^i(p, a), S^w(p) = \text{the supply functions in } i \text{ and } w, \text{ respectively,}$$

where a is a shift parameter representing the cost of pollution control. We may assume:

$$S_a^i = \frac{\partial S^i(p, a)}{\partial a} < 0. \tag{1}$$

That is, all other things being equal, the higher the cost of pollution control, the lower will be the quantity of product supplied by i at any given product price.

---

[8] There is an obvious difference here between the price set by competitive export and import industries and the administered price set by a firm with monopoly power. Ordinarily, the latter will not end up in the inelastic range of the demand curve for his product, but it is perfectly possible for the equilibrium output of the former to fall within the inelastic portion of the industry demand curve. That is why we have the paradoxical result that a country may be able to improve its financial position by "reducing its cost efficiency," as one reader put the issue.

[9] Though it should be noted that those "obvious" conclusions do hold for the classical small country case, the elasticity of demand for whose exports is infinite.

International equilibrium obviously requires equality of total supply and demand for the product in question:

$$S^i(p, a) + S^w(p) = D^i(p) + D^w(p). \tag{2}$$

To determine the effect of a change in the cost of i's production process, assuming that equilibrium is then reestablished, we change the value of a and investigate the equilibrating change in p. Thus, we differentiate (2) totally with respect to a and p to obtain

$$S^i_a \, da - (D^i_p + D^w_p - S^i_p - S^w_p) \, dp = 0$$

where S^i_p represents $\partial S^i(p, a)/\partial p$, and so on,
or

$$dp/da = S^i_a/(D^i_p + D^w_p - S^i_p - S^w_p). \tag{3}$$

With negatively sloping demand curves, we have $D^i_p < 0$, $D^w_p < 0$ and, by (1), $S^i_a < 0$. Hence, if the supply curves are upward sloping, dp/da will certainly be positive. More generally,

$$\frac{dp}{da} > 0 \quad \text{if} \quad S^i_p + S^w_p > D^i_p + D^w_p. \tag{4}$$

We conclude from (4),

Proposition One. If i selects a less expensive process, so that $da < 0$, then the world price of the commodity may be expected to decline. It follows as a corollary that with D^i_p and D^w_p both negative, demand for the item in each of the countries must rise.

It is usually assumed that

$$D^w_p - S^w_p < 0. \tag{5}$$

That is, a rise in price will lead to a decline in w's imports (i's exports) of the item.

Because i's export quantity is $D^w - S^w$, its foreign exchange receipts from its sales of the good will be

$$R^i = p(D^w - S^w). \tag{6}$$

Differentiating, we have

$$dR^i/da = [p(D^w_p - S^w_p) + (D^w - S^w)]\frac{dp}{da}.$$

By (4) and (5), dR^i/da will be negative if $(D^w - S^w)$ is negative (if i is a net importer of the commodity). That is,

Proposition Two(a). If i is a net importer of the commodity, i will always improve its balance of trade by reducing unit costs and price.

However, if $(D^w - S^w) > 0$ so that i is a net exporter of the item, its trade balance may or may not improve from the resulting reduction in the world price of the commodity because dR^i/da may then be either positive or negative. Thus:

Proposition Two(b). If it is a net exporter of the item, country i will gain in its foreign exchange receipts when it keeps down its costs of producing the commodity if and only if w's import demand is elastic, so that a decline in price increases i's receipts as given by expression (6).

We also have

Proposition Three. Output of the commodity in country i can be expected to be higher if it selects the lower cost process of production.

For, in equilibrium, by (2),

$$dS^i/da = [D_p^i + (D_p^w - S_p^w)] \frac{dp}{da} < 0, \qquad (7)$$

whose sign follows from (4), (5), and the negative slope of i's demand curve, $D^i(p)$. By (7), a fall in cost in country i ($da < 0$) will lead to an increase in its equilibrium output, S^i, as asserted.

Finally, we show that

Proposition Four. A decrease in country i's costs of producing output D may not produce a net increase in employment.[10]

If, for example, wages in i remain unchanged, and a constant proportion of expenditure on commodity i is spent on labor, employment in i devoted to commodity D is given by kpS^i for some constant, k. In equilibrium, this employment is equal to

$$kpS^i(p, a) = k[pD^i + p(D^w - S^w)], \qquad (8)$$

where the first term inside the brackets is total revenue from domestic sales of the item, and the remaining expression inside the brackets represents total revenue from exports. Obviously, if both demands are price inelastic, these

---

[10] The decrease in employment will, of course, be accounted for by the decreased use of labor for pollution control, which means that there will be an indirect decline in the quantity of labor utilized per unit of output of D.

will both decline in value when p is reduced as the result of a decrease in a; in that case, employment in this industry in i will decline.

This result is consistent with (7) which requires output to increase when a declines, for the less expensive (more polluting) process may well require less labor (as well as other inputs) per unit of output. Specifically, if we define $L(a)$ as the number of labor hours used per unit of output, our employment demand becomes $L(a)S^i(p, a)$, and $d[L(a)S^i(p, a)]/da = L(a)\, dS^i/da + S^i L_a$. Because L_a may plausibly be taken to be positive, the sign of this expression is indeterminate for, by (7), the first term is negative,[11] but the second will then be positive.

4. LONGER-RUN CONSEQUENCES FOR SPECIALIZATION PATTERNS

The choice of technique of production also has longer-run implications for the international pattern of specialization. We recall that implicit in our model is the production of other goods, some of which presumably are not sources of significant damage to the environment. Let C be the collective designation of such items whose production generates no external costs. By not eliminating its smoke, i will affect the private comparative costs in the two countries: at any given levels of output, w will have less of a comparative cost advantage in the supply of D than it would otherwise. Unless the additional marginal cost of producing D by low pollution methods is completely covered by subsidy, w will be led permanently to produce more of the clean commodity, C, and less of D, than it would [12] if i were to adopt pollution controls for the manufacture of D, and the reverse will be true in country i.

Thus, we have the obvious but very important

Proposition Five. A country that fails to undertake an environmental protection program when other countries do so increases its comparative advantage (decreases its comparative disadvantage) in the production of items that damage its environment; in the absence of offsetting subsidies, this will encourage greater specialization in the production of these polluting outputs.

In sum, as a result of its failure to limit pollution, country i will tend to become specialized more than it would have otherwise in the production of items that generate pollutants. In particular, less-developed countries that choose uncontrolled domestic pollution as a means to improve their economic

[11] Note that the first term contains dS^i/da, not $S^i_a = \partial S^i/\partial a$. It thus includes the indirect effect of a on price, as taken into account in (7).

[12] This is, of course, just a special case of the general proposition on comparative costs and international patterns of specialization.

position will voluntarily become the repository of the world's dirty industries. This means that they will undertake to provide benefits to everyone else by taking on the world's dirty work. The willingness of the poorer nations to bear the social costs produces effects analogous to those that would result from an increase in productivity in the manufacture of polluting outputs. However, this apparent increase in productivity is more accurately described as a peculiar export subsidy, one that conceals, more effectively than most, what the exporting country is giving away to its customers.

5. POLICY FOR EXTERNALITIES THAT CROSS A NATION'S BORDERS

We turn now to the second major issue considered in this chapter: the problem of transnational pollution. In international trade, a tariff plays somewhat the same role as an excise tax for domestic outputs. It would thus seem that, where some import generates costs that are external to the exporting country and that fall on persons in the country in which the good is imported, a tariff on the offending commodity may, at least in principle, become an appropriate instrument to deal with the problem.

It will be argued that such a second-best tariff usually exists, provided the country that is the victim of the externality is also an importer of the commodity whose production process generates it, and that the victim nation has market power sufficient to influence, through its tariffs, the prices (outputs) in the generating country.

As we will see, the tariff that best protects the interests of the importing country is not necessarily the one that yields an (second-best) optimal allocation of resources for the world as a whole. In part, this is just an extension of the observation that, in the absence of externalities, a tariff may be beneficial to the country that imposes it even if it should be undesirable when considered from a more cosmopolitan point of view. We turn consequently to an examination, first, of the tariff level that best protects the victim of a transnational externality, and, second, to the tariff levels that can help to sustain a (second-best) Pareto optimum when the polluting country does not attempt to regulate its emissions or at least does not take adequate account of the effects on the victim nation.

We begin by observing that although a tariff can play somewhat the same role for transnational externalities that a Pigouvian tax performs within a single political jurisdiction, the former will generally not be a perfectly satisfactory substitute for the latter. Thus, suppose that the polluting country enacts an emissions tax based on marginal damage within its borders, and each other affected country imposes a tariff equal to the marginal damage suffered by its own nationals. The resulting set of taxes and tariffs will not generally yield the prices and the allocation of resources that would have resulted if the polluting country had imposed an internationally optimal Pigouvian tax on its emissions—a tax equal to marginal damage in all countries together.

There are several reasons why the two will not be equivalent. First, in the emitting country, prices will not be affected *directly* by duties in countries that import the product.[13] Hence, domestic prices in the producing nation will be different (usually lower) than if producers had been taxed for damage they impose anywhere in the world.[14] Second, the duty in any importing nation will also reflect only those detrimental effects of the externality that fall within its borders, so that its nationals, too, will pay less than the full social costs of their consumption. An extreme case is that in which country *A* produces the externality, country *B* suffers from the externality but imports none of the item whose manufacture generates it, and country *C* imports the item from *A* but receives none of the damage. In that case, there will be no tariff levied on the item in response to its emissions, despite the transnational character of its effects.

Thus, our analysis of appropriate tariff policy will generally be a discussion falling within the theory of the second-best, for no set of tariffs will be capable of sustaining the Pareto optimum that would be yielded by the optimal Pigouvian taxes.

For reasons analogous to those for our discussion in Chapter 6 of the quasi-optimal allocation of resources in the presence of a monopoly, we have found a diagrammatic approach to this issue more fruitful than a more formal analysis. For we are dealing with a second-best problem in which resource allocation is constrained by the nonoptimal behavior of one of the countries, and so any maximization calculation will be complicated considerably by the behavioral relations that must consequently be included among its constraints.

Even the diagrammatic construction is not completely elementary, because the problem is one in which consumption in one country increases *production* in another, and that, in turn, raises the transnational flow of pollutants. As a result, we cannot use an Edgworth-Bowley box diagram that takes the total quantities of commodities produced to be given. After all, the purpose of the tariff is to control the flow of pollutants via its effect on the polluting output, and so an analysis of the problem cannot assume away the possibility of output changes. Fortunately, Meade has provided an ingenious

[13] Of course, the tariff will affect excess demand in the world as a whole and so it will influence prices in other countries, but although this effect can be important, it is an indirect consequence of the duty, differing fundamentally from that of an equal tax imposed on all consumers.

[14] Put in a different way, with optimal Pigouvian taxes, relative commodity prices are the same for all consumers, but with any tariff, relative prices will differ in the exporting and the importing country and that is clearly inconsistent with Pareto optimality.

modification of the box diagram that permits production changes to be taken into account.[15] For this purpose, he transforms the social consumption indifference curves into what have been described as *trade indifference curves* corresponding to the possible exchange positions of the two countries after both their exchange and their production decisions have been made.

Because the device is not as widely known as the ordinary box diagram, it will perhaps be useful to summarize its construction briefly. In Figure 14–2, let the points in quadrant I represent the consumption of the two goods

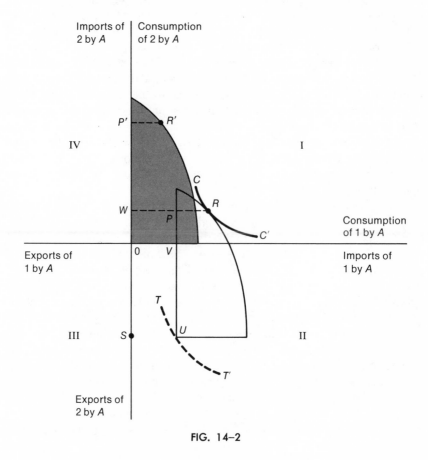

FIG. 14–2

in country A, and let the shaded area represent A's production-possibility set. Now consider any point in this quadrant, such as R. If R is to be an equilibrium point, the ratio of prices of the two goods must be given by the

[15] See James E. Meade, *A Geometry of International Trade* (London: Allen and Unwin, 1952), Chapters i–iv.

slope at that point of CC', the consumption indifference curve of A through R. Similarly, the equilibrium outputs of the two commodities in A will be given by R', the point with the same slope on A's possibility locus. To determine what exports and imports will be required to permit the consumption represented by R when production is represented by R', we now interpret the axes of the diagram to represent imports and exports (negative imports) of the two items. Next, we shift the axes of the production-possibility set until the set is tangent to CC' at R. We see at once that, because at the equilibrium corresponding to R, quantity $P'R' = PR$ of item 1 is produced while WR is consumed, the difference $WP = SU$ of item 1 must be imported.

In exactly the same way, it follows at once that in these circumstances A can export VU of item 2. Hence point U, the shifted origin of the production-possibility set, indicates the export-import combination corresponding to consumption at point R in country A. Repeating this construction for other points on the consumption indifference curve CC', we obtain the locus TT', which is the corresponding trade indifference curve that we wanted to construct. That is, any point on TT' represents a combination of imports and exports that permits A to consume a combination of goods represented by a corresponding point on CC'.

6. ALTERNATIVE TARIFF POLICIES FOR TRANSNATIONAL POLLUTION [16]

In the following discussion, it will be assumed that item 1 is a good whose output produces transnational pollution affecting A, and that A is an

[16] A simplified formalization of the issue may help to clarify the nature of the discussion that follows. We have two commodities, 1 and 2, and two countries, A and B, and we let

x_{1a} = consumption of good 1 in country A, and so on,
$z = z(x_{1a}, x_{1b})$ = the output of pollutant,
$U^a = U^a(x_{1a}, x_{2a}, z)$ and
$U^b = U^b(x_{1b}, x_{2b}, z)$ be social utility functions for countries A and B respectively.

We will examine, at least cursorily, each of the following three maximization problems for country A acting alone:
    (i) Maximization of A's welfare with no consideration of effects on B; this involves the choice of a tariff level by A by simply maximizing U^a;
    (ii) Imposition of a "Pareto-optimal" tariff. This is the second-best tariff that

$$\text{maximizes } U^a(\cdot)$$
$$\text{subject to } U^b(x_{1b}, x_{2b}, z) \geq U^{*b} \text{ (some constant);}$$

    (iii) Imposition of a *quasi*-Pareto-optimal tariff that takes no account of the social cost of the externality in B, on the grounds that, by adopting no externality control measures, B has, in effect, chosen politically the utility function $U^b(x_{1b}, x_{2b}, 0)$, which assumes away emissions damage. This then calls for

importer of good 1 and an exporter of 2. Hence, the following diagrams will correspond to quadrant II of Figure 14–2.

In Figure 14–3, an abscissa, q_{1a}, represents A's imports of 1, the ex-

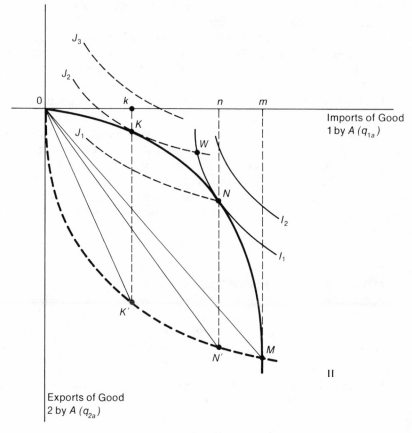

FIG. 14–3

ternality-generating good,[17] and q_{2a} represents its exports of good 2. The initial (zero trade) point is, of course, the origin. The lower, broken offer

maximization of $U^a(\cdot)$
subject to $U^b(x_{1b}, x_{2b}, 0) \geq U^{*b}$ (constant).

For reasons that will be indicated later, most of our discussions will deal with cases (i) and (iii) because there is relatively little we are able to say about case (ii).

[17] We deliberately change our notation from that used in earlier sections in this chapter to emphasize that 1 is an output that generates *transnational* pollution; in contrast, the effects of D, the polluting good of Sections 1–4, were taken to remain entirely within the boundaries of the country that produces it.

curve, $OK'N'M$, is that of A, the importer[18] of 1, and the solid upper offer curve, $OKNM$, is that of the exporting country. Point M is, as usual, the free-trade equilibrium point, and m is then the quantity of item 1 imported.

First, suppose that A decides to levy a tariff that is designed to exploit B but that does not take pollution into account. Let the curves labelled I_i represent the family of A's trade indifference curves relating exclusively to the private benefits of the imports to A's consumers of 1. Given the shape of B's offer curve, and assuming, as is usual in such models, that the exporting country is passive and does nothing to protect itself from exploitation by the importing nation, it follows that country A maximizes its own welfare at N, the point of tangency between the exporting country's offer curve and one of A's indifference curves. This point can be attained by A's imposing an import duty sufficient to restrict the import demand to n. This involves a change in relative prices from that given by the slope of price line OM to that given by ON', where N' is the point on A's offer curve corresponding to import level n.

So far, this is all review of the standard analysis of the "optimum" [19] tariff. Now let us see what happens if the pollution (say, smoke) arising from the externalities is taken into account. We can construct a new family of community indifference curves taking cognizance of *all* of the costs imposed by q_{1a}. The external cost (indirectly) generated by q_{1a} can be interpreted to mean that the relative social marginal utility of 1 is smaller than its relative private

[18] The importing country's offer curve, of course, represents what it *would* be willing to exchange if its international trade were carried out under conditions of pure competition without governmental interference. Because the remainder of the discussion examines the effects of a tariff by the importing country, its offer curve is relevant largely as a standard of comparison to show how the free-trade solution differs from that in which a tariff is imposed. Assuming that industry in A is competitive, however, the offer curve continues to indicate the internal prices (after payment of duty) necessary to restrict the import demand for 1 to any given level.

[19] In the literature, the tariff level that maximizes a country's monopolistic gains from trade is often referred to as *the optimum tariff*. Obviously, this does not correspond to a universal welfare maximum of any sort. In the remainder of the chapter, when we refer to a tariff as optimal we will mean that it can sustain a Pareto-optimal position for the affected countries, or at least one that is second-best.

One advantage in using the standard *optimum tariff* as a starting point for our discussion of the second-best tariff level in the presence of externalities is that it does suggest an important relationship between the two. Both of them require a degree of influence on international prices by the country that imposes them. If that country is so small that its actions do not affect the prices of the countries that export to it, then both the optimum and the second-best tariff levels will be zero.

The method of analysis adopted here, comparing levels of optimal protection, is the method employed by Bhagwati and others to examine a variety of problems in trade theory. There is, indeed, a large class of problems that can best be explored by starting with an optimum tariff rather than free trade, in order to avoid confusing the consequences of departing from free trade with the consequences of the particular problem under study. See Jagdish N. Bhagwati, "Optimal Policies and Immiserizing Growth," *American Economic Review* LIX, no. 5 (December, 1969), 967–70.

utility,[20] because an increase in q_{1a} induces greater *production* of good 1 by the exporter, B, and hence increases the transnational pollution suffered in A.

Because the slope of an indifference curve for two commodities 1 and 2 at any point is equal in absolute value to mu_1/mu_2, the ratio of the marginal utilities of the two commodities at that point, it follows that through any point W in Figure 14–3, there will be what we may call the *social* indifference curve J_i (the curve that takes externalities into account), which will be flatter[21] than the *private* community indifference curve, I_i, through that point. Figure 14–3 depicts a family of such social indifference curves, the curves labelled $J_i(i = 1, 2, 3)$. The exporter's offer curve, $0KNM$, has, on the usual assumptions, been drawn concave downward. This implies that the point of tangency, K, between this offer curve and one of the social indifference curves must lie to the left of N, the point of tangency with a private community indifference curve. Curve J_1, the J curve through point N, lies below the offer curve to the left of point N, and so better points from the importer's point of view must also lie to the left of N. The tariff corresponding to K is, as before, indicated by the relative slope of $0K'$, the price line through K'. Because $0K'$ is steeper than $0N'$, the tariff for A now generates an even greater departure from the price ratio than would emerge under free trade. That is,

Proposition Six.   The tariff that maximizes the importing nation's net gain in the presence of external costs imposed by the imports is higher than that which would do so in the absence of externalities, all other things being equal.

So much for the interests of the country that levies the tariff. We turn now to a somewhat less parochial view of the matter. Figure 14–4 depicts two contract curves—the locus of what may be called "quasi-Pareto-optimal points" corresponding to the cases where the transnational externalities are not, and that in which they are, taken into account. The curves labelled E are the community indifference curves of the exporting country, which are taken to be based on private preferences in B and to ignore external damage in that country.[22] Once again, the I and the J curves are the community indifference curves of A, the importing country, corresponding respectively

---

[20] Here it seems easier to take the pollution resulting from increased output of item 1 to affect the indifference curves through the disutility it imposes on consumers rather than the production of other goods. Of course, the externalities may also affect the production-possibility locus by increasing the resources cost of some (or all) outputs.

[21] Reverting to the notation of an earlier footnote, $U^a[x_{1a},x_{2a},z(x_{1a},x_{1b})]$ is A's utility function. Then the absolute value of the slope of the indifference curves II' that ignore the externality is U_1^a/U_2^a. That of the JJ' indifference curves is $(U_1^a + U_z^a \partial z/\partial x_{1a})/U_2^a$, which takes into account the smoke damage resulting from increased production of good 1. Because smoke creates a disutility, $U_z^a < 0$, so we may expect the second fraction to be smaller than the first; that is, the JJ' curves can be expected to be flatter than the II'.

[22] In terms of the first footnote of this section, we are dealing with case (iii) in which B's (implicit?) political decision to ignore domestic external effects is respected.

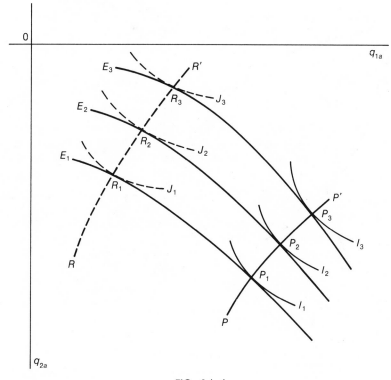

FIG. 14–4

to the cases where externalities are not, and are, included in A's welfare calculations. Because the former are steeper than the latter, the tangency point, P_i, of one of the I curves with an E curve will lie to the right of R_i, the point of tangency of a J curve with the same E curve. Hence, contract curve RR', the locus of all the R_i tangency points that take externalities into account, will be entirely to the left of PP', the contract curve that ignores the externalities.[23]

In Figure 14–5, these two contract curves are brought together with the two offer curves. In accord with the usual argument, the free-market equilibrium point, M, at which the two offer curves intersect, lies on the zero externalities contract curve, PP'. But because externalities *are* in fact present,

[23] As we have noted, this argument takes into account only the externalities that fall on the importing country, A. By showing the effects of the externalities on the E curves, we can also take account of effect on B. It follows by the same argument as before that the external damage yielded by production of item 1 will flatten B's as well as A's indifference curves, so that it becomes very difficult to say much about the position of RR'. The argument of Chapter 7 shows that, with appropriate convexity assumptions, RR' will still lie *somewhere* to the left of PP' (that is, some reduction in use of commodity 1 will be required for Pareto optimality). Hence, some positive tariff will still be appropriate.

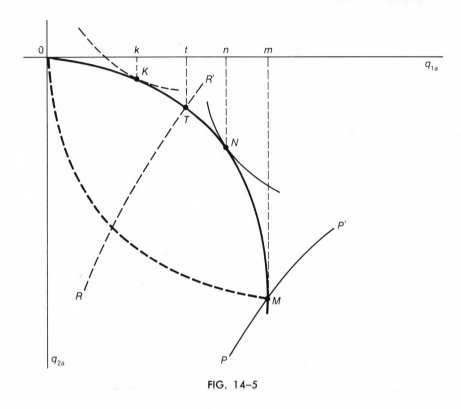

FIG. 14–5

there is nothing optimal or necessarily desirable about points on this pseudo-contract locus. The optimal point on the exporting country's offer curve (which we continue to take as given) is T, the intersection point of that offer curve with RR', the true locus of Pareto-optimal points. Clearly, this must lie to the left of the market-equilibrium point, M.

As a final step in our diagrammatic discussion of tariffs and externalities, we can now relate these two points, M and T, to the points N and K of Figure 14-3 that ignored the interests of country B. As we know, point N must lie to the left of M. For exactly the same reason, K must lie to the left of T. For T is simply the market-equilibrium point that would prevail (with an appropriate distribution of income) if market prices were adjusted to reflect the full values of the social costs of goods 1 and 2, and K is the point that corresponds to N in these circumstances.[24] It follows that k, the level of

---

[24] Incidentally, there seems to be no general statement that we can offer about the relative positions of points N and T. Both must lie on $MNK0$ between points M and K, but which will lie to the right of the other depends upon the comparative shapes of the families of indifference curves I and J in a manner that is not generally predictable. In brief, we cannot say whether the tariff that maximizes A's welfare (with externalities ignored) by

importation that best serves the importing country's interests, will be smaller than t, the internationally optimal level of imports. Thus we obtain

Proposition Seven. If the external effects fall entirely on the importing country, the internationally quasi-optimal tariff (corresponding to T) will be smaller than that (associated with point K) which maximizes the importing country's total gain from exploitation of its monopoly position.

We see from this rather lengthy diagrammatic discussion that the presence of external costs can, at least in principle, affect the role of tariffs. We have the basic result

Proposition Eight. In the presence of transnational pollution with no collective regulation, zero tariff levels are generally not optimal.

In the presence of external costs, a tariff sufficient to reduce imports from m to t in Figure 14–5 will be required for the purpose.[25] Moreover, the narrow self-interests of the importing country will also call for a tariff higher than that which would be appropriate in the absence of externalities. In Figure 14–5, the tariff level must exceed that which would apply in the absence of externalities by an amount sufficient to reduce the imports of good 1 from n to k. In general, if the externalities generated by the imports affect only the importing country, the tariff that is best from the point of view of both countries together will be less than that which maximizes the returns to the importing country alone.[26]

It should be noted once again, in concluding, that even the Pareto-optimal tariff, that corresponding to point T in our discussion, will only sustain a second-best optimum, not the optimum that could have been achieved by a set of internationally optimal Pigouvian taxes in the country where the externality is generated. For the tariff restricts consumption of the externality-generating good in the importing country, but it does not restrict corresponding consumption of the item within the country that exports both the good and the pollution. Consequently, such a duty must inevitably distort international consumption patterns. It is a desirable policy measure only if a more direct attack on the problem is not possible.

---

manipulation of the terms of trade is greater or less than the internationally optimal tariff with external effects accounted for.

[25] This suggests also that where external benefits are present, a negative tariff may be appropriate.

[26] However, even this conclusion can no longer be taken for granted if the exports also impose unregulated pollution costs in the exporting country (for reasons indicated in footnote 23).

7. TRANSNATIONAL POLLUTION CHARGES AS INSTRUMENTS OF PRACTICAL POLICY [27]

We have seen that the adoption of a second-best duty, in principle, will be useful for a country whose transnational pollution problems are in part generated by its own imports, and whose market power is substantial. Moreover, refined optimality calculations, such as those just discussed, are likely to have little bearing in practice on the use of import duties as a means to control transnational environmental damage. But all this does not mean that the approach itself has little relevance in application. Where an exchange process has a relatively small number of participants, as in international trade or in oligopoly situations, prices can affect resource allocation in at least two different ways. First, they influence the pattern of excess demands and, hence, relative outputs in the usual way. Second, pricing policy can serve as part of a strategy in which one participant threatens to undertake price-influencing measures that would be damaging to some other participant in order to force the latter to modify his behavior. This section considers tariffs both in the role normally assigned to taxes in the externalities literature, and as part of a threat strategy designed to induce the generator of transnational pollution to modify its behavior.

Because the record of international cooperation on other critical matters hardly inspires confidence in the prospects for efficacious multilateral measures for the protection of the environment, it may be essential to design instruments whose effectiveness does not require the unanimous consent of those involved. Suppose half the nations bordering a body of water were to agree on some set of emission standards. Without unanimous consent, the remaining countries in the group might well continue to pour their wastes into the waterway as before, unless someone were to produce some device to induce a change in their behavior.

The pollution tariff (which may give less offense if called something like "a transnational resources charge") is such a device. It does not require the consent of the polluting country. Indeed, if several countries decide (jointly or independently) to adopt such a measure, they need not agree to use a similar schedule of charges or on uniformity of other provisions. Thus, the danger that the process of negotiation will preclude any effective program is minimized because little or no negotiation or coordination is required.

This approach also has several characteristics that distinguish it from protective tariffs of the classic beggar-my-neighbor variety. First, although the usual tariff is likely to lead to a misallocation of resources and reduced economic efficiency, a well designed transnational resources charge can be expected to improve them.

---

[27] We are grateful to Bertil Ohlin for suggesting to us the general ideas of this section.

But there are other significant differences. The ordinary tariff depends for its effectiveness on the absence of similar action by other countries. If everyone builds a system of protective tariffs against everyone else, all countries are likely to lose in the process. In the case of the transnational resources charge, the more widely it is adopted the more salutary it is likely to be. If polluting country B finds its exports subject to an environmental charge only by (small) country A, then it need not give the matter much attention. But if a large number of importers of its products adopt such a measure, the costs of its damage to the international environment will effectively come home to roost.[28]

Suddenly, its exporters will find their financial interests reversed. In the absence of a widely accepted resources charge, they can be depended upon to resist any substantial program for the protection of the environment for fear that its cost will reduce their ability to compete on the international market. But with duties levied on their products in many of the world's markets so long as they *fail* to adopt an appropriate program, they will recognize soon enough that promotion of their foreign sales in fact requires environmental protection measures at home.

Of course, one hesitates to provide any argument to the opponents of free trade and to open the doors to new rounds of restrictive measures brought in under the banner of environmental protection. Perhaps the threat of such measures may help to facilitate the process of direct negotiation and may lead to cooperative steps that will be effective in controlling transnational pollution. Thus the notion of transnational resources charges may help in one of two ways: either as a threat that helps to stimulate effective cooperation, or by serving as an instrument of second resort in the event some countries, by refusing cooperation, continue to pose a threat to health and welfare in other nations.

As a final point, one should be under no illusion that any transnational pollution charges adopted in practice will bear a marked resemblance to the quasi-optimal levies emerging from the theoretical models of the preceding sections. They will presumably work in the right direction, and serve primarily as a stimulus for a change in practices by a polluting country, not as an instrument for the fine tuning of international resource allocation. This suggests that other economic penalties, such as quotas and outright import prohibitions, may be able to do the job as well and that they will perhaps run into fewer practical difficulties. That may be so, though it is unlikely that they will have the sanction of theoretical analysis, for whatever it may be worth.

---

[28] Of course, if the prime objective of the tariff is to coerce the transnational polluter to take remedial action, there is no reason to levy it only on the commodity that generates it. Any exports of the offending country may be fair game for the purpose.

part 3

THE PROVISION
OF
PUBLIC SERVICES

chapter **15**

Introduction
to Part 3

In the final chapters of this book, we turn to a second, but related, class of problems influencing the quality of life. The members of society consume jointly, not only many of the natural, physical amenities offered by the environment, but also a wide range of services provided largely through the public sector. As we argued in the introduction to this book, the level and the quality of these services, in conjunction with individual activities affecting the state of the physical environment, profoundly influence the prevailing quality of life. In some instances, the interaction may be very direct: the cleanliness of our streets is the result both of individual disposal activities (some possibly involving external effects) and the public provision of sanitation services. In other cases, the link is less direct but nevertheless, we believe, of great importance: the quality of life (or "the environment," broadly interpreted) surely depends in fundamental ways, for example, on the safety of an individual on our streets, on the attractiveness of the neighborhood in which he lives, and on the access he has to a good education. Here again the public sector plays a central role. The point is simply that the environment is, to a large extent, a public good; its quality depends both on how it is influenced by private, individual decisions (a matter explored in the earlier chapters) and on the amenities provided collectively through the public sector. The first influence may be described loosely as the damage man unintentionally brings to his environment as a side effect of his private activities, while the second is made up of collective acts with the explicit purpose of enhancing the quality of life. The formal character of the problem of providing public services is quite different in key respects from our analysis in Parts I and II. Chapter 16 presents a highly simplified model of an economy that provides two goods: a technologically progressive commodity and one that we will call a *personal service*. Because of its technical properties, the personal service exhibits a characteristic of critical importance: *a tendency toward persistent and cumulative increases over time in its costs relative to those of other outputs.* Although admittedly unrealistic in a number of respects, this model allows us to see clearly the nature of the cost-disease problem; there are, we are convinced, a number of important services that are technological laggards to a significant degree. Our model provides some insight into the trends in their relative costs.

Although such services are present both in the private and public sectors, the focus of our attention is the public sector for two reasons. First, rising costs of particular services in the private sector can presumably be handled appropriately by the market system; in fact, one of the supposed virtues of a market economy is that it tends to channel resources into their most efficient use. A commodity whose relative cost rises over time will either largely be priced out of the market or, if it is valued sufficiently, will continue to be produced in significant quantities, at an increasing price, in response to consumer demands. Second, our concern with the rising costs of public services stems from the dominance of services subject to this cost disease in the government sector and the failure, we suspect, of collective decision (that is, political) processes and existing tax systems to deal adequately with this source of pressure on public budgets. Many observers attribute rapidly increasing public expenditures to corruption or inefficiency in the public sector. Although there is, no doubt, some truth to these contentions, we will argue that the technological characteristics of many public services (even in a perfectly efficient and virtuous government sector) imply that their costs will rise more rapidly than the general level of prices.

In Chapter 17, we explore the implications of rising unit costs for the provision of public services with particular attention to the revenue system. The presence of a kind of fiscal illusion or simply of legislative impediments to fiscal change *may* prevent the collection of revenues sufficient to maintain the supply of key public services at levels and of a quality called for by the preferences of the members of the community. One possible solution to this problem may lie in the adoption of more income-elastic revenue structures so that appropriate increments to the funds directed into the public sector are generated automatically through a given rate structure in response to growth in the economy. In this chapter, we discuss the desirability of such tax structures and also analyze formally the design and properties of a tax system that is sufficiently income-elastic to meet the needs of, first, a stationary and, second, a growing level of public output.

We stress that, like the earlier chapters, the analysis of Chapters 16 and

17 is mainly theoretical. For example, we construct and study a model of rising costs of personal services. However, we do not attempt here to document in any depth the applicability of this model to particular public services or to measure the magnitudes of rises in their relative costs. There is some existing empirical work (which is cited) on these problems. In addition, the companion volume to this book documents extensively the relative increase in the costs of the personal services and, in particular, those provided by the public sector. There we present time-series data for a number of public (and nonpublic) services along with some reflections on prospective cost trends and their implications for public budgets.

chapter 16

Outputs of Services and the Quality of Life[1]

The quality of life is not a matter only of the purity of the air we breathe or the cleanliness of our waterways. It depends significantly on the supplies of a variety of services, some provided by the public sector and others by profit and nonprofit private institutions. We have read of the intense and growing financial difficulties associated with the provision of many of these services. Rapidly rising municipal budgets to meet the increasing costs of public elementary and secondary education and of police and fire protection have encountered strong taxpayer opposition. A wide range of nonprofit institutions have also found themselves subject to increasing pressures from the swiftly rising costs of the services they support: hospital care, higher education and research, libraries, and orchestras. More luxurious services, such as those provided by transatlantic liners and restaurants offering haute cuisine, are disappearing altogether. If, as we will suggest, these problems are manifestations of long-term structural relations in our economy and not merely transitory phenomena, it should be clear that they have profound implications for the character of life in the future.

We will argue in this chapter that there are two distinct, but related, difficulties besetting the provision of a multitude of services that influence fundamentally the quality of life. The first is a problem on the supply side: the persistent and cumulative rising costs of a category of activities that we

---

[1] Portions of this chapter draw directly upon W. J. Baumol, "Macroeconomics of Unbalanced Growth: The Anatomy of Urban Crisis," *American Economic Review* LVII (June, 1967), 415–26.

will call *the personal services.* The model presented in the first sections of this chapter is designed to help in explaining the nature of the "cost disease" afflicting these personal services. The model suggests that inherent in the technological structure of these activities as they relate to the rest of the economy are forces generating continuing increases in their *relative* costs. As a consequence, efforts to offset these cost increases—although they may, in practice, succeed temporarily (or perhaps even for more extended periods in particular activities) cannot, in the long run, succeed in reversing the rising comparative costs that characterize this economic sector as a whole.

The second difficulty is a demand phenomenon. Many of these services also encounter, over time, what we may call a rising consumption "cost." This is described in a second model later in the chapter; it also has its source in the technological properties of the activity. The result is likely to be a downward shift in demand for certain services that accompanies but arises independently of their increasing relative cost of supply; paradoxically, this decline in demand will be ascribable, at least in part, to the secular growth in personal income. Both these phenomena then can help to explain the apparent decline in the quality of the services provided to society despite the continuing growth in its productivity and its per-capita income.

1. UNBALANCED PRODUCTIVITY GROWTH AND RISING SERVICE COSTS: THE PREMISES

The central premise of our argument asserts that economic activities can be grouped, not entirely arbitrarily, into two types: technologically progressive activities, in which innovations, capital accumulation, and economies of scale all make for a cumulative rise in output per man hour; and nonprogressive activities that, by their very nature, permit only sporadic increases in productivity.[2]

Activities in this second class (which includes the personal services) typically possess one or both of two closely related characteristics that constitute serious obstacles to significant increases in output per man. First, some of their outputs are inherently unstandardized so that it is hard to introduce techniques for their mass production. For example, children in various phases

---

[2] One point must be made clear at once: nothing in our discussion is meant to imply that any particular activity is incapable of profiting from significant technological changes. The great increases in productivity that arose out of the agricultural revolution, the mechanization of the kitchen, and the truly spectacular productivity increases in the performing arts made possible by the electronic media all have belied arguments that purported to show that there was little room for innovation in these fields. We fully expect that the future will provide other technological revolutions in areas in which we do not anticipate them. Nevertheless, the technical characteristics of certain general types of services do suggest that, for them, rapid and continuing increases in productivity will be relatively difficult to come by.

of their education, such as the acquisition of writing skills, require individual attention because of the diversity of their problems. This illustration also points to the second differentiating characteristic of the personal services: the role of labor. For these services, there is frequently an intimate connection between the quantity of labor used in supplying them and the quality of the end product. Educational activities again provide a variety of examples in which reduced personal supervision appears to mean a poorer product. Illustrations that are even stronger are found in the performing arts where, for example, a creditable rendition of a string quartet written for a thirty-minute performance obviously requires at least a two-hour labor input.

We do not want to exaggerate the difference between the two types of activity in the flexibility of their processes of production; this is clearly a matter of degree rather than an absolute dichotomy. There are all sorts of intermediate activities that fall between the two extreme varieties. Yet, the distinction between the relatively constant productivity industries and those in which productivity can rise more easily is a very real one.

Besides separating activities into our two basic categories, we utilize four additional assumptions to facilitate the analysis in the next section. The first is that all outlays other than labor costs can be ignored; this is patently unrealistic, but it greatly simplifies our mathematical model. Second, we assume that both commodities in our two-good model are produced under conditions of constant returns to scale. The third premise is that wages in the two sectors of the economy go up and down together. In the long run, there is some degree of mobility in all labor markets, and consequently, although wages in one activity can lag behind those in another, unless the former is in the process of disappearing altogether, we cannot expect the disparity to continue indefinitely. For simplicity in the next section, we take hourly wages to be precisely the same in both sectors, but the model can easily be extended to allow for some diversity in wage levels and their movements.

A final inessential assumption, that is, however, not altogether unrealistic, asserts that money wages will rise as rapidly as output per man hour in the sector where productivity is increasing. Because organized labor is not slow to learn of increases in its productivity, unions are likely to adjust their wage demands accordingly. This premise, as will become evident, affects only the absolute price level in our model and does not influence the relative costs and prices that are the critical elements in the analysis.

It must be recognized that the formal validity of some of the propositions in the next section does depend upon two of our assumptions, both of which are clearly restrictive: the premises that there is only a single input and that there are constant returns to scale everywhere. In Section 3, we will relax these assumptions and indicate how this affects the results. However, although under certain conditions our conclusions do require modification, in most cases, the conditions seem sufficiently improbable to leave the thrust of the argument largely undisturbed.

2. THE COST-DISEASE MODEL

As just mentioned, we assume that the economy is divided into two sectors, sector 1, which provides a personal service for which the productivity of labor is constant, and sector 2, in which output per man hour grows cumulatively at a constant compounded rate, r. The respective levels of outputs y_{1t} and y_{2t} in the two sectors at time t are, therefore,

$$y_{1t} = aL_{1t} \tag{1}$$

$$y_{2t} = bL_{2t}e^{rt}, \tag{2}$$

where L_{1t} and L_{2t} are the quantities of labor employed in the two sectors and a and b are constants.

To begin with, we suppose that wages are equal in the two sectors at a level w_t dollars per unit of labor, where w_t itself grows in accord with the productivity of sector 2, our technologically progressive sector, so that

$$w_t = w_0 e^{rt} \ (w_0 = \text{some constant}). \tag{3}$$

We can now derive several properties of such a system. The first and most fundamental is

Proposition One. The cost per unit of output of sector 1, c_{1t}, will rise without limit, while c_{2t}, the unit cost of sector 2, will remain constant.

Proof:

$$c_{1t} = w_t L_{1t}/y_{1t} = w_0 e^{rt} L_{1t}/aL_{1t} = w_0 e^{rt}/a.$$

$$c_{2t} = w_t L_{2t}/y_{2t} = w_0 e^{rt} L_{2t}/bL_{2t}e^{rt} = w_0/b.$$

Note that the *relative* costs will behave in this manner whether or not wages increase in accord with (3), for we have

$$c_{1t}/c_{2t} = be^{rt}/a.$$

In practice, it is possible in these circumstances that the market demand for the output of sector 1 may decline in response to its increasing relative price. Suppose, for example, that the price and income elasticities of demand for the two outputs were such that relative outlays on the two commodities remained constant. If we assume that prices are proportionate to costs, then this means that

$$\frac{p_{1t}y_{1t}}{p_{2t}y_{2t}} = \frac{c_{1t}y_{1t}}{c_{2t}y_{2t}} = \frac{w_t L_{1t}}{w_t L_{2t}} = \frac{L_{1t}}{L_{2t}} = A \text{ (a constant)}. \tag{4}$$

The ratio of outputs of the two sectors would then be given by

$$y_{1t}/y_{2t} = aL_{1t}/bL_{2t}e^{rt} = aA/be^{rt},$$

which declines toward zero with the passage of time. We have, then

Proposition Two. In the model of unbalanced productivity growth, the relative outputs of those products of the nonprogressive sector (the personal services) whose demands are not highly price inelastic and not very income elastic will tend to decline and perhaps ultimately to vanish.[3]

We can inquire, however, what would happen if, despite the change in their relative costs and prices, the relative outputs of the two sectors were maintained, perhaps with the aid of government subsidy or if demand for the personal service were sufficiently price inelastic and income elastic. Then, we would have

$$(b/a)y_{1t}/y_{2t} = L_{1t}/L_{2t}e^{rt} = K.$$

That is,

$$L_{1t}/L_{2t} = Ke^{rt}. \tag{5}$$

This gives us

Proposition Three. In the unbalanced productivity model, if the ratio of the outputs of the two sectors is held constant, more and more of the total labor force must be transferred to the provision of the personal services and the relative amount of labor in the progressive sector will approach zero.

We can also show that a determination to retain a fixed ratio between the outputs of the progressive and nonprogressive sectors can act as a drag on economic growth, causing it to level off over time (unless one revalues sufficiently the outputs of the nonprogressive sector whose increasing absorption of the labor force is, of course, the source of difficulty).[4]

---

[3] Note that with the elasticities posited and with a constant labor force, the output of the nonprogressive sector would not decline; it would remain absolutely constant. For by (4), $L_{1t}/L_{2t} = A$; with total labor supply fixed (that is, $L_{1t} + L_{2t}$ constant), it follows that L_{1t} and, therefore, y_{1t} will not vary with time. However, if expenditures on y_{1t} rise at a rate an iota slower, y_{1t} will, indeed, fall over time absolutely as well as relatively.

[4] Ultimately, even revaluation cannot prevent the leveling-off of any growth index, because there is an absolute limit to the outputs of both sectors if growth is absolutely proportionate. For setting $y_{2t} = ky_{1t}$, output of sector 1 per member of the labor force ($= y_{1t}/L_t$) can be no greater than $aL_t/L_t = a$ where L_t is the total labor supply in period t. Thus, we must have $y_{1t} \le a$, $y_{2t} \le ka$.

To prove the growth proposition, form the following index of output of the two sectors, with constant weights, m_1 and m_2;

$$I_t = m_1 y_{1t} + m_2 y_{2t} = m_1 a L_{1t} + m_2 b L_{2t} e^{rt}. \tag{6}$$

Now from (5) note that

$$L_{2t} = V L_{1t} e^{-rt}, \tag{7}$$

where $V = 1/K$. Substituting this into (6), we obtain

$$I_t = (m_1 a + m_2 b V) L_{1t} = R L_{1t}, \tag{8}$$

where the expression in parentheses, which we have called R, is a constant.

Let us now examine the path over time of output per capita. Assuming population to be proportionate to the total labor supply, we can, by (7), write $L_{1t} + L_{2t} = L_{1t}(1 + V e^{-rt})$, and our index of output per capita becomes, by (8),

$$I_t/(L_{1t} + L_{2t}) = R L_{1t}/L_{1t}(1 + V e^{-rt}) = R/(1 + V e^{-rt}). \tag{9}$$

We see, from (9), that the *level* of output per capita increases with t, but at a declining rate, as it approaches the value R asymptotically. We have, then, arrived at

Proposition Four. An attempt to achieve balanced growth in a world of unbalanced increases in productivity must lead to a declining rate of growth of output per capita. In particular, if productivity in one sector remains constant, the rate of growth of output per head will approach zero asymptotically.

3. A DIAGRAMMATIC ANALYSIS

A number of commentators have found it helpful to restate the preceding argument in geometric terms.[5] In particular, this permits us to use somewhat more general assumptions and to see how they modify the preceding propositions. If we assume that there is a fixed set of input quantities, we can describe the division of the economy into a progressive and a nonprogressive sector by a sequence of production-possibility loci with y_1 and y_2 on the two

[5] The diagram used in this section was first constructed by David Bradford, and the discussion follows his work; see his "Balance on Unbalanced Growth," *Zeitschrift für Nationalökonomie* XXIV (December, 1969), 291–304. Another diagrammatic translation of the argument has been provided by D. A. Worcester, Jr., *American Economic Review* LVIII (September, 1968), 886–93.

axes of the diagram. Our earlier assumptions of a single factor and constant returns to scale implied that the frontier is linear, but we now relax these assumptions and permit curvature in the production-possibility locus. As productivity in industry 2 increases, the vertical intercept of the production-possibility curve will, with the passage of time, shift further and further from the origin. The right-hand end, representing full utilization of resources by the nonprogressive sector alone, will not change its position. Thus, in Figure 16-1 the production-possibility curve shifts over time from an initial position A_0B to A_1B, then to A_2B, and so on.

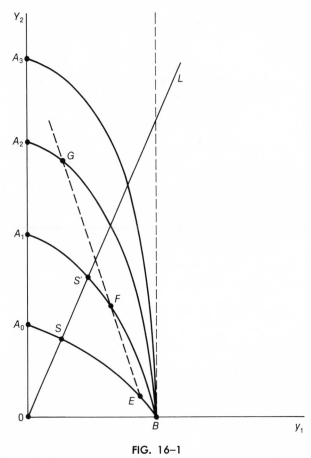

FIG. 16-1

Let us first reexamine our most fundamental proposition (Proposition One), which stated that the relative cost of y_1, the personal service, will rise continuously over time. If the production-possibility curves are linear (as our earlier assumptions implied), this result obviously holds, because successive curves (each with a constant slope throughout) would become continuously steeper over time. However, if the curves are nonlinear, as in Figure 16–1, this need not be the case.[6] For now the relative cost of y_1 depends both on the shape of the expansion path that happens to be followed by the economy and the way in which the frontier alters its shape over time. In Figure 16–1, if the mix of output over time were to follow the path traced out by points E, F, and G, the relative cost of y_1 could actually decline. Note, however, what this outcome implies. It means that the technological advance and the associated potential reduction in the relative cost of y_2 must be more than offset by the resulting shift in factor proportions and factor (shadow) prices. In the case illustrated by points *EFG* in Figure 16–1, the shift in the mix of outputs away from y_1 to y_2 must alter the relative costs of the goods sufficiently to offset the tendency toward the steepening of the frontier. Obviously, such a possibility cannot be ruled out, but as the diagram itself suggests, most expansion paths will encounter rising costs of y_1. This surely must be regarded as the typical case.

Similarly, the other propositions from Section 2 also require some modification either to deal with certain special cases or simply with the presence of multiple factors.[7] Proposition Three, for example, asserts that balanced growth requires a continuously larger proportion of the labor force to be employed in the nonprogressive sector. With more than one factor of production, this proposition needs to be amended. With continuing technological change in the production of y_2 that permits more output from a given bundle of inputs, resources *of some sort* will have to be transferred over time from y_2 to the production of y_1 if balanced growth is to be maintained, but it is possible that the resources shifted will be composed largely of capital rather than labor. The particular composition of the shift in resources will depend on the relative factor intensities in the two industries and on the manner in which this is altered by the particular form of the technological improvement in y_2. In practice, one suspects that extensive substitution of capital for labor as the input to be transferred to the personal services is quite unlikely because much of the problem of those services arises in the first place from the limited opportunities for the use of capital in their provision. In any event, this amendment is fully consistent with the spirit of Proposition Three: balanced growth does necessitate the transfer of resources from the progressive to the nonprogressive sector.

---

[6] Bradford, "Balance on Unbalanced Growth," *Zeitschrift für Nationalökonomie,* explores this possibility (pp. 301–3). See also P. M. Jackson and D. T. Ulph, "The Relative Prices of Public Sector and Private Sector Goods," University of Stirling Discussion Papers in Economics, Finance, and Investment, No. 15 (March, 1973).

[7] Proposition Two requires precisely the same qualification as Proposition One, for it remains valid if relative costs are rising.

4. RISING PURCHASING POWER DESPITE RISING COSTS

One implication of the cost-disease analysis is easily misunderstood. It might seem that, as the costs of the personal services grow ever greater, the community will be forced to consume them in ever-decreasing quantities. This simply is not the case. For although the cost-disease model predicts that the *opportunity cost* of these services in terms of other outputs foregone must rise steadily as productivity elsewhere in the economy increases, the *resources costs* of the personal services, the total labor time, and other inputs required to produce them, certainly need not increase. Indeed, there is evidence that productivity in the personal services does grow, though usually much more slowly than in the remainder of the economy. This means that rising costs do not condemn society to a declining supply of personal services. Because the disease stems from *increases* in productivity, it can hardly require a reduction in output levels.

It is easy to illustrate with the aid of the production functions in our model, equations (1) and (2), that, despite this cost disease, society can increase steadily its consumption of both outputs: the products of both the progressive and the nonprogressive sectors.[8] With r the rate of productivity increase in the progressive sector, let the labor force in the nonprogressive sector approach the total labor force, L, asymptotically at any rate $s < r$, so that

$$L_{1t} = L(1 - 1/e^{st}).$$

To demonstrate that this is sufficient to insure that output in both sectors will grow continually, we note that now

$$L_{2t} = L - L_{1t} = L/e^{st}.$$

Hence, from our two production functions (1) and (2), we obtain at once

$$y_{1t} = aL(1 - 1/e^{st})$$

and

$$y_{2t} = bLe^{(r-s)t},$$

both of which obviously increase without limit with t. We thus have

Proposition Five. The cost disease of the personal services does not

---

[8] This obviously follows by inspection from Figure 16–1. For example, if we move along any ray, such as *OL*, outputs of both sectors must increase as we move to successively higher production-possibilities frontiers over time.

prevent society from consuming ever-increasing quantities of the outputs both of the progressive sector and of the personal services.

The issue is only whether society wishes to do so and, if so, whether institutional obstacles in the form of the fiscal structure of the public sector (and, perhaps, constraints on the private nonprofit sector) will prevent it from achieving this goal.

5. RISING COSTS OF PUBLIC OUTPUTS IN PRACTICE

There seem to be a number of services, some provided in the private and others in the public sector, that we can reasonably associate with the personal service of the cost-disease model. We shall not attempt here to examine costs over time for specific services to which the analysis applies. Several chapters in the companion volume to this book provide a survey of cost trends for a number of services, public and private, as part of a more general appraisal of the importance of the rising costs of the personal services.[9] It will suffice here to point out that the evidence suggests to us that this is a pervasive and important phenomenon. We find, for example, that relative costs of education in particular and of local public services rather generally have risen dramatically and cumulatively over the century as a whole with particularly rapid increases since the end of World War II. Moreover, as the analysis suggests, there has taken place a continuing upward trend in the United States (and elsewhere) in the proportion of the labor force engaged in these service industries.

This is of special importance for the public sector, where disgruntled taxpayers frequently ascribe rising costs to corruption or bureaucratic inefficiency. An apparent result in recent years has been a substantial number of "taxpayer revolts," with residents, for example, simply refusing to approve local school budgets. Because revenue systems at the state and local levels are typically not highly income-elastic, increases in tax *rates* have been necessary to finance the expanding budgets required by the rising costs of public services. It is at least an arguable hypothesis that politicians' reluctance to propose and support adequate increases in tax rates have restricted public-goods supply excessively in terms of the interests of the members of the community. This suggests the importance of an investigation of types of tax structure that can cope more effectively with the problems stemming from the

---

[9] In addition, for relevant materials on higher education see W. G. Bowen, *The Economics of the Major Private Universities* (Berkeley, Calif.: The Carnegie Commission on Higher Education, 1968); on rising costs in the public sector, see D. Bradford, R. Malt, and W. Oates, "The Rising Cost of Local Public Services: Some Evidence and Reflections," *National Tax Journal* XXII (June, 1969), 185–202; and on costs in the performing arts, see W. Baumol and W. Bowen, *Performing Arts: The Economic Dilemma* (New York: The Twentieth Century Fund, 1966).

rising costs of public outputs.[10] Before turning to this issue in the next chapter, we examine another source of growing economic difficulty for some of the personal services often associated closely with the quality of life.

6.   RISING REAL WAGES AND THE DEMAND FOR LEISURELY CONSUMPTION

Pursuing a totally different line of analysis, Linder has recently produced an intriguing set of theorems showing how rising productivity and income, which underlie the cost disease we have been discussing, can also depress effective demands for a certain class of services by increasing the opportunity cost of the consumer's time.[11]

We frequently assume that increasing real wages will make for more leisure, and that this will lead to a greater indulgence in time-utilizing consumption activities. Yet, in his delightful book, Linder offers many observations that cast serious doubt on this assertion. He argues that there exist pressures making for less consumption of goods and services whose utilization require significant amounts of time. Attendance of artistic performances, leisurely eating, and even courtship are among the activities that find themselves at a disadvantage.[12]

The argument rests on a theorem developed by Linder and Karl-Göran Mäler[13] that we have modified somewhat for our purposes. This asserts

Proposition Six.   Because the consumption of commodities requires time as well as money, the substitution effect of a rise in a person's real wages will always work to decrease the consumption of a commodity whose ratio of consumption time to price is relatively high.

In other words, as his rate of real earnings increases, the consumer will be driven to purchase commodities that, although more costly in money

[10] Anyone who doubts that misguided political arrangements can inadvertently impede the flow of resources to the personal services need only consider recent attempts by the federal government to stem inflationary price rises. The program attempted to impose a rate of price rise on the personal services similar to that for the manufacturing sector! If this regulation had been effective and had lasted for any protracted period, it would surely have led to severe reductions in the outputs of these services (compare Proposition One).

[11] Staffan Burenstam Linder, *The Harried Leisure Class* (New York: Columbia University Press, 1970).

[12] This class of services, incidentally, does not coincide precisely with what we have called the personal services. The latter are subject to rising costs of production, while Linder's services exhibit a rising "time-cost" of consumption. A little reflection, however, suggests that there is a considerable overlap in these two sets of services (for example, the performing arts, education).

[13] *Ibid.*, pp. 150–52.

terms, conserve his increasingly scarce resource: time.[14] To derive this result, we use a model that again divides the economy into two sectors, but this time the two outputs are taken to differ not in terms of technological progress in their production, but rather in the amount of time required for their consumption. We use the following notation:

x_1 = the quantity purchased of the commodity under study,

x_2 = the quantity of "all other goods" consumed,

x_3 = the quantity of labor time spent earning income (note the change from our earlier notation where it represented consumption of leisure),

p_1, p_2 = the prices of commodities 1 and 2, respectively,

w = wage rate

t_1, t_2 = consumption time expended per unit of commodities 1 and 2, and

m = nonwage income (if any).

We will show that, neglecting income effects, $\partial x_1 / \partial w > 0$ if, and only if, $t_1/p_1 < t_2/p_2$ (that is, if commodity 1 has an unusually low ratio of consumption time to price). The consumer's objective is to maximize his utility:

$$u(x_1, x_2, x_3),$$

subject to his budget and time-availability constraints:[15]

$$p_1x_1 + p_2x_2 = m + wx_3, \tag{10}$$

$$t_1x_1 + t_2x_2 + x_3 = t. \tag{11}$$

Note that, in this formulation, all leisure is accounted for in the first two terms of (11) as time utilized for consumption. Time spent in complete idleness is easily interpretable in this way, as the consumption of a commodity whose market price is zero, though its opportunity cost is, of course, w per hour.

---

[14] That is, to paraphrase Linder, as his real earnings rate increases, the consumer is driven to seek to spend his money more efficiently (that is, more quickly).

[15] As an alternative approach, it is possible to proceed by eliminating x_3 from the analysis and combining (10) and (11) into the single constraint

$$(p_1 + t_1w)x_1 + (p_2 + t_2w)x_2 = m + tw$$

where, following Becker, $p_i + wt_i$ can be called the *time-price* of i (that is, the sum of the direct and the opportunity costs of its consumption). This alternative procedure is a bit trickier to handle because of the implicit role of x_3. However, it does show clearly that, in this model, time is ultimately the only scarce resource and that income is really congealed time.

We use the standard comparative statics procedure to find our desired expression for $\partial x_1/\partial w$. Our Lagrangian is

$$L = u(x_1, x_2, x_3) + \lambda(m + wx_3 - p_1x_1 - p_2x_2) + \mu(t - t_1x_1 - t_2x_2 - x_3),$$

$$(12)$$

with the first-order conditions (10), (11), and

$$\left.\begin{array}{l} u_1 - \lambda p_1 - \mu t_1 = 0 \\ u_2 - \lambda p_2 - \mu t_2 = 0 \\ u_3 + \lambda w - \mu = 0. \end{array}\right\} \qquad (13)$$

Next, we set equal to zero the total differentials of our first-order conditions (13), (10), and (11) obtaining

$$\left.\begin{array}{l} u_{11}\,dx_1 + u_{12}\,dx_2 + u_{13}\,dx_3 - p_1\,d\lambda - t_1\,d\mu = 0 \\ u_{21}\,dx_1 + u_{22}\,dx_2 + u_{23}\,dx_3 - p_2\,d\lambda - t_2\,d\mu = 0 \\ u_{31}\,dx_1 + u_{32}\,dx_2 + u_{33}\,dx_3 + w\,d\lambda - d\mu = -\lambda\,dw \\ \quad -p_1\,dx_1 - p_2\,dx_2 + w\,dx_3 = -x_3\,dw - dm \\ \quad -t_1\,dx_1 - t_2\,dx_2 - dx_3 = 0. \end{array}\right\} \qquad (14)$$

Letting D represent the determinant of the system (14), we have, by Cramer's rule,

$$D\,dx_1 = \begin{vmatrix} 0 & u_{12} & u_{13} & -p_1 & -t_1 \\ 0 & u_{22} & u_{23} & -p_2 & -t_2 \\ -\lambda\,dw & u_{32} & u_{33} & w & -1 \\ -x_3\,dw - dm & -p_2 & w & 0 & 0 \\ 0 & -t_2 & -1 & 0 & 0 \end{vmatrix}. \qquad (15)$$

Now it is clear that if we were to set $dw = 0$ in (15), dividing through by dm, we would obtain an expression for $D\partial x_1/\partial m$, call it A. Similarly, setting $dm = 0$, we see that, if we solve for $\partial x_1/\partial w$ by expanding the determinant of (15) in terms of its first column, then the expression that multiplies x_3 is also $A = D\partial x_1/\partial m$. Hence, dividing by dw we may write

$$D\partial x_1/\partial w - x_3 D\partial x_1/\partial m = -\lambda \begin{vmatrix} u_{12} & u_{13} & -p_1 & -t_1 \\ u_{22} & u_{23} & -p_2 & -t_2 \\ -p_2 & w & 0 & 0 \\ -t_2 & -1 & 0 & 0 \end{vmatrix} \qquad (16)$$

$$= -\lambda(p_2 + wt_2)(p_1t_2 - p_2t_1).$$

By the second-order conditions, $D < 0$. Moreover, we may interpret λ as the marginal utility of income and therefore positive. Ignoring the income-effect term, $x_3 D(\partial x_1/\partial m)$, we see that $\partial x_1/\partial w$ will be positive if, and only if, $t_1/p_1 < t_2/p_2$ (that is, if the ratio of time-cost to price for commodity 1 is less than that of "all other goods"). This is our desired result.

The intuitive explanation of this result rests in what is, in effect, a rising cost of time. Because the amount of time available to an individual is fixed, it becomes increasingly scarce (and hence, expensive) relative to the expanding quantities of commodities that can be purchased with an ever-rising income (as well as the rising wages that can be earned in each hour). Because consumption requires time, the individual has an incentive to economize on his increasingly scarce resource by consuming relatively more of those goods that require a comparatively small input of time. In contrast, those activities that are time-intensive become correspondingly less attractive.[16] The Linder Theorem thus shows us another way in which rising income over time can influence patterns of consumption and tend to reduce demands for certain categories of services.

7. CONCLUDING COMMENT

We have argued in this chapter that the continued provision of a certain class of services, the personal services, is threatened, with the passage of time, by competition from other outputs that exhibit more rapid increases in productivity; some of these (and other) services may also tend to be displaced by activities whose consumption makes less demand upon the consumer's limited supply of time. Moreover, many of these services are often closely associated with "the quality of life"; they include aspects of education, medicine, the performing arts, libraries, police protection, restaurants, and many others.

In concluding this chapter, we want to indicate with some care the character of our concern with the prospects for these services. First, we stress that, although we have examined together the issues of rising relative resource costs and time costs because of certain convenient analytic similarities, we consider the policy implications of these two phenomena to be quite different. One may bemoan the gradual disappearance of many pleasurable, but time-

---

[16] Our discussion has dealt only with the substitution effect. As usual, the income effect can work either way. Where leisure is not an inferior good, the income effect will make for a secular rise in its demand, offsetting the substitution effect, at least in part. However, casual observation suggests that precisely those individuals with the educational background and occupations associated with attendance at theatrical performances and the utilization of museums and libraries are the persons who have not demanded more free time as their incomes have risen—if anything, they have tended to grow increasingly busy at their "responsible" jobs.

intensive, forms of consumption activity, and regard the increased pace of modern life as a real deterioration in its quality. However, such a view depends upon a very particular set of value judgments and, as such, can hardly be used as an *economic* justification for public-sector support or encouragement of such pursuits.

The rising relative resource cost of the personal services is, however, another matter. Certainly the rising relative costs and prices of many such services will induce appropriate reductions in demand with perhaps the ultimate extinction of some; the fate of these services (including such activities as dining in high-quality restaurants) is no doubt best left to the operation of the market mechanism. However, there are other personal services, many provided in the public and the private, nonprofit sectors, for which (for a number of reasons) the institutional structure may fail to provide the proper response to continuing increases in unit costs. Our concern is that the mechanism we have chosen to finance outputs of many of these services may respond inadequately to the *real preferences* of the public. Our fiscal structure, for example, *may* itself tend to generate levels of certain important public services that are less than optimal. We turn to this issue and its policy implications in the concluding chapter.

chapter 17

Tax Structure
and the Provision
of Public Services

In analyses of the allocative and distributive effects of the public budget, the tax and expenditure sides typically are treated separately. One popular approach is to assume that the level of spending is determined by consideration of efficiency in serving the general welfare, perhaps using a benefit-cost criterion. Then the tax authority designs a revenue structure that will generate budget funds in a way that allocates the tax burden fairly and minimizes interference with the functioning of the price system (that is, minimizes "excess burden"). What this approach overlooks—and this may be of central importance in dealing with the rising costs of public services—is the dependence of expenditures on the revenue system: *the tax structure may itself have important consequences both for the level of public spending and for its composition.*[1]

This can occur in any of several ways. First, alternative revenue systems will produce different patterns of tax burdens and disposable incomes among taxpayers. An individual's demand for public services, whether expressed directly in a vote on the budget or, more indirectly, through his elected representatives, depends to a significant extent on the "tax-price" he must pay. The differing sets of tax-prices associated with various revenue structures will generate different patterns of individual demands for public services, which, depending on existing institutions for fiscal choice, can be expected to result in varying levels of expenditure on particular public services.

Second, in addition to these effects resulting from explicit and recog-

---

[1] This is a central theme in James Buchanan's *Public Finance in Democratic Process* (Chapel Hill, N.C.: University of North Carolina Press, 1967).

nized differences in the *distribution* of tax burdens, alternative tax systems may involve differences in *perceived* burdens. Under some forms of taxation (perhaps a tax on corporation profits), the individual who actually bears the burden of the tax (in terms, for example, of a higher price for products of corporations) may not even be aware that he is, effectively, paying the tax. Thus, even though an individual may in fact pay the same tax per unit of public service under two different tax structures, he may perceive his tax-price to be higher under one system than another and, therefore, may demand different quantities of public services under the two revenue systems. This has been termed *fiscal illusion*.[2] Where an individual's tax burden is disguised so that he does not recognize the extent of the true tax-price he will pay per unit of public service, he will, in general, support a larger public expenditure than he would otherwise.

Third, the structure of the institutions that determine the level of tax receipts may influence profoundly the level of public spending. Of particular interest here is the income-elasticity of the revenue system. If increases in tax *rates* require the explicit approval of taxpayer-voters or their elected representatives, public officials may be far more reluctant to expand their budgets and may find it more difficult to obtain authorization for increased outlays than they would if additional revenues flow in automatically from an expanding revenue base under a given set of tax rates.

A frequent objective of the widespread reforms of state and local revenue systems over the last two decades has been the modification of tax structures to permit revenues to grow more rapidly with rising incomes so that the automatic increments in public revenues will more easily keep pace with the expansion in public expenditure. In some respects, this must seem peculiar to economists who work largely with models of rational economic choice. What this seems to say is that individuals are more willing to support increases in public expenditure if they can be financed without an increase in tax rates: it says that individuals care about tax *rates*, not tax *bills!*

Although in its extreme form this statement is, doubtless, not entirely true, the reluctance of politicians to impose new taxes or raise rates of current taxes does suggest that this form of the fiscal-illusion hypothesis may well have some validity. On the other hand, it is true that states and localities have instituted increased rates and new forms of taxation with striking frequency since 1950; budgetary pressures, stemming largely from rising costs, have proved sufficiently intense to overcome this resistance.

It is thus not entirely clear just how great an influence the elasticity of the revenue system exerts on public spending. We are inclined to believe that it has a substantial effect. It is, nevertheless, an empirical issue. One hypothesis

---

[2] A provocative examination of fiscal illusion appears in Buchanan, *Public Finance in Democratic Process*, Chapter 10.

the argument suggests is that, if this type of fiscal illusion is important, one should expect to observe more rapid rates of growth in spending in states with more income-elastic revenue structures. This is a proposition we are currently investigating.

1. RISING COSTS AND FISCAL RESOURCES

What does all this imply about the problem of rising costs and the provision of public services? In the discussion of unbalanced productivity growth in the preceding chapter, we saw that, for technological laggards, relative costs tend to rise persistently over time. Because it appears that a number of important public services probably qualify for the laggard category, we can expect public budgets to be subject to expansionary pressures simply as a result of rising unit costs.

Before turning to the financing of the public budget, we want to emphasize again a critical property of the cost-disease model. The rising cost of the personal services is a phenomenon of increasing *relative* costs. The problem is not one in which ever-larger input quantities are required over time to provide a unit of these services; rather, it resides in the growing opportunity cost of these inputs stemming from rising productivity in other sectors. Somewhat paradoxically, it is thus a process of increases in productivity and the associated growth in real income that seems to make it more difficult for the community to afford the personal services. This is important, because it means that, *if desired*, the supplies of the personal services can be maintained or even increased in quantity and quality along with a continual growth of output in the progressive sectors.

Just how much of its expanding real income the members of society want to devote to personal services, in view of their increasing relative expense, depends on the relevant price and income elasticities of demand, which can be expected to vary from service to service. If the demand for some such service is highly price inelastic but sufficiently income elastic, then the rise in real income will generate an increase in demand for the service despite the rise in its relative cost.

For services provided in the private sector, we can generally rely upon the normal processes of market adjustment to changing costs and incomes to generate appropriate levels of output.[3] For reasons discussed earlier, how-

---

[3] That is, we can rely on them in the absence of government intervention. There is evidence that regulation by the public sector is likely to produce distortions in prices by attempting to be even-handed in its treatment of the progressive and nonprogressive sectors. This has been true in the regulation of public utility rates and, as already mentioned, in the recent attempts to limit inflationary price increases by controls on the prices of the manufacturing and service sectors. In the public utility sector, the problem has occurred most characteristically in noninflationary periods when the costs of regulated firms in the non-

ever, the problem may be of a somewhat different character in the public sector; here, there may exist real obstacles, perhaps a kind of fiscal illusion, that add to the impediments besetting the provision of Pareto-optimal quantities of certain public services. If this is true, it may be far easier to meet the rising costs of those public services if the tax system is sufficiently income-elastic to generate revenues adequate to meet their rising costs (along, perhaps, with desired increases in outputs) with no increase in tax rates. Otherwise, taxpayer opposition to periodic proposals for rises in tax rates or the timidity of politicians in imposing them, is likely to force cutbacks in services, whether or not they are justified by the preferences of individuals. In the next section, we consider formally the design of such revenue systems. In a concluding section, we will then speculate on their desirability.

2.   TAX STRUCTURE AND THE PUBLIC BUDGET

To illustrate the structure of a tax system that adapts itself automatically to rising service costs and intertemporal demand patterns, let us turn to the simple model of the preceding chapter involving one output in the public sector, Y_1, and one in the private sector, Y_2, where only the latter exhibits technological advance. As before, we will assume for simplicity that productivity in the nonprogressive (here the public) sector is absolutely stationary, and that in the progressive (private) sector it grows exponentially. With labor our only input, we again have

$$Y_{1t} = aL_{1t}, \tag{1}$$

$$Y_{2t} = bL_{2t}e^{rt}, \tag{2}$$

where r is the rate of increase of productivity in the production of Y_2. The total supply of labor is assumed fixed at L so that

$$L_{1t} + L_{2t} = L. \tag{3}$$

Finally, we assume the wage rate, w_t, to be the same in both sectors and to rise at some rate u:

$$w_t = w_0e^{ut}, \tag{4}$$

where u may or may not equal the rate of increase in productivity in the private sector (r).

---

progressive sector, such as automotive insurance companies, have continued to rise, while the costs of electricity and long distance telecommunications have frequently fallen. Regulators of insurance rates were obviously unhappy about matching prices to rising costs, particularly in a period when other regulated rates were falling.

Case a: Fixed Output in the Public Sector.   Within this framework, we consider first the case where the price and income elasticities of demand for the public good offset one another precisely. Thus, the reduced demand for output 1 resulting from its rising relative cost is exactly counterbalanced by the rise in demand generated from the increase in real income, so that the desired level of output of the public good remains unchanged over time. To maintain the same output from one period to the next, the public sector will obviously require precisely the same quantity of labor. From this and (3), it follows that

$$L_{1t} = L_1 \quad \text{and} \quad L_{2t} = L_2 \text{ are constants.} \tag{5}$$

The public budget in period t will thus be

$$B_t = w_t L_1. \tag{6}$$

Consider next the construction of a tax system that will generate the required tax revenues, $T_t = B_t$, and that does this with no need for rate increases over time. Suppose that a tax *rate*, v_t, were applied to the *total* wage bill, $w_t L$, at a level sufficient to cover expenditures in the public sector in period t. We thus have for any period t,

$$B_t = T_t(v) = v_t w_t L \quad \text{or} \quad v_t = \frac{B_t}{w_t L}. \tag{7}$$

By substituting (6) for B_t in (7), we find that

$$v_t = \frac{w_t L_1}{w_t L} = \frac{L_1}{L} = \text{constant [by (5)].} \tag{8}$$

Thus, by (7),

$$v_t = v_0 = B_0/w_0 L. \tag{9}$$

The initial tax rate, v_0, will therefore automatically bring in sufficient revenues to finance the public budget in all future years. We have thus shown that there is a tax rate on wages (or, equivalently, a proportional income tax because, in this model, all income takes the form of wages) that will generate exactly the level of receipts required to maintain public output at its initial level in all successive periods. Note that, in reaching this conclusion, we have not used the assumption in (4) concerning the rate of increase of wages; our result holds regardless of the behavior of the overall level of wages, so long as wages in both sectors vary proportionately. If, for example, wages were to double from one period to the next, the public budget would double; but so would the revenues from a proportional tax on wage income.

The necessary funds could also be generated by an *ad valorem* sales tax on private output, if we assume there is a fixed price markup over costs. With a fractional markup of m on each unit of Y_2, the total revenue from a sales tax of rate s_t on private (sector 2) output would equal

$$T_t(s) = s_t[(1 + m)w_t L_2], \tag{10}$$

because the cost of producing Y_{2t} is $w_t L_2$. In period t, with public expenditures B_t, the necessary sales tax is

$$B_t = w_t L_1 = T_t(s) = s_t[(1 + m)w_t L_2], \quad \text{or}$$

$$s_t = \frac{w_t L_1}{(1 + m)w_t L_2} = \frac{L_1}{(1 + m)L_2} = \text{constant.} \tag{11}$$

From (11), we see that there is a single sales tax that will, without future changes in magnitude, automatically provide the increased revenues necessary to keep output in the public sector at its desired initial level. Note again that this conclusion is independent of the rate of increase, u, of the overall level of wages.[4] Proportional wage or sales taxes are thus adequate to finance the public budget in our first case, that in which the level of public output is fixed.[5]

Case b: Proportionate Expansion in the Two Sectors. We consider next a case in which a positive income elasticity of demand for the public good more than offsets the reduction in quantity demanded resulting from its higher cost. This will obviously require a tax system capable of producing revenues that grow more rapidly than those in the preceding case, because the community must pay not only for rising labor costs, but also for the additional units of public output. To keep the analysis simple, we will assume a pattern of balanced growth: over time, output in the public sector grows at the same rate as that in the private sector.

As Proposition Three in the preceding chapter indicated, this implies a continuing transfer of labor from the private to the public sector. More

---

[4] In the case where wages do rise at the rate of increase of productivity in the private sector, r, it can be shown that there is a *fixed* tax per unit of *physical output* in the private sector that will generate revenues sufficient to maintain public output over time. This is not true, however, if the rate of wage increase diverges from r.

[5] We have reached these conclusions in a model with a stationary population (or, more precisely, labor force). If the labor force is itself growing, the conclusions still hold if we require public output *per capita* (Y_{1t}/L_t) to remain unchanged. If however, Y_{1t} were a pure Samuelsonian public good, whose output requires no increase in outlays as population grows, the tax rate v (or, alternatively, s) could actually fall over time. With L_{1t} constant but L_{2t} now expanding, we can see from (8) that $v_t = (L_1/L)$ would decline with the rise over time in L. However, for most public services (such as education), it seems to us more reasonable to assume that constant inputs *per capita* are needed to maintain a given level of the service.

specifically, we see from equation (5) in the preceding chapter that, to maintain balanced growth in output, the labor engaged in the provision of public output at time t must equal:

$$L_{1t} = L_{2t}Ke^{rt}, \tag{12}$$

where $K = [(b/a)(Y_{1t}/Y_{2t})]$ is a constant whose value depends on the parameters a and b in the production functions and on the given ratio of public to private output. Noting that with the labor force fixed at L so that

$$L_{2t} = L - L_{1t},$$

we can express (12) as

$$L_{1t} = L \frac{Ke^{rt}}{(1 + Ke^{rt})}. \tag{13}$$

The level of public expenditure, as before, is given by (6) as $B_t = w_t L_{1t}$, but, in this case, L_{1t} is no longer a constant. If we assume that wages rise at some constant rate u, by (13) we can rewrite (6) as

$$B_t = w_t L_{1t} = w_0 e^{ut} L \frac{Ke^{rt}}{(1 + Ke^{rt})}. \tag{14}$$

Let us again suppose that we levy a proportional tax on wage income. We then have

$$T^t(v) = v_t w_t L = v_t w_0 e^{ut} L, \tag{15}$$

where v_t is the tax rate and $T_t(v)$ is tax revenue at time t. If revenues are to be sufficient to meet expenditures, (15) must equal (14). Solving the resulting equation for v_t, we obtain:

$$v_t = \frac{Ke^{rt}}{(1 + Ke^{rt})}. \tag{16}$$

Equation (16) has several noteworthy properties. First, it is clear that the required tax rate is no longer constant over time; to finance the public budget, the tax rate on wage income must rise over time and, in the limit as t goes to infinity, it must approach unity.[6] Second, we find again that the pat-

---

[6] For a retail sales tax on private output, the rate s would also have to rise continually over time, approaching infinity in the limit. But these dramatic rate increases do *not* decrease the *real* disposable income of the wage earner. On the contrary, in this model, his real command over output of the private sector, sector 2, increases in strict proportion with public-sector output. That is the basic premise on which the model is built. The declining share of tax-free income reflects the decreased relative cost of private sector output resulting from its growing productivity.

tern of desired tax rates *over time* in no way depends on the rate at which wages rise (or, for that matter, fall). The required increase in the tax rate depends on r, the rate of increase of productivity in the private sector, not on u.[7]

This does, however, create a curious problem in the design of the appropriate rate structure. An obvious approach to our problem is a progressive tax that will yield higher revenues automatically as the community income grows. But such a tax on income (or wages) defines its rates as a function of income level, not as a function of time as in (16). Thus, our next step must be to translate (16) into a particular schedule of tax rates *defined as a function of wage levels* that will be operative in all periods and that will generate in each period the revenues needed to finance the public budget. Assuming rising wages (that is, $u > 0$), this calls for a progressive rate schedule so that, as wages rise over time, the tax rate will *automatically* increase also.[8] The difficulty is that, although we know from equation (16) what the tax rate, v_t, *should be* at time t, we cannot establish in advance the appropriate rate schedule defined over wages without knowing what the level of wages will be at t; under a progressive rate structure, the *actual* value of v_t depends on w_t.

The structure of tax rates *defined as a function of wages* in our simple model with balanced growth thus does depend on the rate of increase of wages. To make the relationship between v_t and w_t explicit, suppose that the level of wages rises at a continuous rate, u, so that (4) holds (that is, $w_t = w_0 e^{ut}$). We can now express (16) as a function of w_t rather than t. For simplicity, using the notation

$$W_t = w_t/w_0, \tag{17}$$

we may rewrite (4) as $W_t = e^{ut}$ and solve for t as

$$t = (\ln W_t)/u. \tag{18}$$

We can now express the tax rate, v_t, as a function of wages by substitution of (18) into (16).

For this purpose we note that

$$e^{rt} = e^{r/u \ln W_t} = e^{\ln W_t^{r/u}} = W_t^{r/u}.$$

[7] The intuitive rationale for this result is apparent from equation (8): the income tax *rate* needed to finance the public budget will always be equal to L_{1t}/L. For example, when 20 percent of the labor force is employed in the public sector (assuming equal wage rates in both sectors), the tax rate will have to be 0.2; the revenue system will have to collect 20 percent of national income to pay public employees. This result is clearly independent of the level of wage rates at time t. The need for rising tax rates in the case of balanced growth stems solely from the continued expansion in employment in the public sector: L_{1t}/L rises over time at a rate dependent on the value of r.

[8] Note that, if *money* wages were falling over time (that is, if $u < 0$), a regressive rate schedule would be required to generate the prescribed increase in v_t!

Hence, (16) becomes

$$v_t(w_t) = \frac{KW_t^{r/u}}{1 + KW_t^{r/u}}. \tag{19}$$

To determine the marginal tax rate associated with each level of wages, we differentiate (19) with respect to W_t obtaining

$$\frac{dv_t}{dW_t} = \frac{\dfrac{r}{u} KW_t^{(r/u)-1}}{(1 + KW_t^{r/u})^2}. \tag{20}$$

Because all the terms on the right-hand side of (20) are positive, we confirm that, as wages rise over time, the tax rate, v_t, must also increase. Assuming we know the values of the parameters, w_0, K, r, and u, we can use equation (19) or (20) to compute a progressive schedule of tax rates that, if instituted at time $t = 0$, would generate the additional revenues required for the public budget under balanced growth.[9]

Should wages increase more rapidly than anticipated (that is, at a rate exceeding u), this rate structure will generate a budgetary surplus, because the unexpectedly high wage levels will trigger a tax rate higher than is necessary to finance public outputs. Conversely, if wages rise at a rate less than u, the tax rate will not increase sufficiently rapidly to fund the projected expansion in public expenditure.

In summary, we find in our simple model of zero-productivity growth in the public sector that proportional income or sales taxes are required simply to maintain, over time, the initial level of public output. To increase these outputs along with the growth in private output necessitates the adoption of a rate structure that will produce a rising average tax rate over time. In both cases, these conclusions and, more precisely, the level of tax rates, over time, needed to finance the public budget are independent of the rate of increase in the level of wages. We did see, however, that to derive a progressive rate structure defined over income or wage levels that can finance balanced growth is somewhat complicated and does require estimates of the rate of wage increases in future periods. These results are, of course, only illustrative: they suggest that it is possible, at least in principle, to design a tax system that, with a given structure of tax rates, will automatically generate

[9] All this is admittedly quite oversimplified. A crucial assumption implicit in the discussion is that all individuals earn the same income (all in the form of wages) in any given time period. Where this is not true, the rate schedule described may not, for some periods, generate the necessary level of revenues. The rate v_t is to be interpreted as the *average* tax rate to apply to income in period t; differing distributions of income under a progressive tax schedule will, in general, produce different average tax rates. Moreover, as has been noted, construction of even this simplified tax schedule requires a great deal of information concerning values of parameters, information that is not easy to come by.

the revenues needed to finance the desired time-stream of public output. However, we must still examine a bit further the utility of such an income-elastic revenue system.

3. SOME REFLECTIONS ON TAX ELASTICITY

What, if anything, can we conclude from all this about the desirability of relatively income-elastic revenue structures? The appeal of such tax systems appears to rest on two premises. First, the budgetary cost of providing the *desired* level of public outputs must increase more rapidly than aggregate income; otherwise, an elastic tax system is obviously unnecessary because it would simply produce budgetary surpluses (or, alternatively, wasteful expenditure). And second (as discussed earlier), there must exist some sort of fiscal illusion or some other political impediments to the financing process; there must be some obstacles to increases in tax rates, even those fully warranted on the basis of desired levels of public output. If this second condition were not satisfied, then taxpayers and legislators would willingly support and enact the increases in tax rates needed to finance the optimal public budget.

There is some fragmentary evidence that bears on the first premise. As suggested in the preceding chapter, in spite of formidable difficulties in measuring units of public output, the available data do suggest that the *relative* costs per unit of providing a wide range of public services have risen at a substantial rate in this century; formal education, for example, seems to fit our case of a personal service reasonably well. This, however, would not in itself imply that rising public expenditures are desirable; people might well prefer to respond to rising costs by cutting back on quantity so that the public budget need not expand. However, this seems not to have been the case. What evidence we have suggests that demands for most public services are highly price-inelastic. In the most sophisticated of such studies, Bergstrom and Goodman have recently used a large body of cross-sectional data to estimate individuals' demand functions for the public services (other than education) provided by local governments in the United States.[10] Their results suggest, in practically every case, that demand is highly price-inelastic, usually on the order of -0.2. Studies of the demand for public elementary and secondary education also find that the price elasticity is very low; two independent cross-sectional studies (using rather different measures for the price variable) produced estimates of the price elasticity of demand for education of -0.36 and -0.34.[11] Similarly, a time-series study of the demand for higher

[10] Theodore Bergstrom and Robert Goodman, "Private Demands for Public Goods," *American Economic Review* LXIII (June, 1973), 280–96.

[11] D. Bradford and W. Oates, "Suburban Exploitation of Central Cities and Governmental Structure," in H. Hochman and G. Peterson, eds., *Redistribution Through Public*

education by Campbell and Siegel [12] (using tuition charges as a price variable) generated a price elasticity of only $-.44$. These results indicate that the demand for most public services is not highly responsive to rising unit costs.

By assuming a specific form for the demand function, we can illustrate how one might generate a rough estimate of the influence of changing prices and incomes upon individual demands for public expenditures. Suppose, for example, that our representative consumer has a multiplicative demand function for public services of the form

$$q_t = ay_t^\alpha p_t^\beta, \tag{21}$$

where q_t is quantity of public services demanded at time t, y_t is his income, p_t is his tax-price, and a, α, and β are parameters. Taking logs and differentiating with respect to time, we find the rate of growth of his most desired output of public services to be

$$\frac{\dot{q}}{q} = \alpha \frac{\dot{y}}{y} + \beta \frac{\dot{p}}{p}, \tag{22}$$

where $\dot{q} = (dq/dt)$, and so on. His most desired expenditure at time t is

$$E_t = q_t p_t. \tag{23}$$

Again taking logs and differentiating with respect to time, we have

$$\frac{\dot{E}}{E} = \frac{\dot{q}}{q} + \frac{\dot{p}}{p}. \tag{24}$$

Substituting (22) for $(\dot{q}/q)$ in (24) yields

$$\frac{\dot{E}}{E} = (1 + \beta)\frac{\dot{p}}{p} + \alpha \frac{\dot{y}}{y}. \tag{25}$$

Equation (25) thus gives us the representative consumer's desired rate of increase in his tax liability. Let us next substitute into (25) a "typical" value of $-.3$ for the parameter β, the price elasticity. These same studies (see Bergstrom and Goodman, and Bradford and Oates) yield estimates for α, the income elasticity of demand, on the order of 0.7. For the annual rate of increase in p, the tax-price, we use 3 percent, which is an estimate of the

Choice (New York: Columbia University Press, 1974); and Bruce Gensemer, *Determinants of the Fiscal Policy Decisions of Local Governments in Urban Areas: Public Safety and Public Education* (Ph.D. dissertation, University of Michigan, 1966).

[12] Robert Campbell and B. N. Siegel, "The Demand for Higher Education in the United States, 1919–1964," *American Economic Review* LVII (June, 1967), 482–94.

average annual rate of rise in the *relative* costs of the local public services (see Bradford, Malt, and Oates, "The Rising Cost of Local Public Services," *National Tax Journal*). Finally, for $(\dot{y}/y)$, we take the average annual increase in real income per capita in the United States over the period 1950–70, which was about 2 percent. Substitution of these values into (25) gives us

$$\frac{\dot{E}}{E} = (1 - .3).03 + .7(.02) = .035. \tag{26}$$

This means that, for typical values of our variables, our representative consumer desires a growth in real public spending close to double the rate of expansion in his real income. These results are obviously not very reliable, as they depend on the form assumed for the demand function and the particular values used for the parameters and the variables (along with certain implicit assumptions concerning the aggregation of demand functions). However, similar qualitative results have been yielded by a number of alternative conceptual experiments we have undertaken; the reader, of course, is encouraged to test the sensitivity of this illustrative finding to alternative specifications with his own values of the variables. At any rate, the evidence we have been able to assemble suggests to us that the first of our premises is probably valid: the demand for public spending (at least for many public services) can be expected to rise more rapidly than aggregate income.

The issue, then, becomes whether there are built into the fiscal system systematic tendencies toward underfinancing of the public services relative to the apparently growing demand for public expenditure. The source of the problem is not the same as the bias toward undersupply by the private sector of outputs with public-good attributes. Where fiscal decisions are made by ballot, directly or indirectly, there need be no incentive to the individual to understate his demand for an output; with everyone paying his share of the taxes, the free-rider problem need not be pertinent.[13]

But there are other reasons why the political system may provide fewer resources for the public services than would a free market. For one thing, rapidly rising costs mean that the public frequently finds itself paying more every year for smaller quantities of services. The source of the difficulty not being obvious, this observation soon leads to the inference that one does not get more or better services by adding to the funds flowing into the public sector. The public becomes exasperated and refuses to sanction the expenditures requisite for the quantities of services it desires, because it feels gov-

---

[13] However, where public services supplied by a municipality offer benefits to non-residents, the free-rider issue becomes very real. This can certainly be an impediment to adequate supplies of public services by local governments, and one suspects that it is often significant.

ernmental inefficiency and corruption make the authorization of additional funds pointless.

Casual observation also suggests that price rises that must be sanctioned explicitly by a public body are peculiarly difficult to obtain even where the price increases are comparatively modest. Somehow, a price increase decided upon *in camera* by a private firm does not normally attract the notice and the opposition that public discussion often calls forth. This observation draws some support from the fate of proposed increases in public utility rates during inflationary periods. For reasons that are just the obverse of those underlying the cost disease of the public services, many public utilities have been able to increase their productivity at a rate more rapid than that of the remainder of the economy. Consequently, their costs have risen much more slowly than costs elsewhere, and their proposals for price increases to the regulatory agencies have typically been smaller than rates of increases in prices generally. The great opposition that has nevertheless greeted these proposals suggests that it is far more difficult to institute upward price adjustments that are introduced openly than those that are shielded from public discussion.

Certainly, the political process encourages politicians to compete with one another in their self-proclaimed dedication to bargain basement government. Few candidates are willing to advocate taxes higher than their opponents are prepared to institute.

All of these influences then do seem to work in the direction of underfinancing of the public services (at least those provided at state and local levels where revenue systems are not highly income elastic). One may suspect, therefore, that a more rapid flow of funds to the public sector to help it keep abreast of rising costs is desirable in terms of the wishes of the members of the community. If so, it is appropriate to look for modifications in our fiscal institutions that will make it easier to generate these funds. That is the ultimate reason for our concern with increased elasticity of the tax system and greater automaticity in the adjustment of tax receipts.

If the demand for public expenditure does in fact increase more than proportionately with income, we then have the choice of adopting income-elastic revenue systems that will automatically provide (at least, the bulk of) the necessary increments in revenues, or alternatively, of periodic discretionary increases in tax rates.[14] At a pragmatic level, the latter option does have one attraction: it forces the populace to reevaluate from time to time its desired level of public outputs in relation to their costs. On the other hand,

---

[14] An alternative to the adoption of more elastic state-local tax structures is the introduction of revenue sharing by which the federal government shares the growing increments in revenues from its highly income-elastic progressive income tax with state and local governments.

this alternative brings with it the possibility of revenue shortages and less-than-optimal supplies of services associated with the frequent delays and the political obstacles to increases in tax rates (or the institution of new taxes). Some sort of fiscal illusion may well be present, and it may impede seriously the adoption of socially desirable increases in tax rates. In the absence of any systematic and persuasive evidence, it is difficult to do much more than speculate about the matter,[15] but it seems to us that the presence of such fiscal illusion and other political constraints is quite plausible, and that the adoption of more income-elastic revenue systems, notably by state and local governments, would provide a fiscal system better able to meet the demands on the public sector.

[15] We are investigating the effects of the income-elasticity of the tax structure on the size and composition of public budgets and plan to report our findings in the companion volume to this one.

Index